FOOD NEEDS LABELLING, PEOPLE DON'T

For my partner.
This book is dedicated to you.
I love you.

Acknowledgements

I would like to thank all of the following.

Vanessa Fox O'Loughlin for her advice throughout the process, Aifric McGlinchy and Maria McGuinness for their editing skills, Chenile Keogh from Kazoo, Jenny Sharif from Katie Bowe PR.

I would also like to thank the following people who have helped me to this point: Pippa Worthington, Patricia Banks, Ash Matthews, Martin Duffy, Annette Peard, Shane O'Donoghue, Jo-Anne McMillan, Siobhan Johnson, Mary Kennedy, Bernice McKenna and her wonderful group, Andrew Smith, Maura Harmon and Maureen Bushe.

In terms of helping me personally with the writing of this book, I would like to thank my mother and sisters and especially my two wonderful children for all their support.

Lastly, huge thanks to my partner for giving me the support to do everything daring in my life.

In all affairs it's a healthy thing now and then to hang a question mark on the things you have long taken for granted.

~ Bertrand Russell

Labels are for filing. Labels are for clothing. Labels are not for people.

~ Martina Navratilova

A journey from gender confusion to self-acceptance

FOOD NEEDS LABELLING, PEOPLE DON'T

CHRIS RICKETTS

First published in 2016 by
Little Singing Bear Publishing
Dalkey, Co. Dublin, Ireland

www.genderidentitydisorder.ie
www.shamanicliving.ie

Paperback	ISBN: 978-1-911013-242
Ebook – Mobi format	ISBN: 978-1-911013-259
Ebook – epub format	ISBN: 978-1-911013-266
CreateSpace	ISBN: 978-1-911013-273

Produced by Kazoo Independent Publishing Services
222 Beech Park, Lucan, Co. Dublin
www.kazoopublishing.com

Kazoo Independent Publishing Services is not the publisher of this work. All rights and responsibilities pertaining to this work remain with Little Singing Bear Publishing.

Kazoo offers independent authors a full range of publishing services. For further details visit www.kazoopublishing.com

Cover design by Andrew Brown
Printed in the EU

Contents

Prologue		ix
Chapter 1	*The canvas*	11
Chapter 2	*Alwyn and Gwladys*	18
Chapter 3	*Tom and Miriam*	23
Chapter 4	*John and Mair*	26
Chapter 5	*Susan*	30
Chapter 6	*Christine/Chris*	33
Chapter 7	*Moving from Nanty*	36
Chapter 8	*Confusion mounts*	39
Chapter 9	*Leaving the homeland*	43
Chapter 10	*National school*	51
Chapter 11	*Outside perfect, inside turmoil*	55
Chapter 12	*Bad blood*	59
Chapter 13	*Desires*	63
Chapter 14	*Battlegrounds*	68
Chapter 15	*The good times*	72
Chapter 16	*Friendships*	76
Chapter 17	*The inside out*	78
Chapter 18	*A shock and a revelation*	88
Chapter 19	*It all goes pear-shaped*	93

Chapter 20	*Hiding in plain view*	100
Chapter 21	*Rising waters*	105
Chapter 22	*A girl*	114
Chapter 23	*Pandora's box opened*	116
Chapter 24	*History repeats itself*	119
Chapter 25	*Beginning the healing*	125
Chapter 26	*Ending the life of a woman*	132
Chapter 27	*Writing out my confusion*	138
Chapter 28	*One foot on the path to healing*	141
Chapter 29	*Feeling not thinking: The second piece*	144
Chapter 30	*The French connection*	155
Chapter 31	*The journey*	158
Chapter 32	*Living alone with my children*	171
Chapter 33	*A link to my past*	180
Chapter 34	*Meeting Ash*	185
Chapter 35	*Spiritual shopping*	189
Chapter 36	*Training with Ash*	194
Chapter 37	*Pippa*	199
Chapter 38	*The greatest lessons*	204
Chapter 39	*Life with Alex*	209
Chapter 40	*Dunderry Park: The last piece of the jigsaw*	214
Chapter 41	*Breathing into balance*	222
Chapter 42	*Opening to the new: 2012*	227
Epilogue		231

Prologue

The problem with labels is that we attach them firmly when they should only be temporary.

I once attached the label 'gender identity disorder' (GID) to myself. Never happy with being a woman, preferring to have been born a male, I waged war on my body and was classified as a gender dysphoric person. I was offered the route of gender reassignment surgery but I refused this path, not because I thought it was wrong but because it wasn't right for me. I knew I wasn't feminine, but I was in a female body.

I needed to be told that this was not a disorder nor a problem, but just an alternative existence, a natural diversity. However, this diversity was not open to me at that time. Society was polarised into biological men and women, with gender identity firmly welded to both sexes. Being a feminine man or a masculine woman was not seen as a valuable part of natural diversity, but as a disorder that could be corrected with surgery. We tend to do that with everything in our modern society. If we don't like it, we alter it through expensive medical surgery, rather than accepting it as part of a natural and beautiful diversity. Magazines and television are always extolling the perfect image. There is no allowance for diversity. In this image-driven world, I once felt my existence was disordered.

Today I don't feel that this label is accurate or necessary. If I am a gender man inside a female body, then it is an existence that I may choose to alter through gender surgery, but it is also an existence that I may choose to keep, as a person who now lives in a world that is more gender fluid and less polarised than in the past thirty years.

When I was growing up, the labels of my surrounding world were firmly fixed into binary roles of male and female, masculine and feminine. Today the non-binary is being accepted and supported. We have begun to understand that it is not accurate to have just two sexes or two genders.

I have outgrown the label of gender identity disorder. I was never really completely happy with it, but at the time it was the closest label that I could find to describe how I felt, and it gave me a group to belong to.

Today I associate more with the term non-binary, as I do not fit into the polarised acceptable norms of male or female, but I am not in the wrong body or disordered. This term has less negativity for me and more freedom. However, as society evolves, maybe even this label of non-binary will be replaced.

The reason why I have written this book is to show that society has changed from when I was young. Labels and perspectives have shifted. It is now easier to be accepted in this world as a person who does not fit into either polarised ends of the biological compass – male or female. Reaching this self-acceptance has not been an easy path, but it has been an interesting one.

As I see it, everyone lives inside a holographic universe where each of us has created our own unique picture of life. My picture is different from yours, as no two pictures are ever the same, but we all add to the bigger picture. The difficulty in life is being an individual whilst also being one with the rest of humanity. Labels can limit us or separate us. We need to see any label as a temporary part of our existence rather than a permanent fixture. The problem is that we become too attached to our labels and we let them define us. Sometimes we even choose the wrong label. As with our clothing, we can grow and the label can become too small for us.

Chapter 1
The canvas

I was born in a Welsh valley dominated by the coal industry, in a town of narrow streets and small houses, where outside lavatories were the norm. My parents bought a house on the same road as my aunt and uncle. The house had only two bedrooms upstairs and two rooms downstairs. The toilet was in the back yard – a small shed-like outhouse. My mother and father converted a pantry area by the kitchen into a shower room, otherwise it would have been a bathtub in front of the fire, as was the case with most of the houses around us.

From the side of the valley, our house looked over a dark hill of impurity, left behind from the mining. Slag is what remains from the constant digging under the surface, when the coal is taken away. The slag heap of my childhood was a dark ominous mound. It sat heavily on the landscape and dictated the mood of everything around it. To me it was a large tombstone for all the miners who had perished below.

I was born into a family of moles. As I slept at night in my cot, my grandfathers scrabbled around hundreds of feet under the earth, excavating the coal that had once been the bedrock of the economy of an empire. In truth, these lowly paid men were the true empire builders. With the coal from their hard shifts, steel furnaces were powered, giving birth to railways, ships, armaments and thus conquest. My grandfathers were hard-grafting, working-class men. One of them took night shifts so that he could at least see the sun during the daytime hours. My other grandfather worked 'days'. He went into the pit in the dark and came home in the dark. It was a twilight existence.

My family was archetypically Welsh – living in a valley, working down the mines and supporting rugby. I had relatives who were bus drivers, shopkeepers and cleaners. Although financially limited, they had a great deal of social interaction and family interdependence. It was impossible to walk around the community without someone calling out your name or mentioning your family. Everyone knew everyone. It was a small, insular, tight-knit community. Mining towns are like little volcanic islands in a sea of valleys, erupting to the surface with ash and dust.

Most of my memories have faded concerning those early days in Wales. A few monochrome images remain and those are rapidly diminishing in detail and intensity. It is a running joke in my family that my memory is appalling. While my older sister regales our family with stories from our childhood, I usually listen in mild admiration as my memory provides so few of these moments. In fact, most of my remaining memories of the past are based around the smell and taste of the food from the fish and chip shop across the road from my gran's – cod in thick, crispy batter, hot steaming steak and kidney pies in little foil tins, with more gravy than meat, and more kidney than steak; chips, greasy but tasty, wrapped in yesterday's news and covered in salt and vinegar from large plastic bottles sitting on the counter. The chipper was where hardened arteries were created and lovingly fostered. Any trip back to Wales had to include a visit to this bastion of Britishness. My father used to say that the Irish could not do pies. They didn't taste the same. My father had a very rosy view of life in the valleys.

Other smells of my childhood include the earthy smells emanating from the small vegetable patch kept by Pop, my grandfather. It was in a little wedge-shaped garden, awkwardly sandwiched between two main roads that ran through the village. He would bend over the cabbages and beetroot and tug out the weeds interfering with their growth, his braces holding up his trousers as he worked. If the heat of the work became too much, he would take out a handkerchief from his pocket and mop his brow.

'It's those damn slugs I can't stand.'

Then he would pick one up and toss it over the garden wall. The poor offending slug would sail on to the road where a passing truck would end its life in a mess of shell and slime.

'Salt gets them too. They hate salt.'

As a young child, in shorts and T-shirt, I would watch him bending over with a little plastic bottle of Saxo salt, saving his vegetables from the thieving hordes of slugs. And on his head was always a flat cap. He talked to me while he gardened, but I rarely answered him. He scared me. Pop was his name to us. With all his five grandchildren, he had the odd habit of spelling out Pop in a little phrase, as if to explain where it came from. It was his one playful link to us as children.

'I don't want cold water. I want P-O-P, Pop!'

He would laugh at our puzzled little faces, as if he had delivered the funniest joke. Then he would take out his comb, brush back his hair and roll another cigarette between his chiselled fingers. Every time we called to visit, we had to recite the little phrase with him, as if reconnecting to his grand-parenting.

He wasn't a big talker. He didn't read stories, as other grandparents did. He would just sit in his favourite chair and frown. He did a great deal of frowning, especially when reading the newspaper. Even as a child, I saw him as this dark, menacing figure in the corner. I wouldn't dare sit too close in case he took a swipe at me with his words.

'What are you doing? Stop messing the floor with those puzzles. Go and do them elsewhere.'

My cousin Andrew and I would always run away and play away from view.

'What will we be today?'

'Let's be pilots or train drivers.'

There was a train track behind the village. You couldn't see it from Pop's house but you could hear it pulling the heavy loads of weight through the valley. I used to imagine it taking me to the places I saw in the cinema.

Memories of my very early childhood also come in the taste and smell of ice cream and sweets. Sometimes we would be asked to go to the nearest shop for cigarette wrappers or matches. If I had enough money I would buy a Strawberry Split made by Walls. It was a delicious flavour – strawberry, wrapped around a creamy, yellow, Devon ice cream. We called it a Mivy. We could buy them at Minnie's.

My dad's cousin, Minnie, ran a shop up the road from Pop. It was safe for us to go to as it was only about fourteen buildings up the same street. You didn't even have to cross the road. It was my favourite experience to walk through the front door and listen to the little bell tinkle. Minnie would come out from behind the counter and wrap Andrew and me in the biggest hugs.

'Oh hello, cariads, you're back again.'

She had the warmest manner. She was a big woman, full-bosomed and round of face. She always welcomed us as if she would never clap eyes on us again. She was an adult I never feared.

'Now, how much money do you have there? Let's see what we can stretch that to.'

She would disappear behind the counter and start filling small brown paper bags with sweets from jars that lined the shelves. They were exotic delicacies to a small child – round and hard apple pies; lemon sherbets, the shape of real lemons; black sticky liquorice in spirals; and hard toffees that rendered you dumb while eating. The bag in my little hand would be like a pot of gold. I would sit on the doorstep and happily chew my way through visits to Nantyffyllon. I still go back to Wales and look for them in the shops. These days I am mostly disappointed. The jars are all gone, the chocolates are wrapped in dull perfection and there are no little bags of surprises.

My memory of Wales is also triggered by music – a small chapel with the sound of Welsh hymns reverberating throughout the building and my gran coming out dressed in her Sunday black. There was no smile on her face for it was a serious business loving God, showing him reverence and respect.

Chapels in Wales are sombre-looking buildings. There are no expressive Gothic pillars or pointed arches and flèches arrowing up to heaven. These buildings are dour and Victorian. They sit like solemn blocks of industrial definition. They anchor the people to the earth, with no exuberance about them. Their tone is serious. Escape from the trials and tribulations of this industrial world will only occur when the adherent rises to heaven. Sadly, most of these chapels are now closed or have been turned into bingo halls or estate agents.

My older sister, Susan, remembers Wales in great detail. It is a completely different world from the one I remember. In her head it has a different hue, coloured by a very bright little girl who loved her grandparents and her life in Penyfai and was happy being Welsh. I liked being Welsh too, but I found parts of my life in Wales very scary and only one person there eased my fears – my gran.

This sweet little woman remains as clear and certain in my memories today as the day before she died. My gran was Pop's second wife and my father's second mother. She is central to this story as she has appeared in my life so many times since her death. She has appeared in spirit form to my friends and to me. She is always with me but unfortunately it took me a long time to realise it. She was the first person to introduce magic into my life, in the form of her spirituality.

It is always easy to recall my gran – stoking her oven in the kitchen, singing hymns as she cooked and the smell of Welsh cakes permeating everything. Welsh cakes are a delight – small, round, almost flat – griddle-cooked flour, butter and sugar, riddled with raisins. They were the Welsh working man's scone, cheaper to make and no oven needed. The sweet aroma they leave behind in a kitchen always reminds me of my upbringing. If I taste one today, the little house in Wales instantly appears before my eyes. They are a time transporter to a fondly remembered past.

'No, don't turn them yet, they're not ready,' Gran would reprimand me.

'But they've been ages, Gran,' I would reply.

'You are so impatient,' she would tut, 'you have to let the heat go through them and the bottom go a golden brown. Now off and play. I will call you when I'm finished and you can have one hot.'

I would sit down quietly in the dining room, pretending to play with a toy, watching her from the corner of my eyes. If I sat in the right place, I could see into the kitchen through the open door. She would stand by the range and sing hymns softly as she waited for the cakes to cook, one hand on her hip, the other holding a spatula. She was a small woman. Her skirt would always come well down over her knees and it was rarely visible underneath the pinny that she constantly wiped her hands on. I never saw my grandmother's legs. Tights were thick and constant.

The only time the pinny ever came off was on a Sunday. Gran loved her church. Every day she would sing hymns, the pure sound floating throughout the house as she cleaned and tidied. She seemed to have a connection with the Divine that went far beyond words. Her whole attitude was of trust and affection for her Maker. Often in my life, I have envied her certitude of the existence of God and the power of Spirit, and the security this brought her. I have found her type of absolute faith in very few of the people that I have encountered since.

However, Gran's life had not been easy. She should not have been my grandmother at all, but my grand-aunt. Her older sister had died in childbirth and left behind a husband and two very small children, aged six and four. At the time, Gwladys, the woman I knew as my grandmother, was still living at home with a parent. She was looking after her own father in his elderly years and was only saved from the life of a spinster by marrying my grandfather and giving my dad and my Aunt Sadie another mother. In marrying my grandfather, she took charge of her sister's children as if they were her own. She was a very good mother to them and they both loved her dearly. And this love was not misplaced, for she was a woman well worth loving.

My father's early life was littered with sadness and Gran was the guardian angel who helped him and his sister feel safe again. However, Gran nearly died too when she suffered problems in childbirth. My grandfather was terrified of losing another wife and did not react well when the birthing process went badly. At home, in their small house in the valleys, with only a midwife for care, my gran lost their baby. My grandfather took the dead baby, put it in a box and gave it to my nine-year-old father to take to the local churchyard to have buried. The baby was not even given a name, and was never mentioned afterwards in the presence of my grandfather or grandmother. My grandfather was told by his in-laws to not even think of trying for another child. My grandmother's family feared losing another sister. My own poor father, who had to take away his dead sibling to be buried, was traumatised by the event.

I think the burden of my father's past weighed heavily with him throughout his life. There was a great deal of pain that he had not processed from those early years – losing his mother, then almost losing a second and taking a sibling for burial. My dad died of cancer – liver cancer, bowel cancer and lung cancer – his body eaten from the inside out. I watched him slowly shrivel away, although he was good at hiding death from us, making jokes at his own expense, when he thought we could see his frailty. It was my mother who was left alone with the darker side of him in those final days. He feared death. He did not have his mother's faith. When we would all go home to our own houses, my mother would sit with my father and have to cope with his fears of death and his bottled emotions. He could not hide them from her. She was his partner for nearly all of his life, except for the first nineteen years, and he was unable to quench his anger at his own demise. He did not want to go; for a year after the verdict of death was given, he fought it bravely. He lasted past their prognosis. However, my mother was well used to his pain; it had been a constant partner in their marriage from the very start, always lurking under the surface. She had been warned about marrying a Ricketts' man. Their tempers were well known. However, my father had a very warm, loving side, when he did not give in to his fears. He was an excellent brother to his little sister, a wonderful son to his parents and a loyal, loving husband who would have done anything for my mother. He was also a doting father. He fought hard against his inner childhood angst to be a good man.

In my dad's young eyes, his birth mother had abandoned him. She had disappeared into a room, for what was anticipated as a joyous event, and had never come out. He had stood on the other side of a closed door and wondered why the world had gone eerily quiet, until the terrible news was broken to him. And at the tender age of six, I doubt he was told much at all. Children were to be seen but not heard.

In those days, the children didn't attend funerals, so my father, my aunt – his little four-year-old sister just sat at home with a relative and absorbed the loneliness on their own. I believe it fuelled my father's mistrust of women. In difficult circumstances, he saw them as weak and the root of his problems. He saw them as incapable of being there for him and he questioned constantly their love for him. Sometimes it seemed he only trusted the love of his sister, as she was there at the time of his mother's death and never left his side. She never abandoned him. She suffered with him. Sadie is still alive and I know that she misses her brother.

My father loved my mother without question, but sometimes she suffered as a result of his unforgiving past. In their marriage, she was rarely given the freedom to make friends or pursue hobbies because they would take her away from him; he could not bear to lose her, either physically or mentally. He was constantly worried about loss. It is a fear that was created in his childhood. I remember when he retired he drove her nuts with his constant nagging for her to accompany him on a morning walk down the pier. She would have housework to do; housework that if she didn't do he would later complain about when the room was untidy or the laundry out on display. She did enjoy the walks with him, but it was always at his convenience. He had to be in control. I think it is a trait passed down through the lineage of my family. We all like to be in control.

Chapter 2
Alwyn and Gwladys

It was not just his mother's death that had caused so much grief for my dad. His father, Pop, was also a drinker and an unpleasant one, by all accounts. Sober, he was fine, but under the influence of alcohol his company was unwanted. When his first wife died, no relative was open to taking him in or giving him support. There was a fear that if they helped him out he would shirk all his responsibilities and rely too heavily on them. Money was also tight in those days and few could afford to pay for two or three extra mouths to feed, especially if it involved putting up with a drunk.

Before my grandmother Gwladys saved them all from a harder life, my father and my aunt were often on the doorstep, sitting all day with nothing to do and nothing to eat, as my grandfather went to work underground. They were out on the streets from morning to evening, looking after each other, but yet not old enough to tie their own shoelaces. They would have ended up being taken in by the authorities and put into care if it happened today. But they were living in the years of the Great Depression and its aftermath, and there was poverty in many places and too many children on street corners.

Gwladys stepped into their lives and saved all three of them. It must have been an odd relationship in the very beginning. My grandfather was happy to have someone to look after his children and she was happy to be out of her previous situation. She was a good cook, a decent woman. I don't know how much love there was between them but I do like to think that it grew stronger as the years passed. My mother said that after my grandfather Pop died she was awoken one night by a sound like a banshee wailing. It put the fear of God across her until she realised that it was coming from my grandmother's room, and she realised that Gwladys was grieving deeply for her husband. Their marriage had obviously produced affection and love, although they had no children of their own – not one that survived childbirth in any case.

Pop was always scary – a strong and domineering character. From his armchair in the corner of the kitchen, he would rule his domain unopposed. But then which aspect of me is writing this book? It's not the adult. It's the scared child that is writing this passage. The child who didn't realise that there were other sides to this man, sides his wife loved and his own children admired. I only saw him from my narrow, young eyes. And to me he was an old, gruff man.

'Cup of tea, woman?'

'Coming, Alwyn.'

His manner with Gran always seemed so rough. I never saw any affection between them. I saw orders – words that were expected to be obeyed, his demeanour never fearing anything but compliance. Smoking his rolled cigarettes, his flat cap hanging in the corner behind him, he would rarely smile at her. He was my first example of an old man. His fingers were always coal-stained from the mines or yellow from the tar, sometimes even both. He also smelled different from any other man I had ever met. It was a smell of coal dust, hair cream, musty clothing and tobacco. The smoking eventually killed him. He lost a leg to gangrene and then it spread elsewhere. As he lay in his bed in the room downstairs, he literally rotted to death. As a child, his death frightened me – the bedclothes flat to the mattress, the lack of leg underneath, the whiteness of his face, the greyness of his eyes and the scent of death. I was so scared of him.

'Come closer and let me see you.'

I just shook my head, hiding behind my sister Susan's legs. She didn't seem scared of Pop. Susan never seemed scared of anything. She was four years older and always clever about things. She would even sit on the bed and talk to him. Not that there was ever much to say. He was sleeping downstairs for a year before he died – in the parlour.

It was a strange house. The front door was never used. It opened straight on to the main road – no gate, no garden. Behind it, a hallway led to a set of stairs that led to the bedrooms. Upstairs there were four bedrooms: two to the front with windows over the main road and a larger bedroom to the back from which there was another door which led to a smaller room that held my biggest fear as a child – the ghost.

In this small room, old trunks and cases, dresses and shoes were kept. It was an attic of a bedroom, filled with the detritus of a lifetime. As a child, pushing through the small door into its dusty confines, it was like crossing a threshold into another world. Nothing in the room lived. It was old, decaying and forgotten. When I had my older sister for company, I would sometimes venture in to look through the yellowed occupants of the photographs scattered in a cupboard drawer: men and women in stiff clothes with stiffer faces, coalminers dressed in their Sunday best, trapped in their suits, bursting out of tight collars and polished shoes; images of babies with chubby faces and cotton clothing, cherubs staring into a lens; women martialling their children, stoically standing over them with an air of Victorian harshness.

'Out of here! What are you doing in here? If Pop found you up here!'

'Sorry Gran.'

'Never come in here. These are not your things.' She would hurriedly push the photographs back into their drawer and shut the door firmly, trapping the memories into their musty coffin.

I was brought up as a small child with outside toilets. I was four when I first lived in a house with an inside bathroom. My grandparents' house had their toilet in the garden. At night, when the house was locked up and everyone was in bed, it was the chamber pot that had to be used. Porcelain and white, with handles at the side, it was a necessity in every bedroom. It was easy as a toddler to climb down from the big bed of heavy blankets and squat over it, although it sometimes was missed when tiredness affected the accuracy. In the morning, the room would have a faint, sweet smell of the chamber pot which would have to be emptied down the end of the garden, mostly down the drain but sometimes on Pop's compost patch.

My grandparents had a strange seat for their chamber pot. It was called a commode. It was a throne for chamber pots as it had a floral pattern lid. I remember theirs being of plush material and carved wood. When closed, it sat in their bedroom like an ordinary piece of furniture, decoratively hiding the effluence within.

Downstairs in the house, there were two rooms hardly ever used. They were situated just off the main hall. One was the front parlour. This room held all the things we were not allowed to touch as children. It was a room for receiving guests but for nothing else, until Pop needed to sleep downstairs. It was full of dark mahogany furniture, old armchairs and standing lamps with tassels. The dining room, where no one ever ate, was equally as brown. A large table dominated the centre of the floor and as young children we would play underneath its protective shadow. There were always pieces of Lego to be found under its solid wooden frame.

My grandmother kept these two reception rooms completely clean and polished. The rooms most frequently lived in and worked in were the kitchen and the outer kitchen. It was a strange amalgamation of two rooms. From the back of the dining room, a door led into a small room with an old coal-fed oven and hob. It was an odd room as it looked out on to the main road but it also had a door into the small wedge-shaped garden, with a gate before the street. Everyone who called came through that small gate and straight into the cosy kitchen. They would be seated at a square kitchen table on firm chairs and brewed a cup of tea from an old black kettle which whistled on the stove. My grandmother was always pleased to see people arriving, always welcoming. My grandfather would sit in the corner, eyeing everyone more suspiciously. The back kitchen off this room was a smaller area occupied by a sink and a pantry for food and storage.

This house is etched clearly in my early years. I have passed this house recently as a middle-aged person and found it oddly small now. It seemed enormous as a child, with a front room, parlour, a kitchen and a garden. But in fact it was very small and very ordinary. It is the memories that are larger than life.

These early memories of the house where my grandparents lived are blurred and incomplete but they take their place in the story of my family. The most important impact of that house in High Street, Nantyffyllon, was the presence of my grandmother – Gwladys. It is such a strong, unusual name. In my mind it always conjures up the times of Arthurian legends with names such as Gwaine and Lancelot. She was a small woman with a big heart and an almost reticent desire to show it. She was never the kind of grandmother who gave you many treats or bought you toys outside of Christmas. Even at Christmas, the presents were sensible and almost austere. Whereas my other grandmother would spoil my sisters and me with visits to the sweet shop and jars filled with 'thrupenny' pieces, saved for our arrival, Gwladys shook her head at such extravagances. She often gave out about the treats my other grandmother bestowed upon us. She was from a different school of grandmothers – the type that did up your coat buttons and pushed you out into the windy day to get your constitutional fresh air;

who wanted your elbows off the table and your shoes polished. A child was to know their place and not be the centre of attention with Gran.

Gwladys was born in 1900, a year of renewed hope with the onset of a new century. She lived through both world wars and the dramas of the Cold War era. She fascinated me from a young age and she was instrumental in bringing me into a greater understanding of spirit. However, her relationship with my grandfather seemed, to my young eyes, to only be one of subservience. This aspect of her life I found difficult to come to terms with, as she was worth so much more to me than just a support for a man.

Not all my father's early years were sad. After Gwladys married Pop and they set up their own home, my father and his sister were given a greater stability and some very happy days. My father has told me stories – of summers that point to a different time, of less food and material things but more happiness and community spirit. Of all these stories, the summer migration has always been my most cherished.

In the summer, when the schools were closed, the whole village, street by street, would leave the ash-covered valley for the clean air of the coast. Trucks would be borrowed or rented and every useful stick of furniture would be placed on board. Double beds, pots and pans, armchairs and washing tubs would make the journey through the valley to the campsite by the beach. Large tents would become the refuge for the summer. Every tent would be placed in the same order as the street at home, rows of neighbours would look out on each other from the morning dew and feel safe and secure in their tented village. The women and children would live there all summer, while the men came down every weekend and for the whole of the miners' holiday.

My father used to tell stories of packing the truck with his father and then sitting in the back, on the sofa beside Sadie, as the truck rumbled and wheezed its way out of the valleys and down the winding roads to the sea. From the back of the truck, they could watch the valley landscape disappear to be replaced by fields and modern houses.

It was always my pleasure to watch my father's face light up as he recounted this past – of sunny, lazy days, filled with memories which are now sadly never repeated. The villagers no longer migrate to the coast for the summer. The people no longer form a tightly-knit community. Families take bus tours to Blackpool and York, London or the Dales, or fly off to Spain.

Chapter 3
Tom and Miriam

My mother can recall the same magical camping excursions. She lived in a different village from my father, but it was less than three miles away. She remembers her mother hosting sing-songs by the camp fire while her father was back in the village. My other grandmother was the gregarious type. In fact my two grandmothers were polar opposites: where Gwladys went to chapel and prayed religiously, Miriam was a party animal and had no faith at all. She was an atheist before the word became popular. She sang songs by her piano, which she played, self-taught, and she drank socially but never to excess.

Grandmother Miriam was married to Grandpa Tom. When I was a teenager, my friends used to laugh at his full name. He was rather simply and repetitiously christened Tom Thomas. I think his parents may have run out of names to give him. He had many brothers and sisters and all the males in his family went down the mines. As a child visiting their home, I remember him coming home from work and my sisters and I being sent out to play. He would strip bare in their small living room and step into an old metal bath in front of the fire. There he would lie, with his arms up on the rim, while my grandmother scrubbed the coal dust from his body with a firm brush and soap, until his pale skin was white again. He was a small wiry man but extremely agile and muscular. Granny seemed nearly twice his size, with her large bosom and full face. They had eloped as youngsters – an eighteen-year-old boy with a ladder and a bicycle rescuing his seventeen-year-old princess from a life with her older sister. Miriam looked after all her nephews and nieces, of which there were a tribe. Auntie Lizzie, as she was known, had seven children. She was my grandmother's older sister and a very kind woman, but for Miriam an escape from the world of all those nephews and nieces would have been a happy thought. So Miriam Hughes married Tom Thomas in a registry office wedding and they devoted their lives to each other until he died of cancer in his seventies. Childhood sweethearts, they were together over sixty years.

Tom and Miriam had only two children, although my grandmother was pregnant on many other occasions. My mother was the elder of the two, and for eight years the only child, something that she was completely used to and happy with it seems. By the time my Uncle Ivor arrived, she was a complete princess in the household. She told me that she was more than happy to have a little sibling to play with and push around in his pram but jealousy soon developed between them. This was mostly due to my grandmother. She had waited so long for another child that she doted on her son and gave him everything that he wanted. The bond between mother and son was strong and, whereas my mother had to make do when times were tough, Ivor was given the moon and stars to keep him happy. He became my grandmother's pride and joy. He was a beautiful child – thick dark hair, smouldering brown eyes and sallow skin. That is not to say that my mother was not attractive. In fact, having seen the photographs, she was an extremely pretty girl, but a mother rarely sees the true beauty in her daughters. All she sees is the reflection of her own imperfections, which she knows too well, so my grandmother rarely flattered my mother unduly. The relationship between my mother and her younger brother became fraught. My mother was jealous of Miriam's willingness to do anything for her little brother. Sadly, Ivor is now dead. He died of emphysema – a smoker all his life. He married another smoker who died the same way. Neither of them survived their sixties.

The stories of our lives are created in the paths of our ancestors. My mother and father were moulded by their years in the valley and I too have become a bead along that string of existence. In their hopes and fears, I have found the origins of my anxieties and desires. And I am sure that my parents birthed their insecurities from their parents.

In shamanism, this passing of fears and issues down through the generations is an ancestral shaping which we can alter and eventually leave behind. The present and future can be healed with an understanding of these inherited patterns. My story contains a great deal of the problems of my childhood. I would not blame my parents for any of this as they did their very best, as any parent does. However, it was important that I learned of this ancestral pain to heal my own. In my ancestral line, there was a great deal of dominance over the feminine by the masculine. The power and ability of women was often subdued.

By healing our own pain from ancestral issues, we can also heal it for our children so that they might escape the same fears and scars. This is mostly achieved by the example that we play in the lives of our children. Parents are role models and this is a heavy burden. My parents were very formative in my life but in ways that are sometimes not obvious.

Chapter 4
John and Mair

My mother first met my father in the immediate aftermath of the Second World War. The war came very close to the Welsh valleys. The bombing of Port Talbot, with its steelworks in Margam, was a high priority for the Luftwaffe. My mother says that she used to lie in bed and watch the night sky fill with flickering lights as the bombs dropped ten miles away. It was exciting in many ways and yet a time of underlying fear.

Rationing was the main way that the war affected my family. Miners didn't have to fight – their work was too important to the war effort and so they all avoided conscription. With coupon cards in hand, my mother went shopping with Miriam and joined the queues for meat and sugar. The recipes that I remember eating as a child had their origins in these war years. Corned beef pie – a little Fray Bentos tin for the whole family – accompanied by carrots, onions and swedes as cheap, locally produced fillers. The vegetables would be cooked off in a stock, with some fresh garden herbs, and then placed at the bottom of a pie dish. Slices of corned beef would be layered on top of the vegetables and then it would be topped off with a floury pastry crust. Cooked in the oven, it was hearty and warming, simple but effective as a meal.

Offal was also used as it was cheaper than cuts of meat and nothing was wasted during the war. My father loved tripe and onions. Tripe is the stomach linings of an ox. It is boiled off and simmered in milk and onions, nutmeg and bay leaf. Other common cheap cuts were the tail and the tongue. Oxtail soup was one of my older sister's favourites from our childhood. The soup contained all the usual cheap vegetables in large chunks, accompanied by pieces of bony oxtail. I hated it. I also disliked tongue. It usually came in the shape of pressed cold meat in an aspic jelly.

I preferred the sweet recipes my mother cooked, in particular iced-sliders. These are known as custard slices elsewhere – lovely flaky pastry filled with thick custard and topped with royal icing. I still salivate and smile when I think of them.

The war brought dances to the valley, with the sounds of the Glen Miller band. On a Saturday night, all the young locals visited the dance hall and courted future husbands or wives. My mother and father were no different. At one dance she noticed him in his uniform, as he had joined the RAF in 1945, but he had no eyes for her as she was too young. He was twenty-one and she was only sixteen. So their time had not yet come. They had a few years living apart before they would be together.

After the war, my mother managed to persuade her whole family to move to Slough so that she could find work and leave the valleys behind. My mother hated living in the valleys. She saw them as narrow and limiting. My grandmother, grandfather and a teenage Ivor packed up their bags and went to live with another of my grandmother's sisters in England. The move didn't last long. My grandmother found her new work too hard. She was employed as a cleaning lady and the steep stairs in the house proved too hard for her chest complaint. She soon wished to be back in the valley.

Back in Wales, older and wiser, my mother was ready for my father the next time they met. It was on a bus. It was nothing romantic and heady but, when recalled by my mother, she still smiles wistfully and remembers the time with deep warmth. Recently she told me about the boy that she had been courting just before she met my father. He was red-haired and quite handsome, but cared more about his rugby club and seeing his friends than being with her. It was why she found herself unaccompanied on a bus one weekend. She had gone dancing with her best friend. On the trip home, they were both sitting on the top of the bus with no male to keep them company. My father did not leave my mother that way for too long.

Although my father had joined the RAF, it was at the end of the war and he didn't see any combat. Colour-blind, he ended up in the ground crew, although it was unlikely that he would ever have had the chance to be a pilot. He spent 1945–46 in Egypt, manning a prisoner-of-war camp and seeing the pyramids. At least he saw them from a distance as they were not on the top of his priorities as a young man. I have seen pictures of him, a broad smile on his face, standing in front of his tent with another recruit, happily showing off their suntans and uniforms. I suppose the experience gave my father a taste for life outside of the valleys.

Oddly enough, onsidering our family's future life, he had a small break in Ireland during this period, a holiday in Wexford. He was amazed at the amount of sausages, rashers and eggs available for his breakfast. Rationing was different in Ireland, or Éire as it was known then. Éire had rationing on coal and oil, tea and sugar and other goods from abroad. Churchill had stopped the British merchant navy delivering to Ireland, in the hope of forcing Ireland to join the war effort. Ireland had no merchant ships of her own and she was thus left without oil and other essential commodities until Seán Lemass, Minister of Supplies, set up the Irish Shipping Company. It was an interesting time in Ireland's history. A train from Dublin to Galway took around eight hours, powered by turf rather than coal, and the country had glimmer men going around making sure that people were not wasting gas. They were inspectors, employed by gas supply companies, to travel around the smaller towns in Ireland. Their job was to detect the use of gas in restricted periods during the years of the Emergency from March 1942. They lasted in some places as late as 1947. My dad loved history.

'It is important to know what happened in the past,' he would say.

We must have listened. Two of us have history degrees and so does one of his grandsons.

However my father's visit to Ireland left him feeling that the war had not impacted on the Irish at all, as food was plentiful in the hotel where he stayed. My father often vented anger towards the Irish for leaving Britain unsupported during the Second World War.

'It was wrong. Selfish buggers just looked after themselves.'

'No Dad, it wasn't that simple. They didn't have the army or navy to fight.'

'Is that what I paid for you to learn in school? Rubbish. Propaganda. Don't be stupid. They were all republicans. Hated us and that is why they didn't help. Simple!'

When we came to live in Ireland, he used to mutter about the damned Irish frequently, refusing to watch RTÉ news and any local television, even though his friends were Irish. It was one of the problems about my general knowledge as a young child. I knew all the leaders of the British parties but could never tell one Irish politician from another. It was not until I went to university in Dublin to study history, geography and politics that I actually bridged some of the gap.

When his service ended, my father went back home to Wales to look for work. He briefly worked down a mine but he couldn't take the darkness, lack of sunlight and claustrophobia, so he applied for a job in the coal board office as a tea boy/ junior clerk. He was good at mathematics and so his career as an accountant started. My mother was instrumental in pushing his career to become so much more.

When John Alwyn Ricketts married Eileen Mair Thomas in September 1954, they moved in with Tom and Miriam Thomas, and lived on one floor of a three-storied house. I remember thinking that it sounded grand, a three-storied house, until I saw it this summer and realised that it was a very compact dwelling. In my imagination, I had created a much bigger home. The reality of its size almost shocked me. I realised how privileged a life my parents had given me compared to the life that they had lived, although my privileges were based on the physical trappings of a larger house, a more expensive car and better family holidays. These trappings of a modern life didn't necessarily make me any happier than my mother or my father in their respective upbringings, but it did open doors for me into a better education.

My maternal grandmother, Miriam, was very good to my parents. On a Friday night she would give my father money to go out for a drink with his friends, knowing that their money was tight. Even though my mother worked, my parents would have been saving hard to buy their own house. She had a job with Revlon, the cosmetic company. Most of the women in the valley worked there, packing lipsticks into boxes, testing for damages and working the belts. They were allowed to take the products which were damaged home and there was a constant stream of goods out of the factory being sold on the black market. Mum worked in the office. She was really good at mathematics and extremely bright so she would have been wasted on the floor packing make-up.

On a Friday night in the local bars, most of the women of the area smelled of Revlon and sported the latest make-up on their eyes and cheeks. The company was a good employer and at Christmas held wonderful parties for workers and their families. Every year they would put on a pantomime or some sort of variety performance. Bosses and factory workers all acted together for the amusement of their spouses and children. It was followed by a dinner, singing and dancing.

Chapter 5
Susan

My sister, Susan, was born in the spring of 1957. As she was my parents' first child there was a great deal of excitement over the birth. I suppose with my grandmother Miriam in the house, there was a certain amount of anxiety, as her own experience of childbirth had not been that easy (again the ancestral lineage). My grandmother had gone through a few miscarriages. On 28 March 1957, my mother entered the small local hospital, but she was not to go home again for another three months. They were dark days for her, days that have affected us all in their pain for her.

After my older sister was born, my mother suffered postnatal depression. The medical world at the time was harsh with their treatment of depression. My older sister was taken home to be nurtured by Granny Miriam, while my father was at work. My mother was put into a psychiatric ward and made to endure electric shock treatment while they tried to spark some life into her beyond her depression. For my mother, these were amongst the worst days of her life. Deprived of contact from her newborn baby and unable to see her husband, she sat day after day in a soulless room weaving baskets and suffering the ignorance of the medical world. I have listened to her describe the harrowing treatment – lying back on the table, the electricity connected to her slim body, the juddering in her arms and legs, her teeth chattering painfully. It is still a horrible memory for her.

I feel anger at the thought of the pain and the loneliness that she felt. It left a deep scar, and one of the fears that runs deep through me – the fear of being locked up. While it's good to be aware of the tendencies in our family history, it can also be dangerous to become too attached to the stories of the past; they can trap us and define who we are and who we become.

Like labels, we must tear them off as we change and outgrow them. Our lives involve so many journeys, and through all these we collect so much baggage, all with different labels. At some point, we must look back fondly at what these journeys have taught us, but then move on and not become consumed by them. Knowing the past can free us but living in the past can trap us.

When my mother eventually returned home, my grandmother had bonded with her baby granddaughter. At the age of forty-four, Miriam was a relatively young grandmother and happy to care for her first grandchild's every need. She was loath to part with the four-month-old that she had cared for since birth. A battle almost ensued over the nurturing of my sister. In many ways she became spoilt, as the two women tried to compete for her favour. Miriam was a strong woman and not capable of letting go of the control that she had been given. There was nothing malicious in it. It was just a matter of bonding and my grandmother had bonded tightly. Susan had also bonded with her. It left my mother feeling quite alienated from her own child. When the family left Wales for Ireland, nine years later, Susan was devastated by the move. She was leaving her grandparents behind for a strange place, with no friends or relatives to comfort her.

It must have been hard for my mother to think of conceiving again. However, she has told me that she didn't want to bring up an only child. My father, understandably, was loath to see her in hospital again. It pressed buttons from his past. It had been extremely difficult for him to watch his own wife disappear from him after childbirth. He had lost a mother to childbirth and his fears in that area were engrained. Susan's birth only cemented them further. He didn't need any more children to bring further tragedy into his life.

Three years after the birth of my sister, my mother told my father that she was ready to try for another child. She was brave enough to become pregnant again. My father was unhappy at the prospect. He was happy enough having one child and concentrating on his blossoming career. However, my mother was obviously persuasive and I was conceived in early spring, and due on Christmas Eve. I was to be called Christopher.

My parents, especially my mother, were sure that they were going to have a son. They planned my name, my room and waited eagerly for the festive season. I was not thought of as anything else but a future son.

I have often thought of those days of my pre-birth. I doubt many do, but I have good reason to understand their possible significance in my life. In the womb, all eggs are first female in their development. The maleness comes as the chromosomes kick in and play their X and Y games with the embryo. The chromosomes create the arrival of testosterone or oestrogen which forms their sexual differences.

In times of great stress, all men and women produce extra testosterone, part of the fight or flight response. My mother was no different. In the months of 1960 as the baby grew inside her, so, possibly, did her subconscious fears. Unbeknownst to her, that underlying fear could have flooded her unborn baby with higher levels of testosterone than normal and there the changes could have started.

At least, this is one explanation of my former gender identity disorder that the medical world has put forward, through understanding those days before my birth. I am not too sure about their validity as I have talked to my mother about that time and she has assured me that she was very happy to be pregnant with me. She was looking forward to having a second child and returning home with her baby. In fact, she said that she was more than happy during this period. Her fears during her first pregnancy had centred on not knowing how to look after and bring up a baby. When I came along, she was four years older and much more confident about raising a child. However, she did think that she was having a boy. In fact, a few women who were deemed to be psychic had told her as much.

Chapter 6
Christine/Chris

Born a week late on New Year's Eve, I arrived to a happy mother and doting father at the end of 1960. As a little baby, I was blissfully unaware of my gender. They must have been such happy days. I didn't know when I was born that I was a female. It was obviously not a concept as a baby that I would have cared about or understood. I was too busy being occupied with feeding and sleeping and learning. And I learned that I was a little girl from everything that happened around me.

When I was a baby, we lived in King's Terrace. It was a row of houses sitting on a hillside above Nantyffyllon. The houses were not shabby, but they were small. The brickwork was ornate, a reddish-brown hue for the main walls, with windows and door mantel outlined in yellow bricks. The houses were terraced, each with its own small front garden, iron railings and four steps up to the front door. They looked like tiny Victorian mansions. They didn't have a garage although later some were added around the corner on open land. My dad built ours in the small back garden. He was not a natural handyman but he never ran away from hard work. Grandfather Tom helped him. He was the manual worker and more confident with tools.

I was not the only new baby in the street that winter. My dad's sister, Sadie, and her husband, Bill, had brought home their second son, Andrew, only three months before my arrival. He was one of my closest friends at an early age. Sadie and Bill lived across the road, a few doors up from our house. Their first child, Ian, was close in age to my sister Susan, but they were never to become as close as Andrew and I were as children. They had a healthy rivalry as the first grandchildren. Susan always thought that Ian was unhappy at having another grandchild to compete with for attention. She may have been right.

Andrew and I just ignored all that and played. We were placed in the same cots and playpens together as babies. My mother remembers that we never kept to the gender toys that we were given. I played with his toys and he played with mine. Growing up from babyhood with Andrew, I didn't see myself as any different from him. I quite often didn't know which were the toys meant for me and which were for him. We were just small children enjoying having someone else to play with and sharing our toys. He learned to play with dolls and I learned to hammer wooden shapes into a box with holes.

As we grew into small children, I was taller than Andrew, although younger. He had a beautiful, cherubic face so he always looked younger than me. I felt more capable when we played games with other children, especially the physical ones. I liked climbing walls, trees and any other obstacles that got in my way. I was rough and tough in my attitude and he was quiet and timid. However, I don't remember ever being faced with my gender until I was with Susan and saw how she behaved.

Four years older than me, she was a reader and not a very boisterous girl. If she was told to take me out and look after me, I was always aware of her happiness to wear dresses and tie her long hair up in bows. I didn't want to be like her. I didn't want to grow up to be someone who sat reading books and couldn't cross the stream at the end of the road without falling into it. She also didn't like me much. I'm afraid the feeling was mutual, but then we were children and ours was the usual sibling rivalry. It wasn't me being the lovely child and her being the bossy older sister. It was her being responsible for me and me being a completely difficult task to manage. As she was four years older than me, she was given that task of looking after me and I didn't want her to succeed. I made her life difficult. Today she is one of my best friends and her friendship is one of the most important things in my life, as she is a wonderfully supportive, kind person. But as children, we had nothing in common. I was just this noisy little kid that she had to take care of. She always seemed very bored with me or very angry with me. She didn't want to play football or any other game, unless it involved sitting down with dice. While I was a young child that kicked stones with my shoes, she was the young child that obediently sat and polished hers. She was always being good. I looked up to her and respected her in many ways but I was not as adept at being good and so I became jealous.

It was a wedding that gave me my first real shock of being female. My mum's cousin Clive was marrying his fiancée Sandra. Susan and I were to be the bridesmaids. A little lemon-coloured dress and small headdress was left on the bed for me. I remember looking at it and wondering would Andrew ever have to wear one of these stupid floral things. My mother came in to dress me and her words were not welcomed.

'Oh won't you look so pretty.'

I just stood there saying nothing.

'It's such a lovely little dress, isn't it? Fit for a princess.'

I refused to smile or look happy.

'Look! Susan has one just the same.'

Susan was beaming, pulling down her dress and happily flattening out any creases with her seven-year-old hands.

Take it off. Take the horrible thing off. In my head I was screaming but there were no words coming out of my lips. Insult was added to injury when my mother brushed my short hair and put the little headdress on her angry princess.

'Oh, now you are so sweet.'

Take it off. Take it all off. But nothing would come out. I just stood there, my face becoming sadder and sadder. By the time we left for the wedding I had managed to give myself tonsillitis.

I have friends now who would see this episode the same way as me. The young Chris could not find her voice to tell her mother how she felt in the dress. She had just swallowed the pain and kept her anger in. The anger came out in tonsillitis. The throat chakra was blocked.

Chapter 7
Moving from Nanty

'Isn't this exciting? We're going to be so happy.' My mum turned around in the passenger seat and beamed at the two of us sitting behind her. My favourite toys were packed in a cardboard box in the boot. Susan was sitting beside me, grinning from ear to ear.

'It's a lovely new house, kids, a bungalow!'

'Will I be able to see Andrew every day?' I asked.

'Not every day, but it's only a few miles away so we will see them often.'

Often wasn't good. Often wasn't even an exact number. It meant nothing to me but not every day, which was my huge problem with it.

We moved from King's Terrace when I was four, nearly five. We left the small valley, with its narrow-terraced streets and the comforting presence of my cousin, and went to a beautiful new build of bungalows outside of Bridgend, in a village called Penyfai. It was in a much brighter area. There were no slag heaps, no dust in the air and no terraced houses. This village was not a mining community. It had the air of an English hamlet about it. There was a beautiful small church, quaint brick houses and fields full of sheep. It was a village where the men commuted to the nearest towns and worked in white-collar jobs. It was a step up for my family in the eyes of my parents.

'Mum, when's Christmas?'

'That's a strange question love.'

'I need Santa to bring me new toys.'

'What's wrong with your old ones?' she laughed.

'They're no fun to play with.' My face was set in a scowl.

My mother looked at me sitting on the floor of my bedroom, emptying toys from a cardboard box.

'But look,' she said, holding up a rag doll with a pink pinafore, 'you've a lovely dolly here from your Auntie Sadie, and your jigsaw puzzle of Sooty and Sweep and a nurse's outfit.'

'I don't want them.'

'But you're lucky to have them. Lots of little children have no toys.'

I didn't care what lots of little children had elsewhere in the world. I knew what I wanted and it wasn't in the cardboard box.

'Can we go to see Andrew?'

'Not now, love, we have to fetch your sister from school soon.'

'I want to play with him and his toys.'

'But you have your own. Just as good.'

I threw the rag doll on to the floor.

Moving house was not the wonderful, happy event that my mother extolled. I had no little boy my age to play with and I also had to go to school in Tondu. The old school house is gone now. I remember very little of this period, except that I was terrified. Susan was in a different school and I was very upset at being cut off from my family all day.

My mother held the little tunic out for me to wear. 'Isn't this lovely, your new school uniform.'

'I don't want to go to school.'

'But you have to, love, every little boy and girl goes to school when they're five.'

'I don't want to go. I want to stay here with you.'

'Well I don't have time to argue with you, so you have to put your uniform on and go to school like everyone else.' My mother held out the tunic and jumper with a cold look.

What if I don't feel like everyone else? What if the tunic is stupid and ridiculous?

Why can't I wear my shorts? At home, I could escape the confines of a dress until church on Sunday, but in school the uniform was mandatory. I started to realise that the world was not accommodating for a child like me. I wasn't the girl with pigtails or the boy with a pocket full of marbles. I felt an outsider with them all. I wanted to go back to King's Terrace and be out in the fields, playing our innocent games. School labelled and defined me.

Wrought iron gates, taller than me and dark and cold, I remember my small fingers wrapped around the metal, my knuckles white; my mother standing the other side, entreating me to go in out of the soft September rain, wanting to see a smile on my face but expecting the worst.

'You'll enjoy it. Don't cry.'

I shook my head, my fingers turning whiter.

A firm hand came down on my shoulder. 'Into class you go now, let your poor mother leave.'

I couldn't breathe then. The world darkened, the sky disappeared, replaced by a flaky painted ceiling, with six large hanging lights, their shades covered in a grey film of dust.

'Christine Ricketts!' a stern voice bellowed out from behind a large table, covered with small copybooks. 'Answer child!'

It was like the wedding again, my voice lost.

'Answer if you are here!'

I don't want to be here. I don't want to talk to you or be in your class in this stupid uniform. Then he was standing in front of me, his hand on my shoulder, his face large and red.

'I presume you are the Ricketts child?'

I nodded.

'Then answer!' His voice was loud, aggressive.

'Sorry.'

'Sorry, sir!'

'Sorry, sir.' I felt it then, a slight wetness. I didn't flood completely but it gave me a damp feeling and I felt like crying. I want to go home, sir. He didn't hear me. I hadn't said anything.

'Did you enjoy school today? What did you do?' My mum was smiling at me as she walked me up the hill towards Penyfai, my hand clenching hers.

I hated it but I'm not going to tell you. Little boys don't cry. The teacher said so when Arthur Jones spilled his bag of crisps and tears came into his eyes.

'It was okay. I liked mathematics. It's easy.'

'Well that's good. I liked maths too when I was in school.'

The mathematics was easy. It was the easiest part of the day. The playground was the hardest. The little girls were showing their dolls to one another that they had brought to school in their bags. The little boys wouldn't play with me.

There was no Andrew.

Chapter 8
Confusion mounts

'Watch the needle when you put it on, careful not to scratch it.' Dad stood so close when he watched you, worried about his new acquisition. He was almost mimicking the movement of placing the needle on the surface of the small vinyl disc.

'This is the latest Beatles single,' he said, his eyes showing excitement, 'only released last week – "Ticket to Ride".'

'What are the Beatles?' I asked.

'They're the best out there,' my father answered enthusiastically. 'Well, it's between them and the Rolling Stones.'

'I prefer the Beatles,' Susan said, smiling at Dad.

'I prefer the Rolling Stones,' I countered.

Susan looked at me. 'Name one of their songs then?'

I coughed slightly and looked at my dad for help.

'Why don't we just listen to "Ticket to Ride"?' he suggested.

Susan dug me and smirked, sitting down close to Dad. 'I do love the Beatles,' she said.

When the record was finished, Dad carefully removed the needle from the black surface and picked up the 45 gently, handing it to Susan. 'Now you put this back into its dust cover so it doesn't get scratched.'

'Can't I do it, Dad?' I asked.

'No, your sister is older and when you're her age you can do it for me.'

Dad religiously stored his records in their little white covers. He put them away neatly after playing, to avoid scratches and dust. He was always instructing both of us about how to take care of them.

'Don't handle them that way! You have to carefully hold them at the very edges, without even placing a finger on them. If they get scratched, the needle will jump.'

Dad never played the records quietly. It was always a noisy, happy experience, with singing and sometimes dancing. It was the one thing Susan and I both enjoyed doing together – listening to 45s with Dad. Dad could sit for hours listening to music and he was happy to share his music with us. My father appears before my eyes every time I hear certain songs.

He was a good father in many ways. My mother has often recalled how he gave up his lawn bowling club on a Saturday so that he could be with us – taking us to the cinema to watch the latest Disney, or for a drive to the park or the beach. We did everything as an extended family. My father's little Mini Cooper would hold my mum, dad, sister, grandparents and me, along with swimming costumes and towels. With no seatbelts and the engine labouring under the weight, we would head off for Port Talbot or Porthcawl with buckets and spades and a picnic all squashed into the boot. It was usually my mother's parents that we took with us. Miriam and Tom were ever-present weekenders.

Picnics were fun. Days at the beach, wearing my shorts and sandals, were manna from heaven. It was at the beach that Dad brought history to life.

'Put the heap of sand to one side, we need a bigger hole than that.'

Aberavon was fantastic for making sandcastles and Dad was a master sandcastle builder. On our knees, we would scoop out buckets of sand to make a large mound. Then delicately, with the straight edges of a little spade, Dad would sculpt out a detailed Norman castle from Welsh sand. It would have a moat, drawbridge, ramparts, turrets – nothing would be overlooked.

'Can I collect shells for windows, Dad?'

'Absolutely! And if you can find a bird's feather we can use it for our flag.'

Susan would sometimes help but usually she would just sit next to Granny and read her book.

My older sister doted on Granny Miriam and thus I always had Grandpa Tom and Dad to myself. If we three weren't building castles, we were playing beach cricket. My grandfather loved sport. He was accomplished at all of the more working-class sports – darts, pool and soccer. He won trophies in the first two but his talent was hidden in the third. He was throwing a ball at me from the time I was two and I eagerly participated. I had inherited his hand-eye coordination and he had forgotten that I was supposed to be a little girl. The latter, of course, I was desperately pleased about. Tom was my favourite grandparent at an early age. Where Gran was austere, sensible and almost frightening, Granny Miriam was womanly and always ready for a natter or a gossip. Grandpa Tom was a young boy at heart. When he was older and we were living in Ireland, he climbed the round Napoleonic tower on Dalkey Island and sat astride, laughing at the others down below, to the sheer panic of my mother. He had no fear. During his working life, he would fix the broken machinery down a mine or clear the shaft after a collapse or accident. He was used to living with danger.

At five I was probably the only kid on the street in Penyfai who knew the football teams in the English and Scottish leagues. Tom played the pools. At the weekend, he would listen carefully to the results of all the matches, marking down the draws and score draws and adding up his points. I never understood the way it worked but I used to memorise each result in case he missed one. There were some strange teams that I had to learn, especially in Scotland where Forfar 4 - Fife 5 was a possible score. Tom made me fanatical about soccer.

I always had a ball with me. Visits to the beach were perfect for playing sport. In the playground, I had still not broken into the ranks of the boys, but on the beach I could play sport with anyone who was happy to be out in the sun.

Grandpa Tom and Dad often played beach cricket with me. We would buy a small set, consisting of stumps, ball and bat, at a beach kiosk and set up our field on the flat sand. Dad loved his cricket and knew all the rules. He would tease my grandpa who wasn't as sure of the terms.

'Now, Tom, no bowling googlies.'

'I wouldn't know if I did,' Tom would laugh.

'Get in close, Christine. I will bowl your poor grandpa out with this one.'

But, more often than not, the ball would fly over our heads and thud softly into the sand, yards away, and Grandpa would grin at my father as he raced from end to end, making runs for his score.

I never seemed to mind being called Christine in my earlier years. It was just a name. It didn't bother me until much later, when I realised that people made distinctions based on my name. However, even at a young age, I was bothered at being called a girl. Mum and Dad persisted on telling others that they had two daughters and I was supposed to be one of them.

'Can we join in your cricket match with you and your son?' a man asked, gesturing to his son, standing quietly alongside him.

'Of course,' my dad replied. 'But this is actually my daughter.'

I would try to hit the ball harder then. I would play with a fierce determination, almost too aggressively.

I am a boy. What is wrong with you people? Don't I look like a boy? I was taller and stronger than the little boy standing by his father. I liked football and guns and train sets. I hated dolls and silly toy handbags with pretend lipsticks and flowery purses. But there was no point. My behaviour never made my parents change their response.

In school they insisted I was a little girl too. What made them so sure? Why was I a girl in their eyes? It was just because someone had decided it. I had never seen my parents naked. I didn't know what anatomical parts they had. I didn't know the physical differences between men and women. I only knew how they were treated.

So, I didn't like meeting new people. It was always where the misrepresentations began – 'This is our youngest/ (or later) middle daughter, Christine.' Even writing these words jar with me. I am Chris, nobody's daughter but my parents' child. I feel the emotion of those words. I feel the sickness in my stomach and the anxiety in my chest. It is a physical manifestation of the emotions of those days. Writing is cathartic, as I have spent a great deal of my life blocking memories of my childhood, memories of being misrepresented and misunderstood. They are jarring times. A lovely day at the beach could be ruined by just one simple introduction.

Even at the age of six, I knew I wanted to be a boy. Actually it ran deeper. I thought I was a boy. There are numerous photos of me holding or kicking a ball, dressed in a variety of shorts and T-shirts with a big grin on my face. It is always strange to look back at them. I can see the happiness in that moment and the lack of physical complication in that prepubescent existence, before my sexual body became more obvious to the world. The child in those photographs doesn't look like a little girl. There is no sign of one, and it makes me happy to see that, even at this stage of my life.

In fact, one of the photos of me that I love the best was taken when I was fourteen. I am gangly and male in my physique and facial expression. If the photograph was shown to a complete stranger, their guessing at the sexuality of that teenager might prove erroneous, as even I cannot see the female that was soon to emerge like an alien.

Chapter 9
Leaving the homeland

The boat lurched across the waves. The trip was four and a half hours of constant thudding, as the hull dropped back into the water. My mother was hanging on to the side of the boat, her face green about the gills. Behind her, my sister Sarah slept in her buggy, oblivious to the nauseated people around her.

'Come on,' Dad said, 'let's go and get something to eat.'

Susan shook her head. She was upset. She didn't want to leave. This was unfair. She thrust her head further into her book. Dad and I disappeared into the bowels of the boat. The canteen was mostly empty, except for hardened truckers.

'Sausage and chips for you?' my father asked.

I nodded.

The sausages were bigger than the ones I had eaten at home. The chips were greasier. Dad ate pudding, egg and bacon with his. It was my first taste of travelling and the food seemed as exciting as the adventure. I was off to a new country and everything had a chance to be better.

My family left Wales when I was six. At home there were five of us in the family now. Sarah had been born the October before we left Wales. She was barely nine months when we moved to Ireland. My dad was moved to Dublin with his work. Many years earlier, my mother had persuaded him to apply for a job vacancy in the company where she worked.

After the mines, Revlon – a large American cosmetics company – was the biggest employer in the valleys. It was a good move. My father progressed through the accountancy side of the business without exams or credentials but through hard work and a pleasant personality. He was a reliable worker, a meticulous accountant and he loved his job. I asked him about it only a year before he died and his eyes almost lit up. They were some of the best days of his life. I was so pleased that he could say that about his working life. We spend so much of our lives in work.

In 1965, my father was offered promotion to Australia. The house, the schools, all the background details were worked out. It seemed as if it was inevitable. My parents knew all the details of the move. It was to be a huge upheaval, leaving grandparents and cousins, but the prospect was also so good for a young family. Rather than the rain and coal dust-covered valleys, we would be growing up in sunny New South Wales with a beach lifestyle and loads of fresh air.

And then my mother found out that she was pregnant with my younger sister.

'I can't go, John.'

My dad paced the kitchen and looked at the floor. He understood, but what would the company say? 'What about my promotion, our new life? Bringing up a new baby in Australia won't be that bad.'

'I can't do it without my mum's support. I can't do it without family around me – moving to a new house, thousands of miles away, no friends, you working all hours. It won't work.'

The whole move to Australia was cancelled. We had all come so close to living a life down under. In those days, it was only £10 each to travel to Australia. It was a ridiculously small price, created as an attraction for people to emigrate there. Instead of the sun and sand of New South Wales, we ended up travelling to rain-soaked Dublin. Our timing couldn't have been worse. The Troubles had just begun in Northern Ireland and we were British citizens, living in the southern Republic.

Growing up in the Republic in the 1960s and 1970s was a strange time. My father had asked the last holder of his post in Dublin where he should send us to school. My family knew little about Ireland and needed the advice. The advice he gave them had long-term ramifications on all our lives.

'Put them in a Protestant school. You'll fit in better there. They're a different breed from the Catholics, more like the British.'

But the people of the Welsh valleys are not like the British, they are more Celtic. They aren't correct in their behaviour, or cautious, but effusive and rebellious. The Protestant Irish at the time were a small circle, with elitist pretensions and a mode of behaviour more suitable to the British Raj than the Irish Republic. The Welsh on the other hand were from the subjugated stock of Britain and behaved more like the Catholic Celts – singing and dancing – not one stiff upper lip in sight. The Protestant Irish were, as coined by D. P. Moran in the nineteenth century, 'West Brits'. They came from moneyed backgrounds, went to private schools and hailed from a rich, Georgian Dublin.

Though we were from Britain, we were from a working-class background and most of the children in our Irish Protestant schools were very middle class. In national school, it was not so blatantly obvious, but it became more so in the private secondary school.

We arrived into Dublin in the summer of 1966. I was six, Susan was nine and Sarah was only nine months old. Tom and Miriam came with us to help with the move. Susan was distraught at leaving behind all her friends and her grandparents. From Dublin onwards, she became even more of a bookworm and we played even less. However, at first, I was less unhappy. Although sad at leaving Andrew and Gran behind, I saw this new move as a chance to make friends of my own age who were boys. In Penyfai, young boys had been sadly lacking.

Our new house had stairs. It was a three-bedroom, semi-detached house with a long back garden. It seemed much bigger than our bungalow in Penyfai, but Mum preferred her smaller Welsh house. She had been happy there. When Australia fell through, Dad was offered a promotion to Ireland instead. My grandparents were all amenable to visiting in the holidays, so it seemed a good compromise.

The first day we moved in, Mick appeared. He was Catholic and Celtic down to his shoelaces. He was the man hired to paint and decorate our new home. He had a mop of premature grey hair and dark black eyebrows that incongruously gave a reflection of youth.

'Ah, you're here! Welcome to Dublin. Let's get some tea on, will we?'

He had about three million cups of tea in our house over the years. He became my dad's best friend. They were like chalk and cheese but inseparable. Although my father disliked nearly everything about Irish politics and Irish religion, he managed to create a life-long friendship with a man who was as Irish as a pint of Guinness. And they both drank a fair few of those together.

Everyone on the street was Catholic except for one couple and us. This other family was very quiet and had only one daughter. She was a pretty little girl and, although close enough to my age, we had nothing in common.

Her family always seemed well-off. She was given every toy, bike or game before the rest of us. The father drove a Jaguar, and the mother had a car before most of the other women on the street could even drive. It was a fashionable Mini. They also had a conservatory when the rest of the street had only small patios or concrete paths. Although they were Irish, they had extremely different accents from the rest of the community around them. To my young ears, they sounded posh. However, they were extremely nice people, even if they were a different culture from the rest of the road. My family didn't seem to fit in with them or the Catholic Irish around us. It didn't help that my mother was not particularly a 'talker'. She was never the type to stand at her garden gate and discuss the problems of the world. She had an antipathy to nosey neighbours, so much so that she disregarded the wheat with the chaff sometimes.

Our first summer in Ireland was one of getting used to the new environment. We lived in a new housing estate in an area that was almost rural. Our address was attached to the nearest local village, which had one pub, one shop, a large Catholic church and a library. Today the whole area is a busy suburb of Dublin, criss-crossed with roads and houses.

My older sister and I could cycle or walk to school in those days. There were fewer cars on the roads and people felt less anxious about allowing their kids out. My mother didn't have a car, but when we were very young, she would walk us to school and back. I played on the street outside my house with the boys. I did fine at school, but not particularly brilliantly.

My older sister was the straight-A student. She was top of most of her classes throughout her schooling. It was her forte – learning. Mine was running around playing sport and irritating her. We didn't have a particularly good relationship. She always had a vocabulary that I couldn't match. It was not so much sibling rivalry but sibling warfare. Mostly I tried to keep out of her way. I think my arrival into the world was difficult for Susan. I was not born into a harrowing situation. Mum didn't go through any medical trauma with my birth, and both parents happily brought me home.

My younger sister, on the other hand, was my little treasure from the start. I shared a room with Sarah and a strong bond developed between us. When I could read, I recited stories to her while my parents were watching TV. But I preferred inventing stories of my own. It was with her that I first developed my love of storytelling. It was an avenue for my imagination. Sarah was also a good listener. She was a very bright, adorable child. That first summer though, she was of no support as a sibling. She was in a playpen or a pushchair or sleeping. I had to make friends of my own. Having Granny and Grandpa with us helped.

My grandfather never took a drink until he was in his thirties and then he developed a rapid fondness for it. Later, my dad christened him 'Two Pint Tom' because after two pints of Guinness he was unable for much more, but without the two he was ill at ease and fidgety. Walks with my grandparents were littered with stops at pubs, but these walks are part of my fondest memories. Susan rarely came with us that first summer. She was still angry at the move and preferred to stay in her bedroom, while Mum cleaned the house and emptied boxes. Granny would push Sarah along in her pram and chat away to her in a language of 'oohs' and 'ahs'.

Neither my Grandpa Tom nor my Granny Miriam ever made me dress like a girl or behave like one, so I loved these walks. They allowed me to be myself and run wild with the boys. I played football at every park we passed and I became friends with more than one young lad from the Noggin.

I think Grandpa felt at home there. Council houses lined the roads, with grey facades of rough cement. Grandpa saw it as his type of community. There were always more men out of work than in work and the bookies had a constant queue. The mid-1960s did not see a roaring economy in Ireland. The betting shops and pubs were a popular venue for those left behind.

'Hi Mister, can we play with your ball?'

Grandpa looked quizzically at the young boy who was chewing gum and kicking the curb with his shoe.

'Well, Christine, will we let them join us?'

'Is she a girl, mister? Jaysus, we thought she was your son.'

Solace and anger at the same time – they saw me at first and then they were told my name.

I'm not a bloody girl. The silent voice again. Why didn't I shout it out?

'So Christine, will we let them play with our ball?'

'We will play, Grandpa, and we will win.'

'You won't win. You're a girl.' It was a lanky, thin boy looking at me curiously, sucking a tube of sherbet. I wanted to ram it down his throat.

'Pass it to me.'

'Pass the ball to me.'

Seven boys played, running around the green field, jumpers for goalposts, enjoying a match with my grandfather. Granny was pushing Sarah around, loudly singing Mary Poppins tracks. Meanwhile, I ran alongside the action consumed with frustration. Grandpa wouldn't notice. He was too busy dribbling around four young boys. The match would usually last until Grandpa was thirsty.

'We won.' Grandpa handed me my ball back and we continued down the road to Dun Laoghaire.

I didn't win, Grandpa, but I will next time.

I was always improving my football skills. When Tom had gone home and there was no one left to play with, I practised at home against the back wall. I always felt that I had a lot to prove. Sometimes, when my hair was cut short and I had the right shorts on, boys would not realise that I was a girl and these were my happiest moments. I could actually fool them. I would play and laugh and joke with them as if I was the most natural boy in the group. My name was helpful too. In my life outside of my family, I started to introduce myself as Chris. My lack of femininity would do the rest. I began to see Christine as a label that I didn't want.

In those early years, I could easily see the boy in me, except for those terrible days when my mother would make me wear a dress. A dress was my idea of personal hell. On days such as those, Sundays and birthdays, I would feel ill, sick and unhappy. There are many family albums containing pictures of a moody Chris in a dress. I couldn't see how I could possibly grow up to be a woman and be expected to wear dresses all the time as my mother did. I just wasn't made the same. Even worse were the tights that I saw my mother struggle into; tights with weird gussets and ladders that frequently appeared following an overlong fingernail accident. My mother would mutter under her breath and dive back into her drawer for a pair without an offending hole. In my view, women's clothes were awkward to wear, awkward to put on and horribly flowery.

It was at night in bed that the dreams of being something different would take shape. I would dream of growing up to play football with Liverpool, Chelsea or Leeds, my three favourite teams. I could remember every player in every position, and in bed I would take out the little shortbread tin from under the wooden frame and look through the pictures on the well-worn football cards. Then I would allow my imagination to take over.

A whole alternative life would play out when I closed my eyes at night.

There were times, especially in my teen years, when I was more than happy to go to bed so that I could go back to my fantasy world. There was one particular fantasy that I used to play through nearly every night when I was thirteen, but the details of it are shadowy now. I only remember that it involved me and a very attractive woman, and I was James Bond.

However, up until I was ten, I was still convinced that I could beat my body into submission if I just worked hard enough at it. Playing sport was how I was going to physically create a strong and muscular physique.

Even the books that I read and the comics that I bought were an obvious clue as to my inner sexuality. I read the '64-pagers', the war comics – macho heroes blowing up the world as they fought for king and country. As a young twelve-year-old in school, I knew far more about the Second World War than any other girl in the class. The planes of the Luftwaffe, the Panzer tanks and the strategy of Blitzkrieg were all in the pages of my comic books. I found them exciting and I identified more with the characters in these war comics than the females running around screeching in the Chalet School books. Actually, to be honest, I don't know what the girls do in these books, as I have never even read one of them. I am just stereotyping which, in itself, is sad.

My partner still keeps her collection of these novels. They remind her of her youth and they remind me of how different we are. She was so happy to be a little girl and read female-themed books and wear feminine clothes. On the other hand, besides the war comics, the books that I loved were more neutral of any gender preference – the Secret Seven or the Famous Five. However, I always identified with the male characters in these books. I never saw myself as one of the girls.

Then there were the football magazines. I would always have a large collection of these under my bed. The information of who was transferring from one club to another and who was in line for top goal scorer was fascinating to me. I also collected every football World Cup coin and the World Cup cards from petrol stations. Ricardo Villa, Osvaldo Ardiles, Gerd Muller and Franz Beckenbauer – along with other lesser-known names that many lesser football fanatics would have well forgotten – were my heroes.

There was no place for anything feminine in my life. I couldn't stand having pathetic, girly stuff anywhere near me. I was a bit like the horrid kid in *Toy Story*. I would prefer to dismember dolls in a game of war, rather than brush their hair or change their clothes. The maternal instinct was non-existent. My heroes were footballers; my dolls were action men. When my mother decided that it was time that I became a girl, ready for puberty, and guns and cars were no longer allowed amongst my toys, I improvised and made them out of Lego. Lego became my favourite toy. Ships, tanks, cars, guns and castles could all be created, brick by little brick. I would often find my macho creations broken into pieces by the time I went to play with them the next day.

Chapter 10
National school

My national schooling in Ireland hurt most days – the skirts I had to wear, the role I had to play and the way my life was suddenly being forced to progress along gender-defined lines. Before schooling, being female hadn't really impacted upon me too often, except for the Sunday dress for church and the introductions to new people. I could happily eat, sleep and dream as I wanted to. In school, however, I was almost segregated by the uniforms and separate gym times. Nonetheless, it didn't deter me from my course.

My friends were all male. I cannot remember one girl from my class, but I can recite the names of many boys. At break and lunchtime, I would play football with them in the school yard. My football skills were often much better than most of the boys. I had been taught well by Grandpa. The boys never left me out in the early days. I was one of the first picked for teams and sometimes I even got to pick the team.

My best friend in national school was a boy called Jeremy. He was the quiet, more thoughtful one and I was the noisier. He was a slimmer build, with a small face and two very prominent front teeth. The boys called him 'Bugs Bunny' but they still liked him. He was too nice not to like. It was just their way.

'Um, our mums have signed us up for ballroom dancing.' Jeremy looked at me with a shrug of his shoulders.

'I don't want to do it.' I looked at him with a furrowed brow. 'I'm ten not sixty. It's for old ones!'

'It might be fun.'

'It's silly.'

'You can be my partner. Then it won't be so bad.'

'Really?' I asked with more furrowing of the brow. 'Dancing around a floor to boring music, with parents watching?'

We danced, but I led. His two left feet prevented it looking anything like a waltz, but our parents enjoyed it. They were laughing enough. I was counting loudly – 'one, two, three, one, two, three, watch the toes, ouch, there's another one.'

We were inseparable in national school. He was the kinder, warmer person. He had more of a feminine side than I did. He was willing to play with a girl as his best friend because hanging around with the boys was too rough. I liked being with Jeremy because he had all the toys that I wanted to play with, and he was not shy about letting me use them. He was never mean.

He died as a teenager from a sudden death, sitting in a chair at home. He had an aneurism – a headache, a look of sympathy from his mum and he was gone. He was such a close friend in my national school days. We drifted apart when we went to secondary school. He was becoming the boy that I wanted to be and in some ways I was jealous of him. I was becoming the feminine figure that I didn't want him to see, and I believed that our relationship couldn't stay the same as my appearance changed. In my mind, our friendship was built on different grounds.

I wasn't always with Jeremy. Playing with him after school had to be done by arrangement. He lived too far for me to walk to on my own. So the rest of the time I played with the numerous children on our estate. Three boys around my age were my closest friends. Two of the boys were brothers. They were also coincidentally from Wales. They were good-looking kids with sallow skin, dark hair and brown eyes. They hung around with a smaller, Irish boy who lived right at the end of my street – Dennis, also known, unoriginally, as 'the Menace'. Dennis was a barrel of a boy with a wide jaw and round cheeks.

'Pass the ball, Stephen, stop hogging it.'

'In yer face, Kev, I'm scoring. Watch out, Menace!'

It was up to me to tackle him. Only I stood in the way of his victory. Dennis wasn't much of a goalie.

'Take him out of it, Chris,' the Menace roared.

I slid into the tackle, we crashed to the floor and then it happened, all too quickly. He rolled on top of me, pinned me down and pulled up my shirt.

'You've got little boobs! You've got little boobs!'

He may as well have told me that I was an alien.

'I don't,' I cried, trying to hold back the tears.

Kevin and Dennis had rushed over and were standing above us, laughing.

'Ha, ha. You've got boobs.'

I struggled to move him off but he was sitting across my stomach with his hands holding on to my T-shirt. I lost it completely. We were all young and our bodies were changing, but mine was changing differently from theirs. I punched him, smacked him on the nose, until it bled.

'Jesus Christ, I was only messing with you. What the hell is wrong with you?' Stephen stood up, his nose pumping.

Kevin and Dennis looked at me.

I ran. I ran home, the tears streaked across my face.

Red-hot anger!

'I hate you.'

I was not shouting at Stephen, Kevin or Dennis. Standing in my bedroom, looking in the mirror, looking at what they had seen, I shouted at my body for betraying me. I kept shouting in my head for the next few months.

'Christine, what are you doing, stand up straight, there's a good girl. You're slouching.'

Shut up Mum! I'm not your girl. And stop calling me Christine!

'Are you okay, is school not going well?'

I tried walking with my shoulders rounded, trying to hide the existence of developing breasts. I tried to bind them but it felt awkward. I withdrew from playing football with boys. I hated them as much as I hated myself. They did not see me as I did. They saw me as another species – a girl.

This was soon backed up by another boy, but in a gentler way.

'Mum, I don't want to go to school tonight. I feel really sick.'

'Oh, but you have your play tonight. You can't let your school down. Dad and I will be there.'

'I know but I'm not well.'

'What's wrong, you look fine enough?'

'My stomach is in pain.'

'Oh, you're just nervous. It will be fine.'

The national school hall was packed with sixth class students, all dressed in costume. Out in front of the curtain, rows of neatly dressed parents sat, eager to see their child on stage. I was standing alone in the wings, watching a scene unfold. The teacher had made the horrifying decision of making me the princess.

'I don't want to be in the play, Mr Rowntree.'

'Nonsense, I've given you the part and I expect you to learn it and do your best.'

'But I'm not a good princess. I don't like princesses.'

'Well it won't hurt you to try. All experiences are worthwhile.'

He wasn't a teacher you argued with over anything, no matter how much it pained you. So I stood in the wings, wearing a dress and lipstick and felt sick to my stomach. I didn't feel beautiful. I felt a freak.

'Hello, Christine.' A boy from my class was standing beside me.

'Hello.'

'I like your costume.'

'I don't.'

'But you look beautiful.'

It wasn't the words that stunned me as much as the small kiss that he planted on my lips. I didn't respond. I just stared at him disbelievingly and then walked on the stage as my cue was given.

Chapter 11
Outside perfect, inside turmoil

It was not long after my starring role as the princess that I started secondary school – ironically an all-girls' school. It was a small, private, fee-paying school, close to 'St. Trinian's' in some of its mannerisms. We had potty school teachers, rickety old buildings and 'jolly hockey stick' students. These girls had a weird preoccupation with anyone who walked through the grounds in trousers. The poor postman was generally unsafe on the school premises, and any visiting brother became a mooned over photograph in a locker.

I hated secondary school. I hated it more than national school. There was no Jeremy, no football and no escape between 9 a.m. and 4 p.m. unless I was sick. I was incarcerated weekly with nothing but girls. I didn't particularly understand them, even though I had two sisters of my own. However, the fact that I was put in a single-sex school did give me some release from things. It meant that I could avoid the existence of boys, except on awkward social occasions. This was the odd blessing of my secondary school days. Whereas I had longed for the company of boys in my pre-teenage years, I now preferred to be away from them. I knew I could no longer exist with them on any level. I was not meant to beat them at football anymore, nor play rough games with them. I was supposed to fancy them and lose sleep over them as prospective boyfriends.

My feelings in my teenage years were very confused. Life became a bit unbearable. It was at this stage that my anger with my body started to manifest in physical ways. I developed asthma and eczema.

We had a very old-fashioned uniform of jumper, blazer and beret. I quite liked the blazer as I felt it looked boyish. So I set off for school on the first day feeling smartly dressed, almost happy to be going somewhere away from the boys in my national school. The gates to our school were quite imposing for a young first year, straight out of national school, where everything was small in comparison. They were wrought iron, firmly standing between two large pillars and embedded in a granite stone wall. Behind the gates, a tree-lined avenue stretched towards a Georgian house, flanked with old stables converted into classrooms. With a pretend air of knowing my way, I walked firmly into the grounds that first day. Susan was three years ahead of me in school and totally uninterested in my arrival. She was happier being there without me. I would become a burden again, which she hadn't missed when she had left national school.

'Show us your knickers.'

It was a very aggressive demand and the two girls asking were much older than me.

'Come on, new one, show us if you're wearing the school-required underwear. We're prefects and it's our job to make sure you're dressed appropriately.'

They may have had a smirk on their faces but I was not laughing. I stood before them timid and ashen-faced. Without waiting for a reply, they pulled up my skirt in the back to reveal the thick, woollen school underwear. I could hear them laughing as I scurried away into the depths of the drab buildings, looking for a friendly face. To me they were no better than the boys out in the garden who had pulled up my T-shirt. I didn't care if they were prefects, I hated them.

'Hello, can I sit here?'

The young girl looked back at me and pushed a straying lock of hair from her forehead. 'Are you meant to be in 1A?' she asked.

'I think so. I'm not sure.'

'Well these desks are actually taken. My friends and I have been in the Junior School together so we are sitting here.'

I sat behind the row and put my bag on the floor. The classroom was old and cold. There were no posters and drawings on the wall as in my national school. There was no colour anywhere. The desks were wooden and scratched. There was a hole in the top for an ink bottle and a lid that could be lifted, for storing books underneath. These storage spaces were to be useful for more than books, but a rotting banana could offend a whole classroom if a girl was careless.

The windows of my first classroom were high and dusty. Little webs hung in the corners and the odd crack ran down a pane. There were no blinds or curtains, no hint of comfort or warmth. As I sat taking in my surroundings, girls filtered in, two or three at a time, all in conversation, all excited. Some had long hair in braids, others had shoulder-length hair, just one or two had short hair like mine.

The teacher was a middle-aged woman, wearing a floral blouse tucked into a woollen skirt. 'Why don't I take the roll call girls and you can all say one or two things about yourself?'

The names began.

'Alexandra.'

'Present, Miss. I live just across the road from the school. I have one older sister in second year.'

'Dawn.'

'Present, Miss. I don't have a sister or brother and I like horses.'

A few girls nodded their heads in appreciation.

'Christine.'

There it was again – that name.

'Present, Miss. I have an older sister in fourth year and I like football.'

'We don't play football here, Miss Ricketts. It's a rough game.'

The girls nodded.

I soon found the interests of the girls were odd to me. At break-time and lunch, their conversations were usually about other girls, or clothes and pop groups. I never knew what to say. I wavered between being flippant to ultra-serious in my tackling of topics. I could never get the mood right. I really had no notion of how to be a girl. The topics that interested me were far from their conversational repertoire – the football, the war comics, the action films. My method of getting attention in class, or socially, was to tell a joke or make some poor girl the butt of my teasing. My teasing came from a place of anger and pain. I really wanted to be accepted and I realised that one particular girl was easy to tease. My tongue ran away with me. I bullied this poor girl in our class. I was not the only one who partook in it but I was probably the most adept at it. In my sad, pathetic way I wanted to belong, and teasing her was my way of pleasing others, although I'm sure many did not find me in the least bit funny. I was one of the best at making her life a misery. I am ashamed of that year of my life. It coincided with my worst period of adolescence and it showed that my anger towards myself could not readily be contained.

Karma did not let me escape its clutches though. I have been the person bullied in many situations since, and I met the same girl again when she was a married woman. She looked at me with the anger of that bullied child within, showing her contempt for me. She shamed me into reliving that horrible past behaviour.

'Do you know you made my life a misery in school?'

She didn't wait for a reply and I was too embarrassed to give one.

'You teased me relentlessly. I went home and cried most days.'

I apologised but it sounded pathetic. My apology didn't give her comfort. My squirming on my chair as an adult gave her far more. The admonishing of her school nemesis made her feel empowered. That was one of the worst moments of my adult life, especially as I had children of my own at that stage. To realise that I had hurt someone so badly was very difficult to take. It was a really hard conversation to forget. I relived my behaviour for years afterwards. Eventually I realised that my young school self was gone and I had to let it go as it was depressing me.

Chapter 12
Bad blood

Blood – sticky, oozy, brown then red – making its way down my inner thigh, the nightmare beginning. I was standing in the bathroom, toilet paper soiled, wondering whether I would die in that moment.

I had heard of periods, but only once.

But this was so much blood, was this healthy?

I cried.

What was happening to me? How do I leave the bathroom?

We only had one toilet in the house – a small room with just a toilet and a window. There was no bin in it. There was no place to hide anything. A roll of toilet paper and a bottle of Dettol was all that occupied the tiny room, except me and all the blood.

I had managed to get used to the growth of breasts but this – I didn't want this. I sat down on the toilet and cried again. I couldn't stay in there all day but I didn't want to leave. I didn't want to talk to my mother. I couldn't talk to Susan. We didn't talk. None of us talked about these things. They just happened.

I packed some tissue paper into my underwear and gingerly stood up. My bedroom door was close. I could escape into there.

No – that was a bad idea. I needed something to stop the blood. Maybe Mum knew something that women could do to stop this. Or maybe I was bleeding more than normal.

I didn't know what was normal.

Was this a period? Or was it a haemorrhage?

'Christine, are you in there?' A small knock on the door accompanied the question.

'Yes, Mum, I'll just be a minute.'

'Okay.'

'Mum?'

'Yes.'

'I'm scared.'

'What's wrong?'

'I'm bleeding.'

I opened the door and stood, tear-stained face looking out at her through the doorway.

'It's okay, don't panic! Remember the book I gave you to read? Didn't you read it?'

The book she gave me to read? It was a Kermit-green pamphlet book with a hopping bunny on the cover, surrounded by birds and bees. She had pushed it into my hand in the kitchen one day and told me to read it. The book would explain everything. I opened the first few pages and nearly puked. It had images of genitalia in it. I had never seen them before – especially a fully formed penis and testicles. I had only ever caught sight of my cousin's little one when we were very young at the beach when he was changing into his bathers. I had wondered at that stage where mine was.

'I didn't read it all. I didn't like it.'

'It's just a period. You've started your periods. You're a woman now.'

Do you hate me? How can you say that?

She couldn't have hurt me more.

I didn't want to have blood running down my legs once a month. What would happen when you bathed? Would the bath fill with blood? And how could I play sport like this?

'I'll get you a sanitary towel for the blood.'

I shut the bathroom door and waited. I felt nauseous. Could life get any worse? But it did. My mother arrived back with a plastic-wrapped package and a pair of strange underpants.

'You wear these pants. They have the hooks needed to attach the sanitary towel. Okay?'

No it's not okay. What part of this would ever be okay?

I shut the bathroom door, put on the strange underwear and opened the plastic wrapper. The towel was huge – long, thick and white with two small looped strings on either end. It was like having a squashed soft banana between your legs. How could anyone walk wearing these? They were definitely going to be obvious in tight jeans or trousers.

I spent the rest of the day in my bedroom. I spent the next two days in my bedroom. I didn't go to school. I had stomach cramps. I had everything imaginable that I could tell my mother. However, on the third day she refused to allow the pretence to go any further.

'You really can't be that bad now.'

'But I am.'

'Well you have to go back to school. This will happen every month and you have to get used to it.'

I wouldn't play sport after school when I returned, and I didn't want to do PE class.

The PE teacher was not very helpful. 'Why are you not wearing your gym uniform?'

'I can't do gym, Miss.'

'Why? Have you broken a leg?' She was known for her sarcasm.

'I'm not well, Miss.' There were little beads of sweat on my upper lip.

'Well, you need a note from your mother.'

'I don't have one.'

'Well that's because you look perfectly fine to me. Get changed!'

I didn't want to tell her why I couldn't put on the small skirt. I didn't want her to know intimate things about me. I didn't want her to think I was a fully operational woman.

So I hid – behind the lockers in a dusty corner of a converted stable, behind the bins in the yard and in the bushes to the side of the hockey pitch. I hid most weeks and waited for the search party to come. I was to have a running battle with that PE teacher every month for five years. I refused to do PE when I had the curse!

The onset of periods affected my life hugely. I didn't want to run around and play any sport with the fear of what might trickle down my leg. I had heavy periods, uncomfortable periods, and my stomach cramped as if I was giving birth to some monster. And for me, it was a monster, a vile evil disgusting monster. I didn't feel that it was my rite of passage as I didn't feel that I *was* a woman. I was a boy. How did my body not know or understand that? How could it be so at odds with my feelings? I began to hate my body more. I hated my breasts the most. They were so obviously female. There was some hope of hiding a period from the rest of the world but the growing breasts were like two beacons of femininity, and all I wanted to do was to cut them off. It was a very destructive thought to have towards my body. I became a very angry person inside.

Chapter 13
Desires

Most teachers in the school added to my unhappiness. It was not really their fault. I just didn't want to be there. However, one particular lady upset me from the very start. My fourth English class was the beginning of my utter dislike of her. She was Deputy Principal and a woman I feared for six years. She was a spinster and dressed like one. She wore woollen skirts and knitted cardigans and well-ironed blouses. She taught us *Romeo and Juliet* by assigning the class parts from the play. I always sat in the front row. I was earnest to please and didn't want to be seen as a naughty, back-row talker.

Her voice was always imperious, the words strongly delivered.

'Now I will give out parts, starting with the front row.'

Her beady eyes looked down imperiously at us through her spectacles.

'You can be Romeo, you can be Juliet, you can be Tybalt and you …' she stared at me pointedly, 'you can be nothing as I can't really understand a word you're saying with that accent.'

I didn't reply. I was twelve and terrified of her. I had been living in Ireland for five years. My accent wasn't that strong. At least I thought it wasn't, but then maybe I seemed uncouth to the teachers and girls around me with their cultured accents. After all, it was a private school.

I did have friends in school, but many were on a temporary basis of a year or two at most; they never really lasted. I would get to know them only to the extent that I would never have to tell them my inner thoughts, as I was pretty sure at this stage that they were not normal thoughts. With the onset of puberty, I had begun to fancy girls.

Luckily, in those early years, I never fancied any girl in my class, as that would have been a disaster. They were so giddy and high-pitched. But there were a few girls in the years above me that made my teenage years difficult, as I tried to hide a crush on them.

My friends in school were either the sporty kids or the academic types. I fitted in with the academics quite well as they were less likely to share their deep emotions and they were generally too busy working to be overly energetic on the social front. Others I bonded with because they were not mainstream thinkers. However, looking back, they were probably all just normal young girls and I was the odd one. I had just transferred my oddness on to them.

The hockey types I could talk to about sport, although their friendship fell off during the latter years of schooling. They were more socially adept than me and I found their constant desire to meet with boys uncomfortable. It was fine at an early age because nothing was attempted. It was all just talk. However, the older we became the more was expected.

And there was a paradox going on – I was an introverted extrovert. I wanted to be socially acceptable and part of the gang but I was scared of social gatherings. I did not understand how to behave with either the girls or the boys. I tried hard to show that I liked the opposite sex. My nickname in school at one stage was 'Flirty Girty' as I 'scored' so many boys in one year.

For me it was all about 'one-night stands'. It created a front of gender normality with my classmates, but it didn't allow for any meaningful relationships to develop, which would have put me in an awkward position. I could never have allowed anything to develop beyond a very innocent first kiss. So I moved through boys with alarming alacrity, earning a ridiculous nickname in the process. It is weird to write all this down. I have no warmth for myself in retrospection.

I always imagined kissing girls while I was kissing boys. When I was with someone they were not really with me at all, as my full self very rarely turned up. It was all a big game, a show for watching society. On dates with boys, I would appear confident, happy and interested but at home later I would reconnect with my fantasies and leave the sham behind. At home, throughout my teenage years, I had constant fantasies of being with girls.

I did have a few exceptions to the constant 'one-nighters'. I kept some boyfriends around for their interesting conversations and cars. Mostly they were the sexually inhibited or shy boys who were nervous about going past first base. It was a running joke in our house that I never went out with anyone who didn't have a car to chauffeur me around in. This was for the most part true, except for my first real boyfriend. I was with him for a year and I liked him a great deal, but it was more as a friend than a boyfriend. In fact I think I even saw him as an older role model where boys were concerned. If I had been in the right body I would have probably had a schoolboy crush on him as an older jock. He was very warm and kind. I broke it off with him as I could not hurt him by continuing a relationship that was false. However, because I liked him so much I had very conflicting issues with regard to my sexuality at that time.

I knew that I wanted to be a boy and I knew that I fancied girls but my body was feminine, and it did have a sexual desire that needed feeding. In fact, it was a very strong desire. I was confused as to how to work out this conundrum because I knew that I was not gay. In fact, the thought of doing anything gay with a girl was out of the question. I knew I had to find sexual fulfilment from boys but I didn't know how to play the girl with them and I also didn't know if I wanted them to touch me, as that would have felt strangely gay. It was a total minefield.

Concentrating on my homework was difficult with the issue of my sexuality often worrying me. I spent most of my nights in my bedroom penning short stories rather than working at mathematics or French. Writing was always a great escape mechanism for me. I wrote many essays for English that took me to foreign countries and exciting situations. Every lead character was a male. Did my teachers ever notice this bias?

At night, with the duvet pulled up high to blank out the world, I escaped into these male fictional characters, kissing the female supporting role before I went off to war or revolution. In fact, I often did more than kiss her. These were the sexualised dreams that fed my sexual preference. I was really no better than a Walter Mitty. I lived in my daydreams. Even during the day, I spent countless hours lying on my bed, with the pretence of a very bad cold, literally acting out a scene from my alternative existences.

However, my sleeping dreams were a completely different world. I would have hated living in them. I still would. From a very young age, I was plagued with nightmares. Even before going to sleep I would believe that there were people in my bedroom – just sitting, walking or talking. Sometimes they were threatening, with abusive bad language, shouting and screaming. My mother would invariably have to rescue me.

'Come on love, you're only dreaming. They're not real. It's just your imagination.'

'No Mum, they're there. Please don't go.'

'Look, the light is on and there's no one in your room. It's cold. You'll be alright. I'll sit here for a while but then I'm going back to bed.'

But when she went, and the light was out, I still saw them. I saw them and I hid from them. I closed my eyes tightly and hid under my blankets. It was not my imagination. They were there. They still are.

My sleepless nights were not just caused by my fear of having bad nightmares, I was also afraid of my habitual sleepwalking. I sleepwalked frequently and to such an extent that my parents feared for my safety. I would leave my bedroom, race down the stairs and attempt to go out into the night, only clothed in my pyjamas. I was very difficult to live with, and I didn't grow out of those frequent nightmares until very recently. They were a constant feature of all my early teenage years right up until I met my present partner. Her soothing presence has given me far more calmness before going to sleep.

I still have the occasional nightmare, but I can control them more now. I have learned to pre-order a good dream or change the vision in a bad dream. However, sometimes the horrible and the macabre sneak through and I wake up in a sweat. The psychiatrist I saw at one stage said that it was probably my fears and anxieties coming out at night in my subconscious. I also have premonitions. These are not frequent but they do happen and they always contain a death.

One such premonition involved dark, deep water, the wind pulling the surface into small waves, a father showing his son how to put a worm on a line, the little boy's hand trembling with the cold. He catches his little finger on the barb. Ouch! His older brother laughs as he holds another rod over the water, hoping to be the first to catch a trout and impress their dad.

A fish!

Reel her in.

The older boy grins as he fights with the fish, the fish fights back, pulling on the line, struggling for life. His younger brother, moving across the seat to take a look, shakes the boat.

Be careful. Sit still. Too late!

The water is icy cold. His body slithers below the surface, eye to eye with the fish. A father's large hand leans over to grab his collar as he sinks. He misses. He tries again, tries too hard.

The boat upturns. The water has them all now. Cold and deep it sucks them in, and refuses to let go of its icy grip. A rod moves on the surface, a fish tugging it along. The black lake is eerily quiet again.

I sat the next day and shuddered when I read the newspaper. 'Three dead in a fishing accident on an Irish lake' was the headline, two boys and their father on a fishing trip.

Chapter 14
Battlegrounds

I hate myself.

I loathe my body.

I hate my life.

Notebooks full of angry words, paper covered with images of painful adolescence.

Having breasts, getting periods and developing into womanhood were all traumatic. A self-loathing started that was very negative both psychologically and physically. I quarrelled constantly with my older sister and sometimes even with my younger sister. I annoyed them with my macho behaviour. I demanded to watch *Match of the Day* on a Saturday night so that I could keep up with the football results; a fact about which I am still chastised by my sisters. It is mentioned most often in the retelling of our childhood years.

'Why does she have to watch *Match of the Day*? There's a good film on UTV. Please Dad?'

'No. We've been through this before. It's the only programme in the week that your sister really likes to watch.'

Then I would get the eyes. The eyes that said I hate you. But I didn't care, I hated her too – her clever mind, her girly looks and her pathetic boyfriends that came around to help her babysit.

Couldn't care less for your problem, Jimmy Hill was waiting!

Today, clashing programmes would not be a problem, the recording function eliminates the issue, but back then it was a constant cause of wars with my sisters. I was also rarely out on a Saturday night as I didn't feel comfortable socialising with boys or girls in a scenario that could become a dating one. I still watch *Match of the Day* with a wry smile for the irritation it caused my siblings.

It wasn't just my siblings that I irritated during my teenage years. I also had a volatile relationship with my father. It is difficult to say whether it was his fault or mine, probably both. I was unhappy being in my body and he was stressed out in work.

Dad worked long hours. He worked hard and expected to come home to a tidy house and three quiet, compliant daughters. I couldn't always be the daughter he wanted. In fact I saw myself as more of a son and I behaved like one.

Due to work, my father travelled abroad, fine dined and drank wine as well as whiskey. He developed diabetes but he was not diagnosed. Dad rarely went to the doctor. After a hard day at work, he would come home and expect my mother to have cooked a meal comparable to restaurant standards. He was more than fussy. Meals became a battleground.

'I'm not eating this. It's overcooked. It's undercooked. It's burnt. It's tasteless. It's smaller than theirs.'

My sisters and I would sit at the table and wait for the hostility to begin. It was always over food. He was a good man, a loving father and husband, but he could not control his irrational moods when he was tired. None of us knew that he was pre-diabetic. We just thought he was an angry man.

I hated the way he talked to my mother over unsatisfactory dinners. I had been there with her before he had arrived home, watching her worry as she cooked the meal, hoping it would be good enough. I would be furious inside when he would put his plate in the sink, the food untouched.

'I'm not eating that.'

'I'm sorry, what's wrong with it, love? Will I cook you something else instead?'

'I will have a fried egg and bacon.' I would see and hear Pop when I looked at him then.

Her own plate of food would go cold as she cooked him the alternative. My sisters and I would sit there while he left for the TV room to watch the news, the kitchen dead quiet, except for my mum dropping an egg into a frying pan, the spit of the oil breaking the stony silence.

I don't want to be a woman. I don't want to be treated this way.

I had seen it with Pop and Gran and now I was seeing it again.

The rest of the night would be silent.

Battles were not always so openly displayed, some were more insidious. We all knew that one of us had done something wrong but it was never mentioned by my father. He just gave us all the silent treatment and sent my mother to be the messenger. She would come into the bedroom and shake her head furiously at one of us.

'Who's done it this time?' she would say, holding a packet of tampons or, even worse, a sanitary towel in its wrapper, obviously left where it shouldn't have been.

'I found this on top of the toilet!'

Nobody would answer.

'You know you can't leave anything in the bathroom like this. Your father lives in this house too and it's unfair to him. It's not pleasant seeing these. It's bad enough he has to live with four women, without putting up with this.'

Three women, only three women! He was not alone. I was in the house too. But my body didn't support my claim and I hated it more.

'Well is one of you going to say something? Whose time of the month is it?'

It was a constant battle, the misuse of the toilet. We wanted to leave tampons and sanitary towels easily to hand, but Dad wanted us to hide them away. We could store them in the bathroom, next door, under the sink with the toilet cleaner and bleach, but otherwise they were not to be seen.

It was as if having a period was a dirty business. Unfortunately, I agreed with my father at the time. It was disgusting and shouldn't happen to me.

It was hardly surprising that during these teenage years I had the most combative years with my father. He didn't realise it but I saw myself as the young male in the household. I was constantly butting with him over issues that were common between young men and their fathers. However, my father didn't see them coming; he was blindsided by my female body to these attacks, especially the attacks in favour of my mother. I was very defensive about her. I was always trying to support her against him, protecting her, even when it was unnecessary. My mother could do no wrong in my eyes, whereas my father was an overbearing male who treated her poorly. I had an Oedipus complex that most young men would have found hard to emulate. Thus, my father and I battled. We battled over everything.

Chapter 15
The good times

There are two parts of my teenage years that I look back on fondly – one was playing hockey and the other was spending time with my grandmother, Gwladys, in Wales. In national school I had learned how to play hockey and was also coached in rudimentary cricket. Although I loved ball sports, I was so very quiet my first few days in secondary school that I completely missed the practices for first year students in those early weeks. I would usually go home straight after the final bell and sit in my bedroom, drawing or writing.

One afternoon, I ventured out to sit on the grass, too close to the hockey pitch. The hockey coach teacher decided that my laziness could not go without remark.

'Hello, you there with the book?'

Was she talking to me? I looked up at the hockey coach standing on the pitch, waving her hand towards me.

'Yes, you! Why aren't you out here playing hockey? You must be in first year.'

I nodded.

'Well, don't you play sport?'

'Yes.'

'And have you played hockey before?'

'Yes in my national school.'

'Then go and get changed. Chop, chop, five minutes. That's all you have to get out here and join us.'

I liked her. She smiled when she talked to me. She was friendly.

In hockey, I found another escape. I could use my skills to show my physical strength and sheer male aggression. I was very competitive. The happiest memory of my schooldays was scoring the winning goal in the final of the Junior Leinster Cup. I was so excited when my name was in the *Irish Times*. I didn't even care that it said Christine and not Chris.

In sport I had found an avenue to acceptance. Hockey became more than just about enjoyment and fitness, it became an outlet for my frustration with the world, and a way of being seen by the world for one aspect of who I was. I played tennis, hockey, table tennis, cricket and squash in school. My academic results were average to say the least but I didn't care. I was now the sporty one in the family – a label that I loved. I was too naïve to understand that this label of sporty could be ripped away from me. At the time I was inconsiderate of the future. My older sister could achieve all the accolades for learning. I didn't care. I had sport.

My father cared about the academics. He wanted me to do well in school. He wanted all of us to have the secondary education that he had not finished, and the university opportunity that had therefore been denied to him. He often questioned me about my slipping grades.

'Your report isn't very good.'

'I'm sorry. I did try.'

'Well you could try a lot harder. Every teacher has either written satisfactory or could try harder.' My father held up the report and looked at me with frustration.

'My maths and English results are good.' I always talked back.

'You have too many C's here and only one A. It's about hard work. And why all the careless spelling mistakes they're mentioning? You need to read more.'

This again! I didn't like reading. The words seemed to swim on the page. D's and H's swopped positions, letters melted into one another. I had to concentrate to keep them still.

'Your mum and I have decided that you won't get the same magazine as your sister. She reads books all the time. So it's alright for her to read lighter stuff.'

'Oh, okay.' I was trying to suppress a smile. There was a God. Who would want to read the magazines Susan enjoyed?

As children, my mother and father always wanted to encourage us to read. As young children, it was a common activity to read magazines on my dad's knee. Susan, being the eldest, was the first to graduate to a magazine to read alone in her bedroom. In the teenage years, these magazines were very gender oriented – magazines such as *Jackie* or *Diana.* All they contained were pictures of different hairstyles and clothes as well as glossy images of young male entertainers.

My father, as a punishment for my slipping grades, thankfully only allowed me to have *Look and Learn* or *World of Wonder* as my weekly magazine because they were more educational in their content. My dad read them more than I did! I usually flicked through them until I found the one page of cartoon, invariably at the back. I couldn't really manage the longer articles. I wanted to be able to read, as I knew that it was important for future success, and I wanted to be clever and knowledgeable. I knew these attributes impressed my father, but the effort of trying was too much.

My older sister and my father used to have such good conversations about facts. I was jealous of their shared knowledge. As I got older and forced myself to concentrate on the letters, reading became easier but I am still a slow reader and it is still tiring. In the light of my issues with the written word, I focused even more on my sport as a teenager. It was the part of my life that I succeeded at. By the time I left school for university, it was more important than anything.

The other parts of my teenage years that I have fond memories of are times spent with Gran. As a lanky awkward teenager, I went to Wales and spent a holiday with her on my own. In coming to terms with my gender issues, being spiritual helped enormously. It was Gwladys who inspired me on this path.

By the time I visited Gran on my own, Pop was already dead. He had died while our family was on holidays in France, an occurrence which wounded my father badly. My father was distraught that he had not been there for Pop's final moments. The funeral was delayed until they could inform us of his death. They had to give us time to return home to Ireland and then back to Wales for the funeral. It was a challenge for my aunt to hold it up that long, but she refused to let Pop be buried without my father present.

Pop's death did not affect me greatly. I had never been that close to him. He was gruff and liked his own space, except when it came to my little sister, Sarah, who could twist him around her little finger. For some reason, she softened him where others couldn't.

Staying alone with my grandmother brought us closer. I got to understand what made her smile and what made her irritated. I heard some of the stories of her past, which she was usually reticent to share with her grandchildren, and I came to understand her implicit trust in God. She entertained no doubts in God but she didn't ever push her beliefs on me. I think she balked sometimes at the lack of churchgoing amongst my family but she never expected us to accompany her to church. I learned about her God through her behaviour, her clothes and her singing.

My grandmother had an effect on me that I didn't really expect when I was a teenager. It was around the time of my confirmation. I was feeling decidedly off with the world – I wanted to be happy but didn't know how to achieve it. As the happiness that most of my peers sought at my age seemed impossible for me, I saw my grandmother's happiness in the security and comfort of her religion as alluring. Maybe I could find some peace with my life through a steadfast belief in God. I started to take an interest in religion. I even managed to persuade my mother to change church so that I could attend a church where more girls from my school attended and where the congregation was younger. Some of these fellow students from my school seemed to have found a place to belong in their church community. They talked about it in class and met in the church hall for youth group during the week. I thought that maybe I could find acceptance in the same church. Of course the whole process failed miserably. I was too young and naïve to understand that acceptance has to come from within first.

Chapter 16
Friendships

I made some good friends in school but never felt that I could totally explain myself to them or that they would understand me if I did. Thus I felt emotionally alienated from them. I kept friendships on a practical level, with trips to the cinema or walks down the pier. I didn't like shopping for clothes or doing the normal things most of my classmates were eager to do. However, four of my friends went out shopping without me one weekend and I cried bitterly at this seeming ostracism. Of course, it was my own fault. I was no fun to go shopping with and showed little interest in their pleasure with clothes or make-up.

I was also too serious. I was often moody and uncommunicative. I had a difficult temperament. I was either up or down, but never on an even keel. If I was playing sport then I was usually in good form, but even on the sports field I could lose my cool and throw tantrums at a poor decision or a loss of a goal. Whereas most could take these setbacks in sport as simply part of a game, it was the only game for me, the only thing that mattered, the thing that I counted on the most. At the time I think most of my friends and teammates just saw me as very competitive, but this competitive streak came from an inner anger that was very difficult to control. It was also an anger that I had no solution for as I didn't even know who I was or how to explain it to anyone else. I just felt different.

In the 1970s, in school in Dublin, I did not even know what gender identity disorder was, and I had never heard of transgender. I had absolutely no clue how to label my feelings. I just knew that they were different from any friend that I had encountered. I desperately wanted to fit in to the norms of male and female but I knew that I didn't. However, I felt pressurised to conform by my family and society as there were only two choices – to be female or male. There was no in-between.

There were some wonderful people in my class in school but, unfortunately, I was too caught up in my own angst to realise their potential as life-long friends. I had this obsession with not allowing them into the awkward world of my feelings. I became a very difficult person to keep as a friend. I pushed friends away and changed them as if they had no feelings. I was so unable to confront my own feelings that I had no time to consider theirs. It is an embarrassing trait to admit. I was very cold and uncaring as a teenager in this area of my life and unfortunately the trait persisted into later years. I was too self-protective, too afraid of being seen for who I really was – a very angry, confused teenager with gender issues that I didn't even understand.

I was happy to leave school and the confines of that small community. I was looking forward to being in university, somewhere bigger where I might be able to reinvent myself. I even pondered the idea of being a lesbian as I did fancy women. However, I felt that jumping into lesbianism would have been false and it was not an acceptable existence in a devoutly Catholic Ireland. Besides, lesbians seemed to have no problem being women.

Chapter 17
The inside out

By the time I was in my final year of school, my relationship with my father was almost one of love/hate. He was kind, supportive and loving towards me but I was unable to accept his male protective energy. I only accepted his fatherly support when I was really low and in need of it. Otherwise, in moments of strength, I threw it back in his face. It must have been very difficult for him. This combative side came from nowhere in his eyes. Although the fact that he was very derogatory towards women in moments of temper didn't help our relationship.

'Bloody women drivers. They're useless. What idiot gave her a license?'

He did get angry with male drivers but the sentiment was different. 'Oh good God, he is a bloody twit,' he'd say.

Home life with Dad was often fiery but friendships were equally difficult.

'Why aren't you putting your name down for Trinity, Christine?' one of my classmates asked one day.

'My sister went to UCD.'

'Yes but she'll be finished by the time you get there. Come with us.'

I wasn't interested in going with them. They didn't really know the real me. They only knew aspects of me. I wanted to be somewhere on my own where I could hopefully become more of myself.

'I won't get good enough results anyway,' I countered.

There was truth in those words. I hadn't worked hard enough. My school work was always coming second to sport, writing and drawing. I had no interest in anything except being creative – creating a world into which I could escape.

'We can still be friends anyway.' Why had I said it? It sounded false to me. I think we all knew that we wouldn't stay friends. I wasn't close enough to any of them. I had kept them all at arm's-length.

I see it as a pattern in my life. I have always changed my friends every four to six years. I think it is because I fear that the longer the relationship continues, the more chance there is that my friend may unearth the reality of my gender issues. It is only recently that I have understood this facet of my nature. I had always excused it before as down to external changes such as jobs, house locations, etc., but in fact these were excuses to avoid opening up my inner fears, to being scrutinised by someone other than myself. I have seen the reality in this through my children and their friendships. Both my son and my daughter have kept friends from childhood through to their university days and beyond. They have shown that this is possible because they have taken these relationships to deeper stages of understanding and intimacy. They have grown with these friends. I was always loath to open up to my friends in case of reproach and so I moved on to new friends constantly and started afresh. It meant a great deal of loneliness and isolation.

University was not all the fun and games that I thought it would be. There were cliques – the girls from Mount Anville, the boys from Blackrock. They sat together in the lecture halls and around the campus. I had not one school friend in University College Dublin and no one that I knew even to say hello to. The first few weeks were very lonely.

In lectures I sat by myself. I was scared of talking to the boys in case they thought that I fancied them. I was wary of talking to the girls as I did fancy quite a few of them, and I was scared that it would show. I was having trouble containing my feelings towards women, as those years are dominated by the drives of our sexual nature.

It took a month for me to find my feet and then it came in a strange way. I found another outsider to the campus. In the fifth week of term, a late arrival came to the lectures – a small girl in a green cardigan and a skirt, who looked less like a student and more like a librarian. She was four foot nothing and had a big smile and an open countenance. I saw her enter the hall and nearly sighed when she sat down beside me. I did not wish for her company. I preferred sitting alone, taking notes assiduously, almost pathetic in my wish to look academic. She sat straight down beside me and introduced herself with the confidence of someone who thought I would want to know her name.

'Hi, I'm Hazel. I've just arrived on the campus. I'm from Monaghan.'

I don't care if you're from Kathmandu! You're in my personal space.

Move away!

Of course, those words didn't come out. They were the words that constantly streamed through my head that never saw the light of day.

'I'm Christine.'

Was that just habit? Did I introduce myself in full?

'So are you enjoying college?'

I'm trying to listen to the lecture if you'd stay quiet. The silent voice was back.

'It's okay,' I squeezed out.

'What other subjects are you doing?'

'Geography and politics.'

'What a coincidence, so am I. That's great! We can go to lectures together. You can show me around. It's awful starting college late. So many people already have made friends and know everything. Then there are the notes to take that you've missed, the reading to catch up on. It's really difficult. But at least I've made a friend now.'

Lucky me!

It was lucky me. She became my closest friend for the four years of college. She was the opposite of me – friendly, talkative and warm. She kept me sane for the whole of my university experience. Hazel was exactly the type of friend that I needed. Coming from a small village where she knew everyone and everyone knew her, she was a world-class conversationalist who could talk profusely when no one else could think of a word to say. She was unashamedly outgoing and chatty. She was a country girl in the city. Her clothes were out of fashion and her openness out of the norm. She was brilliant. With her as a friend, I soon made friends with plenty of others. However, we weren't the cool college kids. We were the alternatives. There was not one Blackrock boy or Mount Anville girl amongst us. We didn't possess designer clothes or drive around in a Golf or Mini. I apologise for the stereotyping but they did almost wear a uniform of their own creating. We never played pool in the Trap and we only sat out by the lake when the weather permitted. We went to all our lectures and always handed in our essays.

It was through Hazel that I became a member of the canoeing society, the judo club and various other groups. She was full of the joys of spring and intended to make the most of her college years. She was working towards becoming a teacher and therefore her history and geography degree was one step on that path. My history and geography degree was purely a way of satisfying my father's insistence on a college education. I did not go to university with a life goal. I went to please my father.

I joined the hockey club, only to find the same cliques more than comfortable there. All the girls had gone to the same schools and knew each other. I had to break into the fold. I had totally expected to make it to the seconds team when I joined the club. I had been a good player in school and I knew that I had ability in the sport, but I was an unknown to the girls and I had no way of making it past their ad hoc methods of selection. So I played for the fourths that first season and even then they played me out of position. I was physically a strong figure so they changed me from a forward to a defender. It happened after our fifth match. I was scoring goals but we were letting more past us in defence than I could score. So they moved me back to defence and we started winning. I kept the goals out aggressively and then I ran up the pitch and scored them at the other end. The level of hockey was not too strenuous so I was having fun, whilst also getting noticed by the coaches and higher team players.

Staying on the fourths was not an option. I was very competitive. I wanted to play on the firsts. So every weekend, when it was raining heavily and teams were hard to field, I would offer to sub-up to any team missing a player at the last notice. I sometimes played three matches at a weekend just by turning up with my kit and my stick hidden at the side of the pitch.

'She's sprained her ankle. Quick, help her off.'

The girl limped slowly to the touchline, two teammates providing support.

'We'll have to continue with ten players. What the hell happened to the subs?'

The captain shrugged her shoulders, raindrops running off her nose. 'Grace called in sick and Mary just hasn't turned up.'

'Well she won't be selected again. This is a cup match!'

I sidled closer to the conversation, trying to get into their view, but they didn't notice me. It was raining heavily and they were preoccupied. I would have to be direct.

'I can play.'

The coach eyed me suspiciously. She was a formidable woman. 'Who are you?'

'I play for the fourths.'

'What position?' The coach was not looking enthusiastic about the offer.

'I can play anywhere.'

'Can you indeed?'

The referee approached the coach and captain.

'We need to restart. Sorry. Get your sub on now.'

I picked up my hockey stick and took off my tracksuit top, revealing the club kit, slightly dirty and damp from my earlier game.

'Okay, you can play, but if you make things worse you're coming off. Just stick to your position, mark your opposite player and listen to those around you.'

I smiled and took my place on the field. A real game, a cup match, a better level of hockey, this would be fun.

By my second year in college I was where I wanted to be – I was on the firsts. Now I could strut my stuff. Now I had a label firmly attached that I could really identify with and I loved it. By the time I was in third year, I was first team captain and club captain as well, and playing for Leinster in the inter-provincials. This was not down to talent so much as sheer graft. I would practise for hours taking penalty corners when others were in the showers. I would even practise my stick skills in the back garden at home.

Playing hockey was the only time that I forgot about my gender identity issue. I was able to hit out my aggression against a ball that would often hit me back. I damaged kneecaps and ankles, shin bones and wrists. The only issue that I had with playing sport was the showering. It was probably why I stayed out on the pitch after the game, practising; I was trying to avoid going into the showers with my teammates. It is not that I looked at them salaciously in the shower; it was that I didn't want to be put in the position of seeing them naked. In school, it had never been a problem. I had always cycled home after each match or my dad had picked me up from away games. However, in university this was not possible. After the games, there were drinks in the bar or long journeys home from odd locations; remaining soaking wet and sweaty was not an option. And thus I developed two alternatives – racing off to the shower first or being the last to go in.

When I was captain, racing off first was never an option. I had to thank the umpires and shake hands with the opposition coach and their substitutes. I had to be polite and do all the formalities. I often remember freezing out on the pitch waiting for most of my teammates to go through the showering process. If I could get into the shower room with maybe only one or two stragglers left behind then I always found it easier to avoid their nakedness and mine.

Hockey and my diminutive friend, Hazel, were my saving graces in college. I did well in my courses because I wanted to stay in college and play for the university. However, there was another aspect of my life that I found more difficult and that was the threat of relationships.

It was not that I did not date. I dated boys throughout college but I never slept with any of them. I tried not to keep them long enough to have to worry about that issue. I also claimed that because of a hockey match the next day I could not stay overnight. The dating of boys was more for show, although I genuinely enjoyed their company and I didn't wish the world to think me gay. I deliberately fostered the semblance of a heterosexual. It is not difficult to do but it does falsify feelings and override emotions. I was lying to the world but more importantly lying to myself.

Sometimes the lying was confronted by the truth. It happened when I was club captain and had to take a group of younger female hockey students for a trip to Galway. I was two years older than them. I was the female answer to the jock, but I didn't realise it. I saw myself as someone completely different to what they perceived. I didn't see any reason for them to admire me. I just worked hard and played hard.

One particular student came to talk to me as I sat on a beach in Galway during some of our free time. She was tall, thin and very feminine. She was not the type of girl that I usually fancied.

'Do you mind if I join you?'

'Yes.' I said it in a joking manner but I still meant it. I was enjoying the peace and quiet of the beach. I felt myself bristle as she sat down quite close to me and pulled her knees close to her chest with long, slender arms.

'I'm Alison.'

'I'm Chris.'

She laughed.

'I don't find my name that amusing,' I said, looking at her with bemusement.

'It's just we all know who you are, Chris Ricketts. You're the best player in the club.'

'Actually, I'm not. One or two of them play for Ireland.'

'You're the first team captain and the club captain and I've watched you play.'

'It's no big deal. I'm just in third year, that's all. They ran out of options.'

'Too modest! You're really admired.'

I blushed.

'Sorry for embarrassing you.'

'It's okay.'

'You are admired you know. I didn't even know whether I'd have enough courage to sit and talk to you.'

'That's silly,' I said. 'Sure, you're more intimidating than me.'

She had a lovely laugh, warm and assured. 'Why is that then, Chris Ricketts?'

'You're a medical student, far cleverer than me. I only do Arts.'

'How do you know that I do medicine?'

'I was asking a girl on the way down in the bus what everyone was studying; just passing the time.'

'Well it doesn't mean that I'm any smarter than you anyway.'

I looked at her disbelievingly. I had always presumed medical students to be arrogant, full of their own self-importance, for having worked their way into the elite of the college. Of course, I was wrong. It was my own insecurities that made me feel that way.

We talked for hours that day on the beach and later in the bus going home from Galway. We became friends. However, for me she was not a Hazel type of friend. We became close in ways that I found uncomfortable. I used to stay over in her house, as all friends in college do when they live a distance away. Hazel had often stayed in my house, but she may as well have been my sister as I had no interest in her sexually. This girl was different though. I ashamedly fell for her without even knowing it.

'Look Chris, the moon is so bright, you could almost reach out your hand and touch it.'

I rolled over in my sleeping bag and looked out of Alison's bedroom window at the night sky.

'Oh it's amazing! You can almost see the man in the moon. Look in the bottom right corner. Can you see him?'

'Ha, yes, he's got a cranky looking face. Just like you when you've lost a hockey match.'

I huffed loudly. 'Cheek of you, I'm not a sore loser.'

'Oh my God, Chris Ricketts, you really are.'

'Well I don't know why you are friends with me then.' I was still lying on my back looking up at the moon.

'Because you are kind, funny and a lovely person.'

And that's when it happened. She abstractedly ran her fingers through my hair. She had never done it before, and sadly neither of us knew how to react. As I lay beside her on the bedroom floor, I felt the frisson from her gentle touch and, obviously, she felt it too. It was the moment that our friendship ended.

She immediately withdrew her hand. 'God, I'm sorry, shouldn't have done that. Sorry.'

'I don't mind. It's not a problem.'

But she fell quiet and in silence we went to sleep.

I never saw her as a friend after that night. She didn't reply to my phone calls and avoided me in college. I was upset that I had lost a friend and upset that she was not able to talk to me about it. She would have been completely safe. I would not have wanted our friendship to have become anything else. I was more terrified of having a physical relationship with a female than she was. I had put up this false illusion of heterosexuality, which even I had almost come to believe.

Many years later, I saw her again in a village street. She refused to meet my gaze and pretended that she didn't know me. I was hurt by her obliteration of me. Relationships like ours were to become the blueprint of many of my friendships with women.

Losing Alison because of the developing feelings between us was a factor in things changing for me emotionally and physically. I was confronted with the fact that my outer body was stopping a relationship from happening. She liked me, I liked her, and in my mind we could have been boyfriend and girlfriend had my outer body matched my inner sexuality. At least that was how I interpreted the event.

Instead, although she had had obvious feelings for me, some other boy was going to be the one to kiss her and spend time with her and take her to the cinema and dinner. This is not an easy passage to write, because it opens up the very core of my pain as I saw it – my inability to have a heterosexual relationship with a woman. Thankfully, I am now in a relationship with a really lovely woman. Both my partner and I see it as a relationship that needs no labelling, as that only puts distance between us. We don't think of ourselves as heterosexuals or homosexuals. We are just two people living happily together. Society always tries to label us but people do not understand who I am or who she is. They only see our outer skins and judge us by that.

The problem of the outer shell not matching the inner mind is the crux of the issue for a gender-disorientated person. All they want is to have a heterosexual relationship with the opposite sex and all that their body can give them is a seemingly gay relationship, which is so far from the truth. Through Alison, this dichotomy reared its ugly head for me in college. It battered me into hating my body, with an anger that was more palpable and focused than in my teenage years.

In teenage years, all relationships are about experimentation but in college years, relationships are about forging partners for the future and possible procreation. What sort of future did I have if I could not be in an open, honest relationship?

My new-found anger manifested itself in the most aggressive eczema. I had cuts on my hands, wrists and arms. I bled from every part of my body that folded or wrinkled, even my eyelids. I remember in particular one episode from my last year in UCD that upset me hugely. I was attending a rag ball and I was standing in the bathroom washing my hands. A girl came out of the cubicles, slightly drunk, and smiled at me.

'I think you're very brave, you know.'

I looked at her puzzled.

'I don't think I could face going out with such a bad rash,' she added.

She left the bathroom then and I stood alone and looked at my face properly in the mirror. There was blood, gently oozing from an eczema scab underneath my right eye, and both my eyelids were red-raw and flaky. I couldn't cry at that moment, the saltiness of my tears would have made my eyes burn even more. I just went home.

It was because of these difficult relationships during college years that my nightmares became more intense and the worst episode was during a hockey trip to an intervarsity competition in Cork. I was staying with a student from Cork whom I had never met before. Our whole team, from Dublin, was billeted with other students in the Cork area to save on costs. I happened to get the best house to have as my lodgings for the tournament. It was a big manor house near the River Lee and the student had an enormous bedroom in which there were two single beds. I went to sleep the first night, tired from the day's hockey but in good form. However, the nightmare I had was of epic proportions. When I awoke in the morning, my host was sitting in bed peering at me strangely from over her bed sheets. I was bright and breezy.

'Good morning,' I said.

She just looked at me nervously from a blanket pulled up to her chin.

I didn't have to think twice when I saw her troubled face. I must have done something in my sleep. I looked around the room. Not one poster was left on her wall. They were on the floor, ripped and crumpled. The door was hanging off her wardrobe at a strange angle and her bedside lamp was broken. I knew what had happened. I didn't have to be told.

'Sorry. Was this me? I get nightmares.'

'It was frightening,' she said angrily. 'You just kept shouting and ripping at everything.'

'I'm sorry.'

I could recall the nightmare – being locked in a room with no door, frantically trying to find an exit behind wardrobes, posters and curtains. It was a constant nightmare that I had – being trapped. It didn't surprise me. I felt trapped inside my whole body.

Chapter 18
A shock and a revelation

In the summer of 1980, in the middle of my college years, my grandmother, Gwladys, celebrated her eightieth birthday. At the time she seemed healthy and relatively happy, although she found the cold Welsh winters difficult to endure.

As a young college student of nineteen, I had my summer of 1980 well planned. I would go cherry picking in Germany. Along with three friends, I interviewed for two farms for summer employment. Fate was to make a divine intervention for which I have always been exceedingly grateful. My friends were all given employment in one factory and I was given work in the other – over three hundred miles away!

'Come on, Chris, you can come with us.'

'No Hazel, I don't have a job in your factory. Mine is two hundred odd miles away.'

'But if you come with us, you can stay in my room and look for a job in the area. It will be no problem.'

'And what if I don't get a job? It's too uncertain. I can't do uncertain.'

I didn't want to take the risk. I was fearful back then too. So I stayed in Ireland and took a job in the Four Courts in the archive department. It was to be the year my grandmother, Gwladys, decided to visit us for two weeks. We had been living in Ireland since 1965 and she had hardly ever left the Welsh valley, so it was a rare visit for her.

My grandmother's visit was a memorable occasion – not for the places that we visited or the dinners out that we enjoyed, but for the very day before she left. I was playing cards with her. It was something that she had rarely done in the past as her religious beliefs had denounced it. Cards were a frivolous pastime and for gamblers and people of ill repute. However, as she got older, she mellowed and allowed the odd game of gin rummy. She sat in the armchair that day in the corner of the living room and we played cards for the last time. I sat on the little round seat in front of her, the coffee table between us.

'Gran you're a real card shark.'

'I am not. I hardly know how to play.'

'Well I'm not happy with the cheating that's going on here,' I teased.

'I'm not cheating,' she replied. 'I wouldn't know how.'

'Well what's this then?' I said, picking up a King of Hearts from under her chair.

'Oh, I only dropped it.'

'No, no, you were saving it for later, and this one too no doubt.' I removed another card from down the side of her seat and held it out for her to see, as a lawyer with his proof of criminality.

She laughed heartily. 'Oh. I'm such a clumsy thing with my old fingers.'

She always dropped cards on the floor, and I would always tease her about her private stash under the table. I loved the laugh that would follow. I loved that I had made the connection with her, the woman that I so admired. However that day, as we laughed and played, her smile faded and her look became earnest and her words were delivered more slowly and deliberately.

'When I go home tomorrow, Chris, it's for the last time. I won't see you again.'

'Don't be silly, Gran, you're perfectly well and you've lots more years ahead of you.'

'No, my time is up, cariad.'

'You can't possibly know that.'

However, she was adamant. 'I'm tired. I can't face another winter and God is ready for me.'

'But I don't want you to go anywhere and I won't believe it.'

It is a life-altering event when your grandmother tells you that she is going home to die and that you should not worry because she is ready to meet her Maker. She was so certain of the timing, so calm about the passing of her own life.

'Don't tell your father. He won't understand.'

'Of course I won't because I don't understand,' I said, hurt and angry with her refusal to alter her mind.

'Oh, you will one day. You are more like me than you realise.'

I wanted to cry. I didn't want this beautiful person to leave me.

She seemed to read my mind as she patted my arm comfortingly. 'I will always be with you in spirit.'

'But Gran, I want you here now, not in spirit. I don't believe in ghosts.'

'I know, but one day you will.'

I shook my head and wiped away a tear.

'It's my time. And I want say goodbye to you. Don't be sad. I'm not sad. I'm going to meet my Maker.'

She was not in any way frightened.

The strange thing was that I believed her. I knew that I would never see her again in this world and I knew that she would be happy in her passing.

The next day she flew home and my parents went with her. They had made the decision to take her back to Wales. It was a spur of the moment decision as they did not always go with her. Again, it was serendipity. My mother and father sat beside her on the plane and journeyed back to the Welsh valley with her. They saw her go to bed, happy to be back in the house where my grandfather had died.

My mother took her the morning cup of tea.

'Mam?' she said, entering her bedroom with a soft knock upon the door, 'here's your morning tea.'

There was no reply.

'Mam?'

In the bed, lying serenely, my grandmother looked peacefully asleep. But she couldn't be woken. It was totally shocking and completely unexpected for my parents and the rest of my family. My grandmother had shown no illness, pain or reason to be sick, let alone die. However, between her and God there had been a bond, a time designated and preordained, and God had taken her as prearranged. Her spirit knew her time of passing.

I have since read books that would confirm the nature of my grandmother's passing. Books that claim that we all decide, as unborn souls, how long we shall spend on this earth, and that we all know the year, day and hour of our death. It is deep inside us, at a soul level. The closer we are to our spiritual self the more we know this day. In the case of my grandmother, she was a very spiritual person and her soul was on the surface of her existence. My grandmother was unafraid of death – for her it was just a passing from one state to another. She knew that when she died, she would be back in spirit with God and in a state of total bliss and awareness.

Less than two days later, as they 'waked' her body in the parlour, I saw her in my dream. She was standing there in front of me in the little bedroom of her house, but I was not scared or perturbed by her appearance. I was comforted by her presence and we talked.

'I am here,' she said.

'You look the same,' I replied. 'But healthier.'

'I feel healthy.'

'What's it like? Being dead?'

'I'm not dead, cariad. I'm more alive now than when I was on earth with you.'

I could feel the tears on my face. 'I miss you.'

'I will always be with you.'

The image faded and I awoke to see the room empty and my breath visible in the cold night air.

Gran has not been far from me ever since. I now understand the world that she inhabits, as my spiritual grandmother. I understand the unshakable faith that she had in God and the world of spirit. Throughout the more recent years of my life, I have encountered many strange episodes that have opened this world up to me, and often my grandmother has been there watching over me.

Not everyone was as calm about her passing as I seemed that day. My aunt was visibly shaken, although she too had a strong faith. She also believed that my grandmother would exist in spirit form. As is the custom of the Welsh in some parts, my aunt asked us to kiss the cheek of my grandmother as she lay in the coffin, as a mark of respect for her passing. I found the act most disconcerting. I didn't believe that it was my gran lying in the coffin, in her best Sunday clothes. Her body was now a mere shell and her soul, her essence, had long since departed. Even then, I realised that her life force had gone.

She was laid out in the front parlour, the same room that my grandfather had slept in after the gangrene had taken his leg. The coffin was smaller than I had anticipated. Her skin was white and almost opaque. The curtains were half-drawn, casting shades of light and dark across her tiny body. She was wearing lipstick, her usual colour, nothing flash, but it looked too bright on her white face. I touched her forehead. It was so deathly cold. My hand recoiled. I couldn't stop it.

'There's nothing to be frightened of, she's still your gran.' My aunt was in the room with me.

I nodded as if I understood but I was terrified. This was the woman that I loved so strongly, lying in a wooden box with a fixed expression.

'You can kiss her. Say goodbye.'

Luckily someone else came in the room and I was saved from kissing the lifeless body.

My grandmother was the first to show me that life was about spirit being embodied (although maybe she was not showing me, but reawakening me). She was a formidable influence in creating the 'me' of today, in creating 'Chris'.

I have talked to her often since her last day with me in the flesh, playing cards. While sitting in a cosy house in County Kildare, she has spoken to me through a medium. I know it is her; it couldn't be anyone else. The medium has described her accurately – the small woman, singing hymns in her kitchen. The first time I heard from my grandmother through this medium I was astounded. It didn't seem real. It couldn't be real. However, the small little details that she knew about my grandmother were amazing. She even knew that she had lost a child in childbirth.

And so I had to believe, I had no other choice, the evidence was too clear. And every time her spirit comes through, and she is around me, I can hear a certain Welsh hymn in my head and I can almost sing every word of it (although it is in Welsh and I can't speak Welsh). The hymn in my head lets me know that she is near me, supporting me, checking in with me.

Gran's presence in my life, from this spiritual dimension, has given me great strength. It is through knowing that we are not just our bodies, but something much greater and more perfect, that my release has come from a defining label. I understand now that my body is just the vehicle in which I travel through this life. If I were to look at my body as the defining part of me then I would still be troubled by my identity, but the fact that my body is only my outer shell gives me the ability to identify myself more with my inner soul.

Chapter 19
It all goes pear-shaped

I left college with a pillar in my life gone. I was also losing friends too frequently. From college days onwards, some of my best friends became too close and I invariably lost them before the relationship became something that I could not handle or before I opened up my feelings to them. Invariably the friends that I kept long term were the ones that I usually never thought about romantically.

I left UCD with a Bachelor of Arts in History and Geography, and a Masters in History. In a bid not to grow up and face the outside world, I decided to do a Higher Diploma in Education and remain in university for yet another year. I had never wanted to be a teacher but it seemed the best way of extending my college days. So I went off to Trinity to achieve this diploma. However, I had not thought the whole teaching thing through. Teaching was not going to be an easy path to follow.

My first year in education was frightening in every aspect of the work.

I went into my first class with six lessons planned and prepared. They should have lasted me two weeks. However, in my fear of stopping for breath and of allowing any questioning, I went through all six pre-prepared lesson plans in my first class. At the end of the forty minutes, a brave young hand went up. Although I taught that class over thirty-three years ago, I still remember the look on that student's face and her name. Andrea was of valuable assistance to me in my developing H. Dip., along with the rest of her class.

'Excuse me, Miss. I don't mean to be rude but are you always going to teach us that fast?'

I looked at the thirteen-year-old girl with fear. I was older, wiser and in power, but I felt two feet high and ridiculous in the light of her comment.

'What's your name?' I asked.

'Andrea, Miss.'

'Well, Andrea, that was just an overview of those topics. We will be going into depth on each of those areas in the next few days.'

Bullshit, such bullshit!

It was one of my best attributes as a teacher. I could make things up on the spot. Although I presume none of them believed me. They were all fairly certain that I was just a 'newbie' who had no clue.

I don't think you ever forget your first class group. I remember going to my first H. Dip. tutorial and feeling blessed to be in such a good school, especially when others recounted their first few weeks of school. One poor trainee teacher encountered an incident involving a protractor and an eye, after one student bullied the other too aggressively. Another had to watch a fire in the back of her classroom being put out with a fire extinguisher, after a class of disgruntled boys left her. All I had to deal with was a low level of impoliteness and noise.

The stresses of doing the Higher Diploma in Education were compounded by the fact that I was still finishing off my Masters in the September of that year, so my workload was enormous. I had lectures, a thesis to write, classes to teach, exercises to correct and my own training. The school also wanted me to coach hockey with them, considering that my CV was packed full of achievements in that area. I soon found myself run ragged with all the commitments. I was getting tired physically and emotionally.

I was also firmly rooted in a decision that I had made whilst in university – to handle my life as straight as possible. My aim, since the star-gazing incident with my friend in college, was to lead the life that my outer physical body dictated. I would get a job, earn money, meet a man, possibly marry and buy a house. Further than that, I did not plan! I only knew that if I could *not* have a heterosexual relationship with a woman then I was going to have a heterosexual future with a man.

I was not a lesbian and that was that, so a relationship with a woman was out of the question. My inner desire to be a man would have to be squashed and ignored. It would have to be pushed down under the surface from where it could never reappear. I saw my only alternative becoming a fully-fledged female. Surely I could persuade my mind, with force of thought, to be more female. Sadly, I could only do it by hiding my true self and my real feelings.

In the background of all these stressors was my wish to find acceptance. In the first years after university, I still held a notion that this could be found within the security of my own religious background. Thus in my early years as a teacher, I became friends with two other teachers who were profoundly religious. They were also living in the boarding house and we formed a small Bible-reading group. I even asked my confused parents to buy me a Bible for Christmas that year.

It is very sad looking back but I was so hungry to find acceptance that church groups seemed to offer the best possibility of achieving my desire. If you told them often and enthusiastically enough that you loved their version of God, then there was every chance that they would show you love too. I am amazed that I didn't end up in a cult at the time.

My two religious friends were brought up in homes where there were strict beliefs, religious devotion and a certainty to faith. I was brought up in a house where questioning the existence of God was seen as intelligent. There was no taking the word of the Bible as gospel in my home, which is exactly what these two women believed. The Bible was above reproach to them. They read it looking only for the words and stories that backed their faith in the Almighty. If other passages clashed with their view of Christianity then they ignored them or made up some excuse.

I read the Bible in the hope of finding a passage that could make me understand the validity of my existence. I was looking for an affirmation of my presence in this body. I liked the idea of dying and becoming spirit which would bring a relief from the sufferings of this world. Even my two new friends seemed to have a morbid acceptance of death as a good thing. At least I saw it as morbid at that stage. The benefit of dying and becoming a spirit was not an aspect of Christianity that they should have told me about with such glee. Suicide rates are high amongst the gender dysphoric and I was becoming too interested in what it would be like to meet my Maker and transcend into spirit. After all, my grandmother had looked forward to it.

In the biblical study that I completed with them, the words that always resonated with me the most were 'the truth shall set you free'. However, I was damned if I could work out what the truth was. I didn't know whether I was a heterosexual or a homosexual. I didn't know whether I was male or female, and I didn't even know back then that gender identity disorder or transsexualism even existed. If the truth could set you free then I was miles from finding out or understanding the truth.

In fact, the Bible classes only confused me more and I ended up throwing a Bible against the wall, as a blasphemous act, to break up our little religious clique. I could not take the Bible as literally as they did. To me, there were too many contradictions in it. I had studied history in college and the Bible was made up of different texts from different people. If it was the ultimate word of God than he was mightily confused about how he wanted those words delivered. The words of John were almost mystical, whereas some of the words of St Paul and others were grave and instructive, demanding and judgemental. There was a thread of God throughout the Bible but the whole book shuddered with the words of men. Where were the women in God's world? Why were all twelve apostles men?

As my masculine side was almost impossible to bring to the surface, I realised the church would not see me as an equal as a woman. It was less than comforting to realise this problem. All women were useful for in ancient Palestine was for whoring or becoming the mothers and daughters of men! In the Bible, the only women mentioned were mostly extras to the story, unless they were causing trouble – Lot's wife, Eve, Delilah. Lot's wife turned into a pillar of salt, Eve ruined everything and got mankind thrown out of the Garden of Eden and Delilah cut off Samson's hair because he had spurned her. I needed to see the worth of being female if I was going to accept my female body and attempt to live my life as a woman. All I could find was the failures of being born a woman and the curse of it. I gave up the Bible classes. The positive and powerful characters were all men – Noah, Moses, Herod, Jesus, Pontius Pilate, John the Baptist and all the disciples. The Bible was a book about men. Today I wonder what the Bible would have told us if it had been written by the women of that time. But their voices were not recorded.

I still have a problem with the Western religions and their subjugation of the female. Islam today, in its most fundamental form, still treats women with less respect than they deserve. It still questions their rights to make their own decisions and have an education. Islam was born out of the same region of the Middle East, and with the same Old Testament beliefs, as Judaism and Christianity. It is not a religion of the East but of the West. It is as patriarchal as the Church in Rome. It is difficult for a woman to follow these churches without in some way subjugating to the male energy. Why not a female Pope or Archbishop of Canterbury? Or a female mullah? My friends were sad for me when I threw the Bible. They believed in some ways that I had almost gone to the devil.

That first year as a young teacher became a disaster as I was so exhausted and confused by everything that was happening around me. On top of the psychological difficulties related to my gender, I had too much on my plate – a Masters to finish, classes to teach and essays to prepare and correct.

So I crashed.

Having a nervous breakdown was a difficult event, especially following the history of my mother and her period spent in hospital after giving birth to Susan. The notion of someone else in our family having a mental health issue was something almost unmentionable and better swept under the carpet. And the reasons for it happening were impossible to share with anyone, let alone my parents.

The first thing I noticed was that I had a lack of energy and kept getting sick. My eczema was compounded with asthma and I developed chest colds and constant headaches. My head started to hurt with the pressure of being someone that I was not. On the outside, I was Ms Ricketts with the boyfriend in London, the hockey successes and a blossoming teaching career but inside I was a chaotic mess. Looking back, even the boyfriend in London was a happy escape from having to be intimate with men. I could tell the world I was heterosexual and in a relationship without having to perform the duties of it.

However, I was carrying too much baggage, balancing too many things at the same time and one day the mess spilled over. Unfortunately it was on a field trip. Instead of walking around the farm with the other five teachers and ninety-two first years, I just sat on a hay bale in a shed and let the hours pass. I still remember that farm trip clearly as if it happened yesterday. I remember not feeling in control of anything anymore.

The barn was almost dark, except for slithers of light streaming through cracks in the wooden walls. There was a malodorous smell of pig dung wafting in through a half open door, and there was me, 1B's geography teacher, slumped on a hay bale looking into the distance, like some vacant cowhand. I spent more than an hour in there as my charges walked around the farm being entertained by fellow members of staff.

And I did nothing. I neither cried nor moved. I just sat. I sat while my brain did somersaults. I sat whilst my mind whirred constantly with the pressures of my ridiculous existence. I knew sitting in that barn that I was cracking up, or in fact I had already cracked.

'Where have you been?' A teacher nudged my elbow as I boarded the bus.

'I was at the back of the group, watching the bold ones.'

'No you weren't. I couldn't see you.'

Shut up. Stop questioning me. I can't tell you the truth.

'Oh well, I did leave for a few minutes to go to the toilet.'

A long stare and a slight raise of the eyebrows. Had I dodged the bullet?

'Come on, 2C, get on quicker or we'll never get back to school.'

He had found others to pick on. I had escaped with my errant behaviour.

I was weeks in my depression. It was very lonely. I still played hockey. I still taught my classes, which were as carefully prepared as usual, but I didn't leave time in anyone's company for questions. I was always too busy. I just kept moving, motoring through the practicalities of everyday life, avoiding the truth. But at night the quietness would overwhelm me and the fears would manifest. How could I live this way? Why was I spiralling out of control? What was wrong? Was I mad? And the bad thoughts led to excessive nightmares. I think my parents were more than concerned by the level of angst I showed in my sleeping state.

At weekends home from boarding school, I would shout and roar like a person possessed in my sleep. My mother even talked about tying me to the bed to avoid hurting myself. It was a distinct possibility in those days that I could have done myself harm. I once ran past her on the landing of our home and vaulted down the stairs three steps at a time. I was nearly out the door when she dragged me back from the brink of escape. I was always trying to break free – from fires, from chasing murderers, from witches or evil spirits.

My nervous breakdown didn't last long. My parents had been concerned about me. They knew that I was emotionally down and they worried about going out and leaving me in the house alone. However, I hadn't noticed their observations of my emotions. I was blissfully unaware that they knew anything of my nervous state. Until one day I overheard them talking about whether they should go out that night to meet their friends.

'Mick has rung. We're going to meet them at eight in the Punchbowl.'

'I don't think we should go out, John.'

'Why not, we always go out midweek?'

'I'm worried about Christine, she's not herself.'

'She'll be fine. It's just the teaching probably. It's stressful.'

'It's more than that. I think we should stay in with her.'

'She's twenty-one, not a child anymore.' My father sounded frustrated. 'She'll be okay, you're over anxious.'

'I know, but I have never seen her this way before.'

I took a breath. I had stopped breathing to listen, afraid that they would hear me.

'You may be right. We should stay in.'

When I heard those words it stung deeply. What were they worried about? I was fine! Go out!

I was so deluded that I had thought my erratic behaviour would have gone unnoticed. I couldn't believe that they were worried about leaving me alone in the house for an evening. It made me angry with myself for putting them under that strain. I was also mortified, embarrassed. I made up my mind that I would turn things around. I would stop having the panic attacks, vocalising my fears and crying in front of them. I would work hard at exuding an air of normality. In fact, I would become normal again.

It was a conscious decision. Although the issues that had caused my depression had not been dealt with, I was going to turn my life around. I was refusing to be a burden on anyone. I decided to throw myself into my work and my sport, as this would be more advantageous to my mental health. It was yet another decision to bury my emotions even further from the surface. I was a ticking time bomb from that moment onwards. I had not uncovered the fuses; they were just sitting there waiting to be lit again.

It is amazing how resilient the human mind is. Once I had decided to be free of depression, I was free of it. I scrubbed myself down emotionally and put all my feelings back into a box. I wrapped this metaphorical box in thick, brown paper and packaged it away. No one would find out what my true feelings were. I would completely toe the line. I would find a husband, find a home and live a perfect 'Stepford wife' existence.

Chapter 20
Hiding in plain view

Often I have wondered if I should write an apology to my ex-husband for marrying him under the delusion of being in love. My true emotions had been buried before I met him and when I became his other half I was only operating on a physical level of existence. If my world expressed only the basics of food or drink, work or sport, home building or finances, then I could handle it. However, there was no room to peek below the surface of these practical everyday issues. I was unemotional, beyond functioning in a life that could be created by thought process alone. In direct contravention to the desires of my heart, I was living as a woman.

In fact, I had shut down my heart in my college days and my early years as a teacher. I had blamed my heart and their deep feelings for causing my depression. The thought process was that if I wanted to get rid of my depression I had to get rid of my feelings. When I married my ex-husband, I wasn't lying to him. I did love him but it was a love born out of the practicalities of the head not from the feelings of the heart.

I sometimes think that we were definitely well matched at the time of our marriage. His deep emotions were as buried as mine. He had encountered a very difficult event in his upbringing. It is his story to tell and therefore of no relevance here, except for the fact that he also lived his life in the practical zone. Together, we were two emotionally compromised individuals looking for respite.

In fact, he possibly ended up marrying me to escape a difficult issue with his former girlfriend. As a Catholic, she was seen by his very Protestant mother as unsuitable marriage material. My ex-husband did not have the emotional bravery to take on this formidable woman. His mother had already displayed a meltdown at the marriage of his younger brother to a Catholic.

My ex-husband possibly saw marriage to his long-time Catholic girlfriend as a fraught proposal. So he married me instead – the ideal Protestant school teacher who loved sports as much as he did. He could happily take me home to his Protestant mother. How deceptive looks can be. The problem in our marriage was that neither of us was responding to our relationship from a healthy heart space. We were both living in our heads where it was safer.

The night before my wedding was a night of weird reflection. Whilst my family was out celebrating the oncoming nuptials, I was lying on the couch at my parents' home listening to the Carpenters – such maudlin music! I nearly talked myself out of walking up the aisle, even though all my relatives were over from Wales and the whole wedding was in less than twenty-four hours.

All the males in my family were out at a stag party. As to where the women were, I cannot remember, except that they were not with me. I didn't have a hen party as far as I was concerned – I wasn't a hen. The idea of having such a thing disagreed with me. Susan assures me that she held one for me anyway, with all my female relatives in attendance.

My younger sister, Sarah, was my bridesmaid for my wedding, and due to the fact that she lived in Spain, she was out with her Irish friends. So I sat alone at home and sulked.

What are you doing?

I'm getting married.

Why?

Because that is what one's supposed to do. And my life is about what I am supposed to do.

But what do you want to do?

I want to get married so that I can be like everyone else. Live like everyone else. Be happy like everyone else.

Do you love him?

I don't know what love is.

Being on that couch was a surreal moment in my life. I was getting married and I was marrying a man! But another weird thing passed through my mind that night before my wedding.

It won't be my last relationship anyway.

What is that supposed to mean?

I don't know why but we are not going to grow old together.

It was a weird thing to process at that time, because I did believe that marrying him was the right thing to do, and strangely, the thing that I was meant to do. But as I sat there on the couch and sang the lyrics of soppy songs, I had a deep knowing that I would not live with him permanently as my partner.

I have to marry him. I do love him in my own way.

And what way is that?

Well obviously enough for him, as he wants to marry me too.

My pre-wedding period was nothing like a normal wedding preparation. I shopped for the dress and the accoutrements with a cavalier attitude. I literally picked the first dress that fitted me, in the first shop that I ventured into. The small headdress was the same. I felt ridiculous in the clothes. Looking back at the photos now, I actually looked quite pretty in my own way, but I felt like a fish out of water in such feminine garments. In fact, I really felt like a cross-dresser.

The day of the wedding I almost gave my mother and sisters a heart attack. I rose early and went into town to get my hair done. It's not that I thought it needed doing, but it was something that everyone had told me to do on the day of my wedding. I was trying to stick to the script. I also wanted to give myself some free time from the whole pantomime that was developing around me. So I booked an appointment and headed into Dublin. I didn't invite my bridesmaid. I saw no reason for taking her along. I had never read glossy magazines or chick lit or watched girly movies so I had no idea of the formalities of a wedding.

I remember the morning of my wedding being warm and almost sunny, not the best day in July, but then Irish summers aren't known for their stunning weather. The service was being held in St Paul's church – a bastion of Protestantism in south county Dublin and a wonderfully elegant building, with its high spire, large stained-glass windows and beautiful cut stone. However, the church was nearly without a bride that day, as I lingered in Dublin for far too long.

'So what do you want done with it today, anything special?'

The hairdresser stood behind me and scooped up my shoulder-length hair in his hands.

'No, nothing special, same as usual.'

'Okay, you're the boss.'

As he cut and brushed, I listened to the radio station and drifted asleep.

My hairdressing appointment finished early so instead of going back home to prepare for my wedding, I decided to go shopping for music. It was the days before CDs and I bought myself a record – *Let's Dance* by Chris Rea. Walking through the streets of Dublin, with my Golden Discs purchase tucked under my arm, I looked like someone out for a shopping trip, rather than a bride-to-be. I walked up Dawson Street, out on to St Stephen's Green and strolled through the park. I even stopped to sit on a bench and watch the ducks. By the time I sauntered home to Cabinteely it was two o'clock and I was 'getting hitched' at three. My mum was apoplectic.

'Where have you been?' She was ashen. 'Don't you know what time it is?'

Where's the fire? How long does it take to put on a dress?

'It's fine. There's plenty of time.'

'You've less than an hour.' I could hear the panic in her voice, backed by the tutting of my sisters. 'You're getting married for God's sake, not going for dinner.'

But I knew that an hour was plenty of time for me. All I had to do was put on a dress and some eyeshadow. I really couldn't understand the panic. Looking back, they were probably just worrying in case I had thought of doing a runner.

I was probably runner material as far as my mother was concerned. Susan once told me that my mother had confided in her about a packet of contraceptives she had found in my bedroom.

'Guess what Mum found cleaning your bedroom?'

'Well it can't be drugs, I don't use them.'

'She found condoms, Chris.'

I went bright red. I had no smart reply to that comment.

'She was hilarious. She showed them to me and said that she was delighted that you were having a sex life.'

More bright red.

'Isn't that hilarious, Chris. I would have been killed if she had found condoms in my bedroom at your age. But you, she was just happy that you weren't frigid.'

I found the whole conversation more than embarrassing. Any conversation about intercourse is extremely difficult for me, but to hear that my mother thought that I was a prude because I never showed any interest in such matters was especially difficult. But, in fact, I did have interests. They were just not interests that I wanted to explain to any of them.

I was not late for my wedding. If it is fashionable to be late, I proved that I knew nothing about fashion. I was there when the church clock struck three. I stepped out of the hired limousine, with my father holding my hand, and I felt as though I was in a strange dream. It did not appear real at all. It was happening to someone else. I suppose the inner me was someone else, and only the outer me was getting married.

The church was packed. Standing at the back, waiting for the processional music to begin, I felt scared. I hated the fact that there were so many faces looking at me, faces that were smiling and happy. What were they smiling at? Was it the memories of their own happy weddings or the notion that they were celebrating a happy event?

I have sat with the picture album from my wedding and seen the fear on my face. There is a look of the proverbial rabbit, shivering in the headlights of a large truck. My face only comes alive at the end of the wedding, when I am sitting in the limousine with a friend, a friend who had oddly become my husband.

And I am alone with him – just two friends together, dressed rather outlandishly for everyone else's benefit. It is in this car that I start to relax. The church is gone, receding into the distance as the car pulls away, and we can go back to hiding our emotions from the rest of the world. We can play our sport, plant our garden and build a high-walled castle. We did find happiness when we were not given roles to play by our family and society. When we were alone with no stereotypes to adhere to, we could just be ourselves in a playful sense.

However, I had married him and that situation was full of assumptions concerning the roles of husband and wife. These assumptions came from my mother-in-law and my own family, and were going to be difficult for me to live with. If I could have taken my husband to a remote island and lived far away from the world for the rest of our lives, our marriage might have survived. I wouldn't have had to play gender roles, I wouldn't have known what I was missing and I wouldn't have believed anything else was possible.

I had married him because my emotional IQ was non-existent. My head forced myself to believe that I was more than just a friend. The mind can create many unreal circumstances. I did believe that we could live together if we focused on certain practical parts of our lives.

Of course, nothing is ever that simple. When we bury our true feelings there is no saying when they will rise to the surface, causing a tsunami and washing everyone and everything away.

Chapter 21
Rising waters

Being married brought with it the issue of having a constant sex life, although it was something that I had undertaken with my husband before our wedding day. Whether in the wrong body or not, my body did need to feel certain things. It needed a physical release as much as any heterosexual body. I had taken the pill assiduously as a precaution against having children, as the idea of being pregnant was a complete anathema to me. I feel very guilty for writing this as my children might read it and think that I did not want them. Nothing is further from the truth. I would have loved to have been a parent to them at any stage of my life. I just didn't want to be pregnant.

I could even cope with the gender role of a mother but not the role of a pregnant woman. I had always wanted to be a father. I had always imagined teaching my son to play rugby and football and taking him to matches. However, being a parent and mother to my wonderful children has in fact been one of the most rewarding things in my life. It is just the pregnancies that brought my gender issues to the surface.

My body dysphoria erupted emotionally when I realised that I was pregnant. I had not factored pregnancies into my plan for the future when I had married. The night that I found out that I was pregnant with my first child, I drove to a friend's house and cried for hours, drowning my sorrows, irresponsibly, in gin.

'Fiona, I'm really upset. Something terrible has happened.'

'Oh God, no. What's wrong? Are you ill?'

'No, it's almost worse.'

'Would you like a drink?'

'Oh God, yes. A gin and tonic, if you have one.'

'You're shaking.'

'I'm pregnant.' I started crying.

She smiled. 'Oh that's not bad, that's good news.'

'No it's not. I will get fat and I won't be able to play hockey.' And I'm not happy being a woman and having a baby growing inside me. But my last thoughts didn't make it to the surface. They just hid, hurting my throat, blocking my release from everything.

'It's only nine months.'

'That's nearly a year.'

'I do understand. I wouldn't want to get pregnant yet. But you're married and happy and you can play again afterwards.'

But I couldn't see past the horror of something growing inside me. There was nothing that reeked more of being in a feminine physique than being pregnant.

Looking in the mirror, wearing jeans and a T-shirt, I had always been able to look into my own eyes and see the man inside of me, but looking into the mirror and being faced with a big bump of a baby, reduced that view into pure womanhood. I hated it. It put me into a state of shock that I could not explain to anyone. Even being married, I had almost managed to convince myself that we were two friends, happily co-existing under the same roof, as any housemates might. I was managing. I was coping. But being pregnant blew that out of the water. There was no pretence that could hide the fact of my outer femininity.

I was also unhappy because I knew that people would look at me and know that I had had sex. The children in my classes, my parents and my siblings would all know that I had slept with my husband. That overwhelming fact made me feel very nauseous. I didn't want anyone to think that I slept with him – that was gay. I would have preferred if they had all thought of me as asexual or even frigid. In being pregnant, my life became a nightmare from which I couldn't awaken for nine months.

The first visit to the gynaecologist was equally as frightening. He insisted on calling me Christine, even though I had left that name behind a long time ago and preferred to be called Chris. He had taken it from my medical records. He also felt that he had the right to examine my body in whatever depth was necessary for his medical notes.

I have never been happy with anybody physically examining me. I have often ignored an illness to avoid a physical examination. In fact, I only did a breast check this year for the first time, having thrown all the letters in the bin for years. And it was just as bad as I had imagined it – extremely embarrassing and humiliating. The young nurses and doctors touched my breasts as if they were the most natural things in the world to have plastered to the front of my body. They did not know the difficulty that I was having with their examination. I was almost in tears every time they touched me. Sitting in the hospital waiting room I had felt physically sick – a room full of middle-aged women, wearing gowns and reading glossy magazines. I was not one of them and shouldn't have been there. At least that is what my mind was screaming at me. The whole afternoon was a horrible event. I went home very angry and realised that I needed to make the circumstances of my life known to others. The world needed to know how difficult it was to be unseen. At least I have now done the mammogram, but at the time of writing this I have still not been able to bring myself to do a cervical smear. It is a step too far for me.

Thus my gynaecologist had his work cut out. I was not going to be his easiest patient. He did his scan, affirmed that I was pregnant and gave me another appointment for a month's time. It was during that second appointment that everything changed for me in my attitude to being pregnant.

'Now Christine, I'm afraid I have a bit of bad news for you.'

I looked at him holding the scan in his hand and wondered what abnormality he had seen.

'You're going to have a spontaneous abortion. It might be a few days but definitely in the next week your pregnancy will terminate. There's nothing to worry about. It won't be painful.'

A spontaneous abortion? What is spontaneous about an abortion? Crowds cheer spontaneously, protests erupt spontaneously but what is spontaneous about sitting at home waiting for your baby to fall out from your vagina, I was horrified.

'It's because of the shape of your womb.' He was still babbling on, even though he had received no reply. 'The womb changes from pear-shaped to apple-shaped when the baby is growing in the lining of the womb. Your womb is still pear-shaped.'

All I could think of was the expression 'things have gone pear-shaped'. Was this where it came from? I doubted it. But who knows.

'I am sorry, Christine. You're young enough to try again.'

I don't want to try again. I didn't try for this one – the withheld commentary.

'It's fine. Thank you. Bye.'

'No, it's not that simple. You have to come back next week for me to see that everything has evacuated successfully.'

I was distraught. The pregnancy that I had originally not wanted now seemed to be robbed from me. And all that would happen would be an abnormally heavy period. But there was nothing to worry about; just the baby would be gone. Dead. It was all very emphatic and conclusive. I went home and I waited.

I didn't even tell my husband or my parents. I just sat in work, at home and waited. At night, lying in bed, I would pray. I prayed for the survival of my baby and I apologised for not being happier at the news of pregnancy. I asked God for forgiveness and to save my pregnancy.

I am sanitising this slightly. I didn't ask, I begged, and I didn't cry, I wept.

For some reason, my antipathy to the whole body-changing experience was replaced by an overwhelming feeling of loss. I was trying to live the life of a woman, as my physical body had dictated, and yet I was spurning the gift of that body. It was no longer good enough to say that I was not happy being a female. I was in the body of a female and this baby was a gift that I had pushed away. It even crossed my mind that the spontaneous abortion might have been a punishment for throwing the Bible. I had a very negative view of God. I saw him as judgemental and unforgiving. I had obviously missed the whole point of the New Testament.

After the long week was up, the spontaneous abortion had not happened. I went back to the doctor and he gave me another ultrasound and examination. He looked at the screen and just sat there smiling.

'I don't believe it. It's a first for me. Your baby is still growing.'

'Does this mean I'm still going to have a baby?'

'Yes. The statistics against this happening are huge. If you don't mind, I will take a photo of the scan to show my colleagues.'

Of course I didn't mind. My prayers had worked. What other reason could there be?

A new life was growing inside me and this time I was respectful of that miracle.

From that moment onwards, I didn't say one negative thing about being pregnant, although I still didn't publicise it or own it with pride. I wore long T-shirts to cover my bump and I hid from people as much as possible, only going out shopping when I had outgrown all my clothes and the food cupboards were bare. The worst part was going to school and facing the students and their teasing. It was always friendly but, for me, it was always embarrassing.

For my parents, I was going to give birth to their first grandchild and they were ecstatically happy, yet nervous. I just wanted to have my body back and then do as I had promised God – be the best mother that any gender-disorientated person could be. Although at that stage, I did not have that label for myself. I still didn't know who I was. I only knew who I wasn't.

The day of the birth was another example for me that I was still fighting being a woman. Giving birth was traumatic. I was in labour for hours and then the baby had to be extracted from my body with a Caesarean. The medical reason given was that I did not have the right size pelvis to give birth to a baby. His head could not come out or some similar gross detail. All I remember is that I was injected with a local anaesthetic and that it didn't entirely work. I was physically aware of the whole procedure. It was thus a birth that was far more painful than it should have been. Something, which straight afterwards, I almost felt that I had deserved for being so angry at the pregnancy.

Seemingly, I have very sensitive nerves and they did not all go to sleep with the administering of the anaesthetic. I felt the entire first five minutes of the operation. I felt the scalpel draw its line across my stomach and the doctor's hands go inside. It was sheer agony. It all happened as I lay wide awake behind a small two-foot-high screen.

'Excuse me. I can feel what you're doing.' My voice was anxiously higher pitched than usual.

The three faces I could see past the screen were peering down ignoring me. I tried again.

'Please it hurts!'

Three faces turned to me, one with a scalpel in his hand.

'Now, Mrs Connolly, I don't think that's possible. Just relax, you've had the anaesthetic. It's all fine.'

The masked faces turned back to their work.

'Jesus, please stop. It's too painful.'

A nurse was now holding my arm, trying to calm me down. A doctor was frowning at me over the screen, exasperated at my utterances.

'Shh now! It's okay,' the nurse said. 'You can't feel it, you just think you can.'

I always hated people telling me what I felt, especially as I didn't express my feelings too often.

'Well, he's just put a hand into the left side of my abdomen and I'm hurting.'

Three doctors and one nurse looked at each other worriedly. It was not a reaction that I was pleased to see. The gynaecologist immediately gave an instruction to the anaesthetist and the pain subsided. To be honest, up until that second dose, I had never felt pain like it in my life. To be cut open without having one's nerves completely numbed was gut-wrenchingly sickening. I had nightmares for weeks about it.

After an interminable amount of time behind the white screen, I was handed a very beautiful baby boy. Caesarean babies sometimes look better, much calmer, as they have not had to force themselves out of a narrow opening and fight to live.

Gareth looked like a little cherub – completely bald and very clean. I loved him on sight, but I hated what I had gone through to have him. There was terrible pain at any attempt to walk in those first few days. The soreness of the stitches was exacerbated by the friction of any nightclothes or sheets. Then there were the annoying matrons who came in and out trying to encourage me to breastfeed and handling my breasts as if they were theirs. I loathed all that process. I just wanted to go home and be left alone with my child. I am sure that I came across as quite a difficult person during those five days in hospital. I was uncommunicative or terse at best. Their prodding at my body and overtures to get on with being a mother were less than pleasant things for me to endure. I just wanted to go home where I could settle into being a parent – not a mother but a parent.

In hospital, they were all completely unaware that I had felt no happiness in giving birth as a fully operational female. It was the last thing that I wanted to be. And thus in my hour of complete joy at the perfection that was my son's birth, there was also paradoxically a complete hurt and pain at the prodding and poking around of my body – a body which I had no attachment to beyond the fact that it allowed me to play sport and hug my family.

My first venture into parenthood was a crazy time. It left me with a difficulty that was more than physical. I now had more concrete evidence that I was not happy being a woman. I found it more difficult to pretend that my marriage was merely life with a close friend. Emotionally I was being let loose!

At home, I cringed when people entered the room when I was attempting to breastfeed. I remember being so angry with my mother one day, although I attempted to hide it from her. All she did was completely natural for a caring mother and grandmother. She arrived in the house and promptly tried to help me breastfeed by helping the baby latch on. I wanted the ground to swallow me up. I wanted her to leave. How dare she touch my breast? Didn't she know that in reality I was not her daughter, I was her son? I was so angry with her for not knowing the real me.

My antipathy to my loved ones was always heightened at moments such as these, because my family and friends were so oblivious to the pain that I was feeling in the paradoxical nature of even the most normal event. How could they not know who I was? I was not their daughter or sister. I was a son and a brother. At least I was in my head. How could they not know how much difficulty I had with the ordinary living of life?

And yet whose fault was that?

I had never told them of any of my problems with my female body so how could I expect any empathy or sympathy for my situation, or any help in overcoming my anxieties? They didn't know. They were blissfully ignorant and my mother and sisters were just being women, doing what they felt natural with another woman.

The moments of extreme pleasure for most people – such as a successful childbirth – can be oddly painful for someone like me. It is why so many of us take the route of treatment and physical transformation. Reading this over, there is a small part of me that wished that I had been able to do that transformation at a young age. It would have saved me from going through so much pain. Although maybe that alternative life would have brought with it pain of its own making. The larger part of me understands how horrible it would have been not to have had my children. I would have missed out on so much joy and learning from two wonderful people. I would have also missed out on having a unique view of the world, no less worthy of understanding than the seemingly perfect male or female.

During the first few years of Gareth's life, I kept my job as a teacher, tiring myself out, as many mothers do. Bringing up children, and looking after a young family, is a full-time job whether we like to admit it or not. I had an au pair for a while but it bothered me that I was leaving the rearing of my only child in the hands of a strange Hungarian whom I knew far less than most people. By the time Gareth was two and a half, I wanted to spend more time with him and look after him myself, rather than leaving him with an au pair, or my mother and father. I had managed to move beyond the horrors of breastfeeding and early motherhood, and was now happily ensconced in being a parent. The issue of being in the wrong body was not rearing its ugly head as much. This was probably because I was too busy chasing my tail and an energetic toddler.

Gareth did not slow down at night. It was like living in permanent wakefulness. I used to get so tired, I could not function properly. I took him into bed with me just to get some shut-eye, when he eventually fell asleep. It was too tiring standing for hours in his bedroom, gently humming songs to him and hoping he would nod off. He would sit up and play all night if he could. However, this practice of putting him in our bed was to change, brought on by a very worrying but almost comic episode.

One morning, I awoke after a very difficult, almost sleepless night, to find Gareth was not in his cot. My husband had already left for work so I was sure that he did not have Gareth. I went back to my bedroom but there was no sign of my baby there either. Starting to panic, as the mind readily does when it is overtired, I went downstairs to look for him. The front door was open. Immediately, I jumped to the most ridiculous conclusion. Someone had kidnapped my baby. It was an irrational thought to jump to, but my baby couldn't walk yet and the front door was open.

I was just about to ring the guards when I heard a muffled noise upstairs. Running up, two steps at a time, I reached my bedroom only to realise that I had fallen asleep with my son in my bed and he had wriggled his way down under the duvet to the bottom of the bed. How he had not suffocated I do not know. I never took him into bed after that night, at least not until he was a toddler and old enough to rescue himself from a heavy duvet and a comatose parent.

Gareth brought many changes to my life. Because I had a child, my commitment to sport could not be so time consuming. I could not hope to play at such a high level and still look after my son. At least that is what I thought, or maybe it was just an excuse for being afraid to go back. I had made my hockey friends as an individual, a person with a particular vision of themselves. That person no longer existed. I didn't want them to see me as a mother. I didn't want them to see me in this new role.

I couldn't bear to see myself changed through their eyes. I didn't want them to comment on my motherhood, or any other part of me that had altered, and so I joined another club where no one knew me, and I would not have to face a changed persona. I joined my husband's hockey club and met new friends and reinvented myself again. I left behind the drinking and hard training and became a quieter me.

I also fell into the company again of two spiritual people, reminiscent of my earlier teaching career. I was still desperately looking for answers to the complexities of my life. I was also still looking for self-acceptance. I rightly or wrongly believed that if God created me then he must surely understand my issues and thus accept them.

The two women I befriended were also mothers of children the same age as Gareth, so we had a great deal in common. We started a deep friendship that was to include family holidays together and church attendance, although I went to their church alone. My husband was a Church of Ireland non-attendee. I told him that I would give up their church if he went to our local Church of Ireland parish but he was more interested in fishing at the weekend than finding redemption. So I went to the spiritualist meetings with Gareth and later with my second child, Lindsay. Our family was starting to break apart in my need to find acceptance.

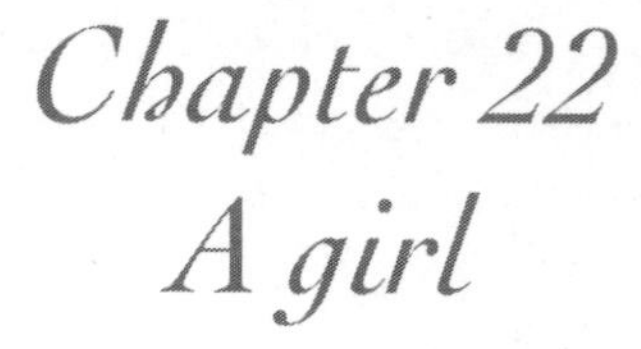

Chapter 22
A girl

Lindsay's birth was not as traumatic. I was prepared for the issues that were to arise and I was ready for the second Caesarean. The doctor felt it necessary to put me under completely, considering the debacle of my first Caesarean, so I was unaware of the birth of my baby girl until I awoke. When I opened my eyes she was simply there, lying in a cot beside me, gurgling away happily.

I had held a deep fear that I would not be able to love this little baby as much as Gareth. I did not think it possible to love two people with such overwhelming depth. I loved my son as a reflection of the masculine that I had never been able to realise. But could I love a little girl and her feminine ways as easily? However, the moment Lindsay smiled at me I was smitten, and I then realised that love was not finite or bound by gender. Real love is genderless. It is only sexual desire that demands a gender preference, and even then some people can see beyond the body to what lies within.

Before Lindsay's birth, I had wanted another boy. For me, bringing up Gareth was a joyful experience. I could do all the things with him that I was prevented from doing as a young child. Footballs, rugby balls, Lego castles, cars and all manner of boyish toys were manna from heaven for me. I could indulge my masculine nature in his world. I enjoyed playing with his toys almost as much as he did.

However, the notion of having a little girl to take care of scared me completely. I didn't know how to raise a girl. I didn't know how to help her grow into a woman. I had only bad memories of being a little girl. How could I give her the example she needed? How could I teach her to be a woman and embrace the feminine? I didn't have to worry.

From the moment she was born Lindsay was the epitome of femininity. She exuded it in whatever she did. She danced like a ballerina, played dress up with numerous dolls and only ever wanted to wear pink or primrose yellow. I spent many Sunday mornings in bed, tired from a hectic Saturday night, entertaining Lindsay by allowing her to put numerous bobbins and ties in my hair. Every Sunday was hairdressing day in our house. I had to undergo a brutal brushing, followed by a perm with fake curlers and then a unique styling with elasticated pain transmitters. My hair was so short that the entire process was always painful. However, it was worth the pain to lie there with my eyes shut and not to have to make the breakfast. Lindsay was the epitome of a girl from an early age and it was not due to my nurturing of her but due to her natural instinct.

My spiritual life was moving rapidly forward, along with my parenting. I spent hours reading books on spirituality. It started with books by mainstream religious writers but then it spread. I read Eckhart Tolle, Marianne Williamson, Anthony de Mello and Deepak Chopra. I was obsessed with finding an answer that could give me self-acceptance.

Unfortunately, with all this appetite for learning also came an appetite for being true to myself. I was finding it difficult keeping a lid on my emotions when the books I read talked about the importance of the truth. I tried talking to my husband but he did not wish to change the parameters of our relationship. He was happy living with the same person he had married. He didn't want things to be analysed, worked on and transmuted. I can understand that now.

I needed to change but he didn't.

Chapter 23
Pandora's box opened

I was operating from a heartfelt space with my children. My emotions had been awakened with their births and I was happy loving them from a very deep level. I wanted that feeling to be extended to other relationships in my life. Except for my children, there was a definite shallowness to my other relationships. None of them knew how I really felt about things. It frightened me.

I was also poor at keeping friendships and yet I was becoming way too close to one of my friends from the hockey club. My thoughts about her were changing. I tried to bury the thoughts but they kept on coming. I didn't want them but I could not make them go away. I would lie awake at night, oddly wishing that I was her partner. I was falling in love with her – something that had not happened to me since university.

I would never have done anything about it, as I would have found any notion of acting upon my feelings distasteful. I was horrified with myself for even thinking them. As a teenager, I had imagined a life as a man, but now I was beginning to want that life as a man, so that I could be with a woman. My inner voice was making itself heard.

You have feelings you know. You can't always hide them.

Yes I can.

I don't think so. They're starting to come to the surface. You can't keep living in a shallow puddle. Remember, the truth shall set you free.

Shut up! I don't know the truth. I'm not gay. So what am I?

Does it matter what you are?

It matters what people think I am.

It shouldn't. Just act upon your feelings.

What, with her? No. It would be wrong. She's married!

Well, if not with her, then find someone else.

I'm married!

Being in love with someone, seeing them nearly every day, was very difficult. I loved being in her company and hated being away from her. So I found all manner of reasons to be with her, to the extent that we were almost living in each other's pockets. She taught aerobics, so I went to her classes. She changed churches, so I did too. She went on holidays with her husband for the weekend, so I stayed in her house to look after her children to help her out. She became an unhealthy obsession.

I don't know whether my husband was jealous or whether he even noticed. He was a man happy in the knowledge that he had a home, a wife and two children, and he could go away fishing whenever he wanted to. I was an unhappy wife who seemed to have everything on the outside but internally was craving to be myself. It was almost impossible to continue with the situation and keep my real self hidden.

Eventually my feelings for her became too much to bear and I ended our friendship, out of a fear of where it might take me. My fear was that I would tell her exactly how I felt, and that she would look at me with horror. I also did not want to cheat on my husband, even in thought, as I had made a vow to him and I was prepared to keep it. But my precarious world was unravelling. The label I had assumed – of dutiful wife – was choking a part of me that I needed to release.

It was one of the most difficult things that I have ever done in my life. From spending every day together as friends, with children who were also friends, I went home one day before Christmas and wrote her a letter. I felt suffocated by her friendship. I needed space for my own life to exist. It was a letter that was horrible for her to receive. However, the truth would have been even more destructive as an alternative. She was happily married to a man that I admired. She was a lovely committed Christian person with a warm, effervescent personality and a very strong faith. I could not have stayed her friend and faced trying to explain my truth to her. I couldn't tell her that I was a man in a woman's body and that I had fallen for her. I had to leave the friendship to preserve my whole false life. My husband, my marriage and the security of my children depended on it. I had to stick to the story that I had invented for myself – I was a happily married woman with a good job, two children and a husband. And I could only be those roles. I could not be anything else.

The fallout from that letter was terrible. She was so hurt and angry with me, especially after all the support that she had given me with childminding and my ever-questioning faith. She had not seen it coming and could not see where it had come from; she even thought that I had gone temporarily mad. She told me that I was incredibly cruel and I was to keep away from her and her children in future.

I never went back to the hockey club. After years of being a player, a captain and a coach, I became an outsider through my own doing. It was as if I had gone through a separation. She kept the hockey club, the friends and the part of my life that had kept my whole precarious situation afloat.

I was set adrift, devastated by the outcome. I had lost everything that I cared about, outside of my children. I had no hockey group, no church group and no friends left, and I had hurt someone deeply. Naturally, she informed others of my selfish act. All our friends in the club knew that I had tossed her aside as a friend. I had no alternative, other than to run away and hide from everything.

For the third time in my life, I cursed the God that I had studied in books and in church. Where was He in all this? Why hadn't He given me the support that I needed to get through it all? I blamed Him entirely. I turned away from the spiritual and I reacted by throwing myself into my work and writing. It took months for me to stop crying – I had thrown away my closest friend and probably the only person at the time to whom I could have told my problem.

During all this, I also changed schools. After Lindsay was born, I started in a new school closer to my home. I could spend more of the day with my children. It was a very good school but smaller than my last place of employment and it was only girls. As before, when I was a teenager, I found myself immersed into the world of women again. There were very few men on the staff and none of them were of interest to me. I suppose I was jealous of them for being something that I was not.

Alwyn and Gwladys Ricketts. My gran was my hero.

My wonderful, fun grandmother, Miriam Thomas.

My father, John Ricketts, in his uniform at the age of nineteen.

Mum and Dad on their wedding day, 4 September 1954.

Dad and me. He was a very loving father.

Happy days in our first house in King's Terrace.
Mum, Dad, Susan and me.

Grandpa Tom, Susan, me and Dad at home.

Susan and I visit Santa.

The terrible flower girl experience. I'm the small, sad one!

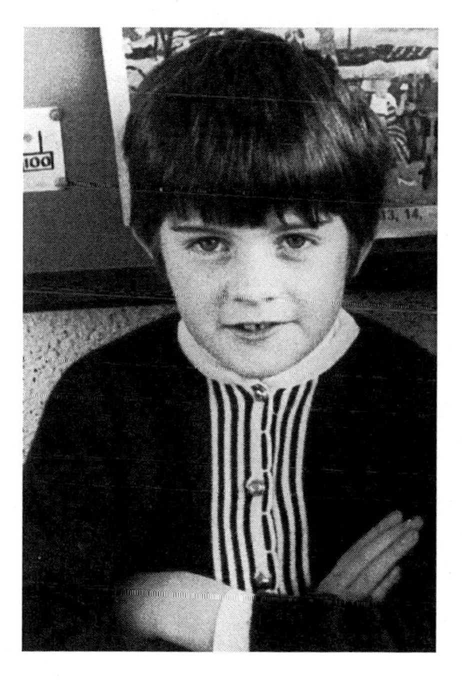

Early national school photograph.
Oh boy!

Fun at Aberavon. Susan, Andrew, me, Ian and Sarah.

At the beach with Mum (right) and a family friend. I was always happy playing football.

Sarah and me at our house gate in Ireland.

Trying to conform, wearing a dress at my BA graduation ceremony.

Happily motorcycling in Ko Yao Noi, Thailand.

My daughter, Lindsay, a beautiful, supportive person.

Chapter 24
History repeats itself

I threw myself into life in my new school. I became the Transition Year co-ordinator after only one year and I challenged myself in every area of work. If I was not getting top results with my classes then I deemed that I was failing. I was driven by deep despondency in my emotional life. I threw myself into work life to hide the failings of my personal life. I disliked everything emotional, heartfelt and sensitive.

However, after the huge loss of this friendship, I did try hard to put my marriage to the forefront. I tried to make myself feel as interested in his company as I had felt in my former friend's. I tried to encourage him to talk about deep issues with me, but he was always happier discussing sport or work. It was just the way our relationship had developed from the outset, and he did not see any reason to change it. It was working fine for him.

The problem was that I had changed. I had found an emotion within me that I had not allowed to exist since childhood, and it was difficult to ignore. It was the emotion of having a deep and expressive connection with another person – a connection that ran to more than the factual musings on life and I did not want that to disappear forever. It was not his fault that our marriage failed. He stayed true to the person that he was when we were first married. I just couldn't stay true to that false me. It wasn't enough anymore and I had to find something better. When Pandora's box is opened, the lid cannot be jammed on again, followed by an 'oops'.

The harder I worked, the more tired I became. I was trapped and yet my life on the outside seemed perfect. I had a lovely house, in a nice area. I had a handsome husband with a very undemanding personality. I had two beautiful children. And yet I was so far from my own true self that it all seemed unreal, fake.

The pressure of keeping up the act was burning me from the inside. My eczema erupted again and a more aggressive asthma and allergic reaction developed. I was becoming a very unhealthy person.

Church had become a no go zone for me after losing my best friend. I vehemently denied any interest in religion and threw all my spiritual books in the attic. However, I was not going to escape that easily.

In ancient Greece, they had a belief that the gods cannot be thwarted. My God proved just as difficult to deny. I was paid a visit by the local rector and he persuaded me that I might find a community through attending his church. Even though it was not necessarily the community that I was looking for, I did not let his words fall entirely on deaf ears. Instead of going to his church, I went back to where I had married and I sat high up in the balcony seats where few could notice me.

At this time, Gareth had just started school and was making friends fast. He was only five but he possessed a very talkative, open personality. He attended the local Protestant national school and I took him there every day and picked him up.

As I sat quietly in the pew, following the sermon, a hand patted my shoulder from behind. When I turned, I saw a friendly face smiling at me. Alongside the woman sat three children, all under the age of six.

'Hi, are you Gareth's mum?'

'Yes.'

'My son recognised you. He plays with Gareth in school.'

'Oh, okay.'

'I'm sorry about the noise. Having three under six is difficult.'

The friendly face that I was looking at became my closest friend. A teacher, the same age as me and overtly outgoing, she was very easy to converse with. She became the first person that I told of my real identity. Her appearance, in the back of church that Sunday, changed my life.

It was on a holiday to Wexford that I told her. We had taken our children away for a week's holiday together. For me, it was always good to leave Dublin behind and spend time on the beach with my children. I was happier away with them than at most other times. In a more relaxed state, it was also easier for me to be more open.

The moment of revelation was to occur in the oddest way. I was never one for watching soaps and thus when I sat down to watch *Coronation Street* that summer's evening, I was unprepared for the character of Hayley appearing on the screen. Here was a woman, who had once been a man, living in a relationship with a man. It was my first exposure to the world of the transsexual. It was a novelty for TV at that stage. The topic was rarely mentioned. I had never even heard of transsexualism. The nearest I had understood was the colourful world of the transvestites.

I can remember sitting there, extremely moved. I wanted to cry but it seemed inappropriate in the circumstance of a holiday. In every conversation in which the TV character, Hayley, explained herself I felt that I was listening to my own feelings. However, where she had longed to be a woman, I longed to be a man. It was as if someone had suddenly opened up a completely new horizon to me. The issue being described was me. I was suffering the same thing – I had found a label. I was gender dysphoric.

My only difficulty with the programme's portrayal of the character's life is that they had made the person Hayley fall in love with the oddest character of the programme – a man who walked around all day with a shopping bag and had rules for every part of his life. A man with no friends to talk to and a method of talking to others that involved staring at the ground or vaguely staring off into space. The overwhelming impression was that the only people that could fall in love with a transsexual were those socially unaccepted themselves – odd people, with psychological problems – thus creating a 'birds of a feather flock together' scenario.

So I was thirty-six when I finally understood who I was. I was a man inside a woman's body and that type of existence was out there. It was a difficult thing to process, but it was also very liberating. I felt suddenly relieved and almost at peace with myself. I knew who I was and I could identify almost entirely with the way Hayley saw the world and it saw her before her sex change. She had been at odds with her gender and it had created a feeling of not belonging. She had been a female inside a male body. She had escaped this unbearable life by having a sex change. The emphatic message of the programme's storyline was that the only escape route for a transgender person was to become a transsexual.

Films, books, television and newspaper articles have been selling that line ever since. Transgender means living in the wrong body. Transsexual is the correction of this state of being, leading to a happy life which is now acceptable and accepted as part of the binary existence forced upon our world in our polarised society.

Unfortunately, I took on the label of gender identity disorder that

Hayley presented, without considering the consequences of my actions. I decided that, as I was like her in my issues, I was also in the wrong body. I also decided, like Hayley, that I was going to denounce one part of my existence and try to completely associate with the inner voice. I was going to be more of a man and discount my femininity as much as possible. I would stop wearing any feminine clothes and playing the pretence of being a woman. In pursuing the persona of a male, I would embody the typical male stereotypes, almost as some gay men act exaggeratedly feminine. I would finally let my male side out of its prison. My feminine side would be ignored, banished. I even thought of having a sex change. I started to fantasise about the life that I could lead in a male body, but I was no longer a teenager with a pen, making up stories, I was now a mother and a wife making life-changing decisions.

The only problem that I had with my new-found transgender identity was that the idea of becoming a transsexual clashed with most of the spiritual teachings that I had acquired over the years. I had to leave behind my spirituality to own this new label. The religions that I followed did not have any place for the transgender at that time. Thankfully it is different now.

However, watching the soap on TV that June summer's day, I soon realised that finding the label was not enough. I had to express my new-found knowledge in order to give it life and make it real.

'What do you think of Hayley?' I asked my friend.

'What do you mean?'

'The idea of someone not being in the right body, have you ever heard of that before?' I looked at her for any curl of the lip or sign of unacceptance but she only shrugged her shoulders.

'It's sad isn't it really – someone being so unhappy in their own body!'

'Yes, it's really sad, but had you ever heard of it before?'

'Not much, why?' She replied.

The words just rushed out before I could grab them back.

'That's me.'

'Sorry?' she looked puzzled.

'I'm like that but before the operation of course. I'm in the wrong body.'

She turned to look at me. 'Are you being serious?'

'Yes. I've always wanted to be male. I don't feel I should be a woman.'

There were tears in my eyes now. It was finally said. I was thirty-six years of age and I had finally given it a voice.

'Oh I'm so sorry. That must be so difficult.'

I was never to regret telling her. I would never have told my sisters, or mother and father if I had not told her first. Without our wine-filled conversations, I would never have had the nerve to spill my truth. She was instrumental in opening the box containing my feelings. She also ensured that I looked for counselling to help me handle them. But that was years in the coming. I still had a great deal of self-loathing to work through and a great deal of angst in controlling my feelings once they were released.

Telling her completely opened the sore and it gathered pus quickly. My body started to show even more signs of the anger I held towards it. Once my hidden self was released, it was even more loath to return to the old patterns. I didn't want to be a wife; I didn't want to be a daughter and I was only happy viewing my mothering as parenting. In fact, I was now so caught up in the persona inside my outer shell that I actually almost forgot that the outside existed and had a reality too. I even went to one of my son's rugby matches and accidently introduced myself as his father. The man to whom I addressed the words looked at me completely perplexed. I died a little at his disbelieving expression.

I wanted the world to see the part of me that I had hidden for so long. I wanted to bring the inside out, especially now that I knew who I was. However, I did not want them to see me as a freak and that is all that I believed they would see if I told him that I was a man inside a woman's body. There were only two genders on display in society and I would have to inhabit one of them. I had tried the female on the outside so now I wanted to try the male living inside. The problem is that neither of them was fully me.

After telling my friend the truth, I thought that everything would be rosy, and that once revealed, everything would slip into place. In fact, it was exactly the opposite. It is undoubtedly true that you can't make an omelette without breaking eggs. By telling her, I had created a desire for an outcome that was still far from achievable. By cracking open the shell, I had left myself open to a beating, and I was to do it to myself. Whenever I tried to tell anyone else that I was gender identity disordered, it sounded false in my mind before I had even the words spoken. It sadly crumbled under my own scrutiny. I had children, I was married and I didn't look or seem 'different' in any way. What was I going to say?

Just because I had told my friend, it did not make telling anyone else any easier. It just made telling them a certainty at some point in the future, as I couldn't put my feelings back into their former protective shell. I had smashed that already. However, telling them took longer than I thought it would.

With my parents and my family the right words would not appear. I found myself growing even more distant from them and even more dependent on my friend. My truth only existed wherever she was. I became almost co-dependent. The problem was my life also centred around my drinking myself into happiness. I was smothering pain with alcohol, namely any type of white wine. I remember telling a friend once that a certain person must have been a heavy drinker as I was always seeing them in the pub. The friend laughed and pointed out that the only reason I saw them there that often was because I was in there drinking too. It made me think at the time that I was probably drinking too much but it didn't stop me doing it. My drinking was an escape mechanism.

I felt a stranger to my family. I didn't even spend holiday times with them and rushed away as soon as celebration dinners were over. I was living a lie with them. I had exposed the truth in one area of my life, and it was souring the rest, especially my marriage. I was sleeping with a man and inside I was a man. There was no part of our relationship that I could accept now. It was all false.

I had spent years living as my outer woman and now the pendulum swung completely in the opposite direction. I wanted to live my life as a man. However, I was incapable of revealing the truth to my family or my husband. It would take something dramatic to push me over the edge and reveal the truth to them. It was to take my own body rejecting me as fast as I was rejecting it. My health became more and more uncertain, from allergic reactions to dramatic bleedings and blinding headaches.

Chapter 25
Beginning the healing

I woke up one morning on a blood-soaked sheet and realised that I needed help. The bathroom floor had been cold. The alcohol had numbed my senses. I was sitting wondering how to move forward but everywhere I found traps. I had a husband, a mortgage and a job. I had responsibilities which confounded any change. At least that is how I saw things.

I don't remember thinking of it. I didn't premeditate the action. Angry with life I just took the razor blade to my left arm and cut through my skin – a long thin cut from wrist to elbow. God it hurt. It was so painful that I nearly blacked out. But it felt relieving.

In a strange way, as I started to bleed, I felt my body's pain was leaking around me. It was no attempt at suicide. I had two children and loved them dearly. I had never contemplated leaving them by taking my own life. However, sadly, many who live with gender dysphoria do take their own lives. This was just a drunken attack on my own body, which had always denied me the life that I had wanted, as far as I was concerned.

The cause of my stupid behaviour that night is still extremely embarrassing. I was again attracted to a woman whom I knew at the time. She was married, not gay, unavailable and very adamant that female bodies were not on her level of sexual desire. It wasn't the desperate need for just this one person that drove me to self-harming but the fact that she was just one of the many that I had hopelessly considered as prospective partners.

In my deluded eyes, a delusion that I have slowly come to understand, she was a woman and I was male. I believed it was natural for me to feel the way that I did towards her, and frustrating that I would never feel it back because of my female body. I wanted to live my life as my mind wished to live it. I wanted to escape my bodily trappings. The desire to be male and to be seen as a man was all that drove my thinking. It drove my thinking to the degree that I could not see the reality of my physical body.

Sheer panic had followed. Seeing the futility of my situation that night and fearing there was no escape route, I had taken out my frustration on my own poor body. I felt trapped. I hated the fact that I could not attract the women that I desired. There are people who have asked me why I didn't pursue a lesbian relationship. But I had no connection to my own body and therefore I couldn't acknowledge its femininity. Lesbians like being with women. I didn't want them to appreciate my body for being female. If they looked on me as a woman, it broke the bubble of the male that existed in my head. I even put on weight to make my body unattractive and to cover up its feminine curves. With rolls of fat, I could hide myself from the world. They were my protective layers. Looking back now they just made me very unhealthy and even less attractive to anyone – male or female.

It was a low point in my life sitting on that bathroom floor. I remember so clearly the coldness of the heater behind my back as I sat crying. I was drunk, not wasted beyond logical thoughts, but melancholy drunk. The night out had been spent with the object of my fantasies appearing in the pub and I felt trapped by the circumstances of my existence. How silly it all looks now, but how deeply unhappy I was then. I was playing the role of a woman. I was attempting to be a mother, a wife, a daughter and a sister, and yet I felt that no one knew me or understood me bar the one friend that I had told.

My marriage came under huge stress from my adoption of the label of gender identity disorder. I almost over identified with it overnight. It made my marriage a mockery, even though there were still parts of it that could have been salvaged. Sadly, to avoid my husband at night-time, I used the children as an excuse, looking after them rather than being with my husband, until eventually we ended up in separate rooms.

Having cut my arms in anger, I knew that my self-loathing was building to a dangerous state and that I needed help. To be honest, when I awoke the next morning to a blood-soaked sheet, I was terrified. I decided to tell the only person that I knew would act upon the knowledge quickly. I told my older sister, Susan.

'Susan, I've done a stupid thing.'

I could sense her gathering her thoughts. It was early in the morning.

'I've cut myself with a razor. I wasn't trying to commit suicide or anything but I've cut myself and I'm scared.'

Her response was so caring.

'It's okay. Don't worry. Are you still bleeding?'

'No, I've wrapped it. It's okay but I'm so sacred.'

'Look, don't worry, I'm here for you. Why don't I come over and we can talk about it together.'

Susan arranged the help I needed immediately. She has always been far more supportive of me than I have sometimes deserved. By twelve the next day I was in a psychiatrist's office facing a barrage of questions.

'Let's take a few background notes first,' suggested the psychiatrist, her pen at the ready.

Name, date of birth, marital status, occupation, children, my life in note form dictated.

'Now, why did you cut your arm?'

A long deep breath – well this was my chance, another person to explain it all to, someone who might understand.

'I am unhappy in my body.'

'Okay. Many people are but they don't take a blade to themselves.'

'I am living a lie – the marriage, the daughter, the sister – I'm in the wrong body.'

'And why would you see yourself as in the wrong body?'

'I should have been a man. I'm not a woman.'

A pause but the pen still scribbling. 'So did you want to end your life because of this?'

'Oh God, no! I was just very angry with my body for stopping me from having the life I want.'

'Have you ever done anything similar before?

'Not in terms of a blade.'

She looked at me intently. She wanted me to continue.

'I've stood on piers and looked into the water. But I love my children, I could never have jumped.'

'Yes, but you hurt yourself when you were drunk last night. You might not have the mental faculty to make the right decision if that happened again. You might act without thinking. I'm going to recommend you see another psychiatrist to evaluate the gender identity issue. He is the top consultant in Ireland for this. I don't think you are a suicide threat but I am worried that if you don't get help for this issue then you could accidentally jeopardise your life.'

My best friend took time off work and drove me to the appointment. I couldn't let my husband take me. I hadn't told him of the cutting or the gender problems. He didn't know the issues that were driving my depressive behaviour. He knew nothing of my newly adopted label. The appointment would have unveiled the truth to him.

The appointment was at St James's Hospital. I was terrified of what to expect. There was even a part of me that feared the psychiatrist would refute my claim and send me home as a delusional woman.

'Good morning, Christine is it?'

'No, Chris.' I shook the hand held out across the large desk.

'Well, Chris. You have been referred to me by my colleague concerning gender identity disorder. It is part of the assessment to ask you a series of questions. There are quite a few so we'll get started.'

There were well over fifty, some very specific. They seemed to go on for ages – questions dealing with the minutiae of life.

'What do you feel about mirrors?'

'I hate mirrors.'

He made a note of it with a silver ballpoint pen.

'Why is that then?' he responded.

'I don't like looking at myself as a woman. I don't like what I see.'

He nodded sagaciously. 'Very few of us like what we see in a mirror. Having a good self-image is difficult to achieve for many.'

'But it's not just my weight, or the size of my nose, it's the whole body. It's wrong.'

When the long list of questions were over, he asked me had I anything to add. I told him about my dreams.

'So what worries you about your dreams?'

'I dream as a man.'

He looked up from his note-taking and fixed me with an ironic, bemused face. 'How would you know how a man dreams, or the types of dream a man has? You're not a man.'

His making light of the issue irritated me. 'You misunderstand me. What I meant was, in my dreams I *am* a man, with a man's body and a man's life. I don't dream *like* a man, I dream *as* a man.'

The psychiatrist apologised and was taken aback with my angrily phrased answer. He made more copious notes on his neatly margined page.

'I think I have heard enough. I am in little doubt that you are gender identity disordered. You answered nearly every question in the fashion of someone with the disorder.'

I felt hugely relieved. I managed a smile.

'It's the usual custom for me to analyse the responses and get back to the patient at a later stage. However, due to your self-harming and the answering of the questions, I think we can proceed with a course of action.'

'So what's next?'

'Have you ever considered gender reassignment surgery?'

'Of course I've thought about it, but I have two children and I don't think it would be right to turn their mother into a father.'

'I understand. Is that the only reason stopping you?'

'No.'

'What else then blocks that as a way forward for you?'

'I just don't think I can. I might not like this body. In fact I hate it. But it is me.'

'To be honest, most people that I see are here because they want to go through with gender reassignment. I see them as a psychiatrist because they want to go further and take the hormones. My support of them is medical. I don't think we need to have another individual session in that case but I do think you should attend the monthly transgender group meeting in the hospital. It will give you support and like-minded people to talk to about how you feel.'

I was disappointed. Once a month – it had taken me nearly thirty years of my life to get to asking for help and now I was only going to have a group meeting once a month which was basically a talk shop.

The psychiatrist held out a piece of paper. 'This is the date and time of the next meeting. They're on Wednesdays at lunchtime. Hopefully, you will be able to get the time off work.'

I stood to leave.

'It is not easy living as a gender dysphoric person,' he looked more sympathetic now, 'although some manage it. However, they rarely cross my path and they live that life usually without telling people. I meet the ones struggling who want the sex change.'

'Well I just can't go down that route at the moment, if ever,' I replied.

'I just need to tell you that those who don't have the surgery do have problems remaining in the same body. The statistics are not good. GID sufferers can often fall into drink or drugs or, even worse, suicide by the time they are fifty. So it is an issue you have to learn to deal with.'

Facing a life of possible drug abuse or attempted suicides was not what I expected to hear. I found it a disturbing insight. I had to find a way out of the mess without resorting to surgery.

I did attend some group sessions in St James's Hospital in Dublin. I told my principal of my new label and surprisingly she reacted very positively and agreed to give me time off once a month to go to these sessions. Unfortunately, I found them more disturbing than helpful. Most of the people there were MTF (male to female) transsexuals. They had gone through the surgery but were still attending sessions. They were still unhappy with their appearance. It was common to hear self-criticism.

'Do you think I should have a bit more taken off my forehead?'

A circle of people would stare back and mutter positive words about the woman's appearance.

'But I still don't look right. I'm not feminine enough. I still wouldn't pass as a female really.'

The group would then rally around further, saying overly positive remarks about her appearance, exaggerating any good feature they could find.

'Yes, but your nose job is great. It's much more feminine than mine.'

What was a feminine nose I wondered? I knew lots of woman with big noses, some famous people amongst them. What were these people looking for, some false perfection?

The praise seemed to help.

'That's good. It's just so hard after all the operations and hormones to still look so male.'

It seemed they all had an image in their head of what they would look like after gender reassignment, and none of them had actually achieved it. Surgery didn't make their hands or feet any smaller. It didn't take inches off their height. I found the whole experience extremely sad. Coupled with which, the only FTM (female to male) that I met was a very aggressive young man who was uncommunicative most of the time. He rarely came to sessions and seemed to have a problem with the MTFs dominating the conversation.

I wanted to belong to this group and find a resonance with them, but I felt a complete outsider. They were all spending money and time trying to be a woman and I was sitting there bemoaning the fact that I was one.

Suddenly, even the label of gender identity disorder felt a misrepresentation. I didn't like being a woman but I really didn't want to go through what they had endured to change my life for the better. Was I losing another label? Where did I fit in?

Why was I was losing the label? It boiled down to the fact that everyone that I had encountered, or talked to, about GID saw sex change as the only outcome to achieve happiness. Their approach was based on the fact that they understood the condition of gender identity disorder as being in 'the wrong body' not as the alternative reality which it can also be – a combination of one gender in body and another in mind. I was starting to reject their version of the label. I was not in the wrong body. I was just in a body that was the polar opposite to my brain. However, I still had to tell my parents and family and GID was the only label that I could find to cover my feelings at the time. Maybe it was the wrong label, but it was the only one I had back then.

My best friend advised me not to leave myself without support so I decided to attend a psychologist with years of experience in America with the transgender community. His office was on the second floor of a Georgian building in the centre of Dublin. He didn't prove to be the support that I needed either.

'So life has been very hard for you so far? Pretending is difficult. Hiding the real you painful.'

I nodded at him as he looked sympathetically at me across his antique table.

'Have you considered having a sex-change?'

Again – the same question! Was there no other solution, less dramatic and less irreversible? I shook my head.

'It's just you would make a really good man.' He was looking at me intently now. 'You have good, broad shoulders, and a face that would easily make the transition into male. You'd be a handsome man you know.'

I didn't know what to say. Was it a compliment? My male side readily accepted it as a positive remark but my feminine exterior, which was also a part of me, found the comment slightly offensive. Why can't I be accepted for who I am? Why do I have to change to be acceptable?

I never returned to his office again.

Chapter 26
Ending the life of a woman

'Where are we going?'

'I've rented a house for us to live in. I know it's not with Dad but it's impossible for me to stay with your dad anymore. I'm sorry.'

How inadequate the word 'sorry' is sometimes. How useless it is when you are radically destroying two lives. Children are those who suffer when parents make poor decisions.

'Is it far?'

'No, it's only a mile from here. You can see your father anytime you want. And it's close to your schools and friends.'

Two faces looked at me anxiously.

'Will you be happier, Mummy?'

How unselfish my children were at that moment.

I packed the last teddy bear and duvet into the car and looked back at the house, my home for seventeen years. It was always going to end in tears. I had never chosen it myself. It was imposed upon me. I married a man who already lived in a house and never wanted to move from it. At the time, it had seemed like a good prospect. It was a very good four-bedroom, semi-detached house in a suburb of Dublin. From the top bedrooms you could see across the sea towards Howth. The back garden was very long and accommodated a children's play area and rows of neatly planted courgettes, potatoes, carrots and onions. We had a seemingly perfect house in which to build a new married life. Except it wasn't perfect! It had belonged to his mother and father. We had bought the family home from his mother and I had bought it not knowing the pain which came with it. His father had committed suicide in the house. It was not a fact that I even knew when I had married him. His emotional past was as buried as mine. The house was almost haunted with his presence. Every time my mother-in-law visited, she moved back the furniture that she had left behind to its original position.

'Why have you moved the copper bucket? It looks much better where it used to be,' she would say.

I lived in a house where the past was protected, preserved and policed. I was an interloper in my own home. I understood their pain at seeing change, but I could not live with my house preserved as a relic to a painful past. So every year, I tried to repaint, redesign and remove the old to create a new atmosphere. It caused many quarrels between us.

'Why have you moved the copper bucket again? It does look so much better where it always was,' he would say.

But I couldn't live in a mausoleum.

'Why don't we move down the country? Buy a bigger and more rural property. You can get a transfer with your company and I can look for a new job.'

I had tried to keep the marriage going. No matter how much I wanted to live a different life, I had made a vow to live with my husband until death us do part and I felt my children deserved to come from more than a broken home.

'But we have good jobs and a lovely house here.'

'Yes, but we could afford so much more down the countryside and life would be better for the children – fresh air and outdoors in nature. You loved that growing up.'

Maybe I was lucky that the move failed. Maybe it would have just prolonged the agony of living a lie and failing to live the truth. However, I did try to fix things between us. We both had tried. We had gone to marriage counselling, but it was never going to be a fixable problem. That was never going to happen after I told him.

'Look I have something to tell you. It may explain my moody state recently and other things between us. It's difficult for me to say and I didn't know it when we married.'

He didn't respond. He just looked at me.

'I think that I'm in the wrong body. I am one of those people that should have been born in the opposite sex. I feel more like a man than a woman.'

My marriage was now in the balance. I had put it out there. I was hoping for some form of acceptance, although that was ridiculous. I had just landed a bombshell on a very reserved man. His response would frame our future together.

'Could you please say something, even if it's angry?'

He looked at me with unsympathetic eyes and said, 'You're mentally insane.'

'Is that what you think?'

'Yes, you're mentally insane. You need help.'

I understood at one level. I had felt that way about myself for years. However, I also felt totally rejected. We never mentioned 'my condition' again, after that one short conversation. So the marriage counselling failed to improve anything and I walked out of my marriage after seventeen years. It was one of the hardest things to do. I left behind my home and my security.

'Can I choose my bedroom first?'

Children are very resilient on one level.

'Yes, of course you can. There are four bedrooms, and just three of us, so go ahead.'

We arrived at our rented house in Flower Grove and my children dashed through the open door and up the stairs. Within minutes they had claimed their domains and were emptying their toys on to shelves.

'It's an okay house, Mum.'

I had rented a big house. It was costing me a fortune on my salary. The solicitor had told me not to leave my marital home. He had told me that I would be relinquishing so much if I walked out. I have never been one to listen to advice if it went against my instinct. I couldn't have expected my husband to leave our family home. It had belonged to his family. Besides, I didn't want to live there with the ghosts of his past and the copper bucket!

The new home was good – four bedrooms and a very large living space – it was a wonderful place for the first six months of our new lives. However, it didn't stop both my children from having a rough ride with the separation. They were so thoughtful in their pain. They hid most of it from me and put on a brave face. They were so unselfish. Talking with them since, I have realised how much they kept inside rather than adding to my burden at the time. On the other hand, I felt so selfish, tearing apart their lives because I had failed in mine.

I was very careful to keep their father in their lives in every other way I could. The first Christmas apart, I invited him for Christmas dinner. I also asked him on our Easter holiday in Galway. In fact, he came to Christmas dinner for the first four years of our separation. I wanted my children to understand that this was not a separation of utter dislike for one another. It was a parting of the ways because I had changed. It was important for them to have their father in their lives. It was a time of huge change for all of us but it was important to keep the lines of communication open as we were all emotionally raw.

I also found myself in a relationship with a woman – an unexpected twist of a casual meeting. It was a strange relationship as it mirrored my pendulum swing away from the feminine and towards the masculine.

I tried dating through online sites. I entered my details into a computer but then hit a huge roadblock. I didn't know what category to enter under. There were only two types of options – heterosexual or gay/lesbian. I did not fit into either category. I didn't want a gay relationship but I definitely did not want another man. It took me ages to pick up the courage to enter lesbian as I thought it had the best chance of a match.

My first blind date was a complete failure. The girl waiting for me with a pint in front of her was dressed in khaki, had piercings in every available part of her body and hair spikier than a hedgehog. She looked at me with the same misgivings. I was in jeans and a jumper, looking like a boring middle-class frump. Our conversation did not help move things any more positively. She was firmly attached to the most expressive form of lesbianism as a label. She hated men.

'So you're not a lesbian?' Her face looked angry.

'No. But I do want to be with women so I had no other box to tick.'

'But you want to be a man?'

'Well not exactly, I don't want a sex change.'

'But you think you are a man in the wrong body.'

'Yes, I suppose you could say that.'

'Are you mad? Why would you want to be a man? Women kick ass!'

This lady wanted woman-on-woman action. She did not want to be with a hybrid! We had one swift drink together and the night was over. I left the hotel deciding that the internet was not going to help me find a new relationship. I was looking for someone to accept my maleness. We should be careful what we ask for in life.

I found a woman who did just that – she looked on me as nothing but my male side. She alienated me from everything feminine. My first relationship with a woman brought even more problems into my life. It was my fault as I had attracted her. She was a heterosexual woman as far as she was concerned and therefore she could not conceive of having a relationship with a woman. Her label of heterosexuality was a badge which she wore clearly. For her, my label of gender identity disorder was an acceptable condition, as it gave her the chance of saying to herself that she was actually with a man. She was with a man who was just in the wrong body, a body that she could ignore and just fully fix on the gender masculinity. To this woman, I became what I thought I wanted to be – I became the male trapped inside.

Our relationship was fundamental in releasing me from the feminine but it also created a false masculine which was equally as injurious. She squashed any feminine instinct or behaviour in me, so that she could fool herself in staying within heterosexual boundaries. She even stopped me wearing earrings as she saw them as a show of femininity. Anything even remotely feminine was removed.

'I'm not going out with you wearing that jumper.'

'I'm sorry?'

'That jumper, where did you get it, did you buy it? I can't imagine you bought it.'

'No, my mother bought it for me for Christmas.'

'I hate it on you, the flowers look ridiculous, it's not you.'

So I put the jumper in the back of my wardrobe and never wore it in her presence again. I wore more manly jumpers, greys and blues, jeans and white shirts.

I had the same problem with my body. She hated seeing its femininity.

'Please don't take off your shirt.'

'Okay.'

I put on six stone during my time with her in order to cover my femininity in a pile of fat. If I was with her romantically, or physically, then my body had to be hidden from view. I felt like one of those unfortunate lepers in India. I became an untouchable, an untouchable for everything female about my body. I had to wear a shirt in every sexual encounter. I had to cover up my sexual body. It caused huge issues for me as I became more, and more, angry with its lack of masculinity. I hated my outer shell in her presence.

Luckily, this woman was not in my life for too long. However, her place in my story is very important. She made me realise that I was my physical body as well as the masculine inside it. I could not divorce myself from my exterior as if it was wrong or horrible. However, this realisation did not come easily. It came after many very wise people gave me good advice. It also came after I wrote out my personal dilemma.

Chapter 27
Writing out my confusion

The first step in my healing came in the writing of a book – not this biographical story but a fictional one. Since I was a child, I had always written. I could be a man on every page that I penned. I could fly aeroplanes in the Second World War, play football for Liverpool and attract the most beautiful women. As a teenager, when my body changed shape to a body that I couldn't accept, I sat on beaches and wrote as if my life depended on it, and, in some ways, my sanity did!

There is one particular time that springs to mind. I was staying with my uncle and aunt in the south of Wales. They took me to a beach in Porthcawl called Rest Bay. It is a horseshoe-shaped beach flanked by rocks and safe for swimming. That day I sat high up on the rocks overlooking the sand. As my cousin and family did the usual sunbathing and swimming, I sat writing. I was filled with the desire to be someone else. I was in another country but I wanted to be in another life altogether. It is strange that, as someone who cannot remember one holiday from the next, or one past story from the rest, this one episode at the beach sticks out so prominently in my mind. It just encapsulates all that I was at the time – moody, reflective, isolated and self-absorbed. You could say that I was a typical hormonal teenager!

Writing was an avenue for my anger, my feelings and my sexual preferences. Those journals, written on beaches, park benches and under the bedclothes at night, have long since gone, scattered through various rubbish dumps, the whimsical thoughts of a teenager in angst. However, they served their purpose well. They gave my alternative side a life of its own.

*

Therefore, it was an obvious option as an adult, angry with the lack of alternatives given by the psychiatrists and counsellors, to write an escape for my gender issue. I incorporated the psychiatrist's unwelcome advice of gender reassignment surgery into the pages of a book, where I turned myself into a transsexual.

In black and white, through words rather than operations, I had the sex change. I felt each word as if it was real. I could not write quickly enough. I wrote the whole book on my laptop and then curiously watched as the walls of that once secretly held dream came tumbling down. I knew, before I had even finished the ending, that I didn't want to become a man any more. The book did not give me the relief that I had expected. The book left me with more questions than answers.

The story revealed the absurdity of my situation. I didn't want to be either fully male or fully female. Being male was not perfect either! In the past I had always felt that I was living a lie – 'pretending' to be a woman, while knowing in my head that, no matter what my body dictated, I was in fact a man; a man rendered impotent by his lack of male body. But, through writing the fictional book, I realised that having a sex change would only create another lie for me. I could medically create the body of a man but I was still not a man from birth. I would only be a man created by surgery and hormone therapy. A man created in a hospital through operations which were painful and difficult.

Who actually was the real me, the real Chris? It seemed I was reaching an understanding that I was neither male nor female but both. I wasn't hermaphrodite with both sexual organs but transgender with two competing parts – a body and a mind. I had to find a way to live both. However, I had spent so much of my life hating my female body that learning now to accept it would be the hardest thing of all.

As much as I believed that I wasn't truly female, no matter how much surgery I would have, I would never be truly male either. I would always be someone who had been born a bit of both and would have to face that fact with the world and with myself. I would have to tell any future partner that I met, any real friends that I made, that I had been born a physical woman. If I hid my past then that would be lying too and thus my male creation would be nothing more than another lie.

Today, I can actually state it. I am not male. I am not a man! How liberating to state that truth. I have come a long way! I had wanted to be accepted by society so I wanted to be fully one or the other of society's polarised genders.

However, I am not only a female either. My body may be female, and it is what people see on the exterior, but in reality I am a complex melding of both male and female. I do not wish to be judged by my cover, as our gender-polarised society does all the time. I wish to be seen for the person that exists within this exterior frame. In fact, I think we all wish to be accepted for the person who lies within the body. It is not just my particular issue. It is universal.

I realised that I would have to find an answer outside of the medical world to help me cope with self-acceptance. Yet again I looked to the world of spirituality for my answers, but this time I looked for an alternative, outside of the mainstream churches. I turned to the alternative healers and their world. Writing a fictional book helped me assess my life from a different perspective, but the alternative therapists gave me the teachings that I needed to go further. They showed me that we are more than just our bodies and that none of us really belong in our bodies. Our bodies are just the vehicles to carry our spirits through life. We all belong in a spirit realm. As Teilhard de Chardin once wrote, 'We are not human beings having a spiritual experience. We are spiritual beings having a human experience.'

Writing the book was a cathartic exercise which made me realise that if the truth was to set me free then I had to live in this body for the rest of my life and simply learn to love it. If I was to acknowledge that truth openly and honestly, then I had to admit that my body was indeed female and there had to be a reason for me being born this way. The problem was that I was a long way from feeling happy in my body and, although my book had shown me a glimpse of the truth, I was still nowhere nearer to understanding how I was to make that peace with my body. That knowledge was to begin during a skiing trip to France, where I met a gifted reflexologist.

Chapter 28
One foot on the path to healing

Healing began in the clear air of the French Alps. My older sister took my two children and me skiing. It was a holiday that changed things for me, because it was when the 'real' world started to come out from behind the veil.

In France, I spent most of my time keeping my older sister company as she didn't ski at that time. We rode on bubbles high up into the Alpine mountains and looked down at the lines of skiers, winding their way down the slopes. In the grandeur of that landscape, it was easy to find God. The craggy peaks and green valleys, hundreds of feet below, were majestic. The air seemed purer and there was a distinct lack of mankind's desecration of nature in this remote landscape. Nature seemed to have the upper hand.

Towards the middle of the week, Susan suggested that we both go for a massage. She chose a full-body massage. The idea of disrobing, to be wrapped only in a towel, and then having strange hands on my skin scared me to the core. The removal of my socks was the only alternative. Even taking my socks and trousers off for a reflexologist was a difficult mental journey in 2004.

Luckily, the reflexologist was a lovely Scottish girl with a happy disposition. I didn't see her face as I was lying on a bed in a room with the curtains closed, but she had a melodic, hypnotic voice and I soon fell into a soporific state. It was my first experience of the power of healing hands. Her hands were gentle but firm on my feet. The massage sent shivers up my spine to the top of my head. To this day, it amazes me how such tiny massaging of the toes can create such a wonderful feeling. I know now that it is the Qi which flows through the body that is being released through the work.

My body had never been given so much pleasure before in a non-sexual way. The flow of energy through me was impressive. She didn't talk as she worked which made the experience even more relaxing. Only now and again did she stop to put more massage oil on her hands. At the end, she gave me a list of issues that were going on in my body. To be fair, she was totally correct. She gave me some tips on healing these issues and told me that alternative treatments were successful for helping most of them. I was so impressed with her work that I asked her for another session later in the week. I was hooked on the experience.

It was in this second session that she emotionally pushed my buttons. As I lay on my stomach, preparing to be cocooned again, she started quietly talking.

'Do you believe in spirit?'

It was an odd opening to a conversation and my mind was in such a relaxed state that I didn't want to reply.

'Yes, I do sometimes. Why?'

'I know this is unusual but it happens the odd time when I do reflexology. I seem to tune into the client's life.'

I began to feel extremely uncomfortable. What could she know about me from twiddling my toes?

'With you I see a woman in spirit around you – your grandmother. She is a lovely person, small and so kind and singing hymns all the time.'

I was not expecting to hear about my grandmother lying on a plinth in the French Alps, especially twenty-four years after her death. I could feel tears welling in my eyes. I couldn't reply.

'I hope you don't mind me telling you this?'

I croaked a faint 'no'.

'She says you need help. You're not happy.'

I did cry then. Not loudly so that she could hear me, but softly, down my cheeks and on to the plinth.

'May I suggest that you look for someone like me when you go home, someone to help you through alternative healing?'

I turned to face her. 'Is there someone like you out there? Is this normal for reflexology?'

She smiled. 'I'm sorry. I'm psychic you see and I don't usually interfere. I usually just do the reflexology which has nothing to do with what I'm saying. Maybe I shouldn't have said anything but your gran was insistent.'

'It's okay. I loved her very much and it's comforting to know that she is still out there somewhere.'

'Oh she is. Definitely! She loves you too but says that it's time now for you to find the truth about things.'

'How do I do that?'

'Go home from this holiday and find someone alternative who connects to spirit and heal with them.'

So I had gone on a non-skiing holiday in the Alps only to find the first piece of the jigsaw of self-acceptance. I arrived back and set out on a mission to find my healer.

Chapter 29
Feeling not thinking: The second piece

I found the second healer, oddly enough, next to the fish shop in my local suburban village after I had spent weeks, possibly months, looking. I had searched the internet, attended some hard-working but less than illuminating reflexologists, and had almost given up on my venture. Then, rather coincidentally, I was standing in a street that I had walked down over half of my life and it was there, in front of my nose, staring out at me. It was not the exact answer to a quest for reflexology but I was immediately drawn to it. The sign read: 'REIKI MASTER, Psycho-Spiritual Healer'. I took down the number, rang the woman and booked an appointment. I had no idea what reiki was. I had never even heard of it before and thus I didn't have a clue how the healing would be conducted. It was literally a step of faith.

The door open and two piercing blue eyes looked out at me. 'So why have you booked this appointment for yourself?' She was a small woman with a firm gaze.

Oddly, I drew a circle in the air. 'I want to be whole.'

'Okay,' she smiled, 'that's a condition which can take a long time to achieve.'

Her smile made me feel at ease.

'Sit down and we will go through some questions to ascertain how best I can help you.'

My first session with her was quite beautiful. After a series of simple questions about my age, background and health, she put me on her plinth. I closed my eyes, she put on her music and then the colours appeared: purples and oranges, reds and greens. It was like flying through a rainbow. My body felt warm and tingly.

She had told me prior to the session that it was a non-contact healing and that she would not be putting a hand on me, so I stole a look when I felt firm, downward pressure on my legs. But I was shocked by what I saw. She was nowhere near my legs, she was standing by my shoulders and yet the feeling of a weight or touch on my leg persisted. This was the pattern of our sessions for many weeks. At times it felt like someone else's hands were actually inside my body, scouring my organs, scrubbing my system, cleansing it all from within. I went every Friday at five after work and she healed me through colour and heat and spiritual energy.

The cost of the sessions was affordable, compared to a local visit to a medical doctor. However, the weekly nature of the visits was a strain on my finances. Nevertheless I had to go. I was hooked. I needed that feeling of energy being pulsed through me and I needed our conversations that were getting further to the root of my problems.

At the beginning and end of each session, we would talk and I would tell her bit by bit about my gender issue and my fears. It was a painful uncovering of layers. It was like scrapping away layers of sticky wallpaper to find more underneath, each one harder to remove than the other. It took six months, but slowly and surely I felt healthier, happier and more self-assured. It was a happiness that I had not felt since I was a child, before puberty took away my smile and I was forced to become one definite sex. She gave me the courage to end the negative relationship with the 'heterosexual' woman.

'You need to bring your life back into balance, Chris. By your own admission, she is no good for you. So why do you persist in staying in a bad relationship?'

I cried a great deal in her healing room.

Years of anger and frustrations exploded after a lifetime of being locked away, and the experience of such outbursts amazed me. Although I knew I had serious gender issues when I began attending her, I also believed that I was a well-rounded and efficient human being in other areas of my life. I thought of myself as successful, and most other people would probably have viewed me that way. However, it was a measuring of success through practical achievements – degrees, medals, honours etc. As an emotional human being, I was a walking disaster, making my way from one wreck to another. And although her healing was profound, I found out later that we were only dealing with the surface wounds and there was far more work to be done to create a happier soul.

'I want you to keep a diary of your feelings for the next two weeks,' she requested.

'No problem, that will be easy, you're dredging up loads here.'

'Oh, I don't think you will find it that easy.'

I ran into problems the first week.

'So did you keep your diary of your feelings?'

I smiled back at her as if I had been the perfect student. 'Yes, I have about thirty pages of them.'

'Excellent, you do surprise me. I thought you'd find this exercise difficult.'

I was really pleased. I liked pleasing this woman. She knew me better than even my family and I was happy to be a good client.

'So give me an example of what you've been feeling during the week.'

I described an example from my notes. Her face fell and she shook her head.

'That's not a feeling,' she said.

'It is,' I countered too quickly and emphatically.

'Chris, it is *not* a feeling, it is a thought.'

It was then my turn to look puzzled. I didn't understand her. As far as I was concerned it was exactly what I was feeling and I reiterated this with even more foolish confidence.

'But I was sitting down for dinner and I realised that being a mother was a really good thing in my life. I want to be their mother. That's good, isn't it?'

'Of course it's good but it's a thought, you are not describing your feelings,' she repeated. 'That is your challenge, Chris, to tell the difference between your thoughts and your feelings because, at the present moment, you really can't.'

It was a painful thing for me to hear but she was completely correct. I had no idea how to talk about my feelings, even alone and to myself in a diary. I had buried them for so long. My head was totally in charge of my life and I had accepted its dominion over me. So much so that when my brain told me that I was a male, I accepted that wholeheartedly. My whole self therefore had to be male, rather than realising that my brain was just one part of who I was.

Now I was scared of what I had created for myself. If I was gender identity disordered then was this purely a thought too, a label created by my thinking? Was it just a tyranny of the mind over the body? What did I really feel about myself?

My brain had always told me who I was, what I needed and how to live my life. But now I was beginning to see my brain was just a very good computer. It could be inputted by any teacher or government or society. Anything society could see as good, I saw as good; anything society dictated as bad, I usually saw as bad. My mind was malleable. She made me question whether it was beneficial to listen to what was inside my head.

'You need to meditate on truthfulness, go to the heart of the matter.'

'What do you mean?'

'Chris, what you feel is really important and you need to access those deep feelings to find the truth in your life.'

'Okay,' I replied defensively. 'I understand what you're saying but I don't know how I feel now, except confused.'

'Then that's a good place to start from. Accept that you are confused and look into why.'

Gandhi once wrote, 'A man is but the product of his thoughts. What he thinks, he becomes.' I needed to watch carefully what I was thinking. I once thought that I should try to be a woman but it failed as it went against my feelings of masculinity. I then see-sawed the other way and dropped my pretence of being a woman in favour of the male, but it was a failure too, as it did not express my true nature either.

My thoughts were now in a spin. I realised that in looking for societal acceptance, I had adopted a label from a TV programme, giving me the false assumption that I was in the wrong body as it had reflected my gender issues. I had taken society's consideration of my existence as the only answer, and I had failed to look for the truth within myself. I had failed to listen to my own feelings. Society as binary had driven me into thinking that I could not be happy staying in a non-binary state. I had to be one or the other to exist happily within society's framework.

We are all living in a holographic universe but, while we reflect the bigger picture, each of us has an individual picture which is different in itself. How can we see this individual picture if we are too busy looking outside of ourselves for the answer and for acceptance? Looking outside of ourselves only makes us doubt who we are, as there is no one like us. We are all individual. So we should not conform to labels that make us less than truthful to our own individual reality. We must truly look at what creates our beliefs.

The six months of healing with my Reiki Master was so powerful that I asked her to train me in reiki. I was hurt when she flatly refused. She used the excuse that she was too busy with her healing practice. She was not the type of woman that you asked twice so I let it go.

Oddly, a month later, she did offer to train me to the first level of reiki but it was to be done properly – no 'fast track' learning. I was to take my time and understand the seriousness of opening myself to such a life.

'You know it worries me how people think they can learn reiki these days. It's not something that you can learn in a weekend course. It takes time. There's a lot to take in and after each level of reiki there should be a period of reflection and absorption to understand the depths of the teachings.'

I nodded in understanding.

'In the Western world we like to fast track everything. It is why we fail to lead meaningful lives. We don't take our time with anything. Everything is rushed. I will not train you if you want to be a fast-track learner.'

'I understand. I don't want that either.'

'Are you sure?'

'Yes, I want to get it right,' I replied.

'It's not about getting it right. Not everyone is supposed to be a reiki healer. Everyone can learn it. Everyone can sit in a class but not everyone's path is to become a reiki healer or a reiki teacher. Besides, the soul needs to heal itself before it can heal others, Chris. So maybe you are ready for stage one but you have more personal healing to do yet.'

Of course I was deflated. I felt as if I was being told that I was not good enough. However, she was right. It is like what the biblical passage expresses – we must remove the stick from our eye before we remove the stick from another's. I have since learned that the wounded warrior, healed of their wounds, makes a good healer because they have more empathy for a client's suffering. However, the wounded warrior must fight a difficult battle before they become healed enough to assist others.

The shed in the garden of her rented house became my school for reiki Level I. It was an amazing location for such training – a small, intimate space, filled with her spiritual paintings. With her daughter as my fellow classmate, we went through the basics of training and the magic started to happen. It is so difficult to explain this magic to anyone who has not experienced it. How does one describe a miracle?

Modern Western society still lives under a Newtonian viewpoint of physics. Quantum physics may have rocked the science world but it has not become the paradigm for society yet. Newtonian physics anchors us to a linear time of existence with its fundamental laws. New quantum physics is challenging this existence that we have taken for gospel; it is a physics of almost spiritual origins – understanding the world through the realms of an intelligent life force that is creative and dynamic, thoughtful and also reactive to thought. The world of our scientific awareness is closing in on the world of our spiritual understanding. This is a very exciting time in history.

One of my strongest memories from my first training in reiki started my experiential learning of the world of spirit and it still makes me feel happy when I think about it. It proved to me, more than anything else at that time, that the universe of conscious interaction was out there and I was part of it, wrapped up in its survival, playing out my story in its growth to self-awareness.

As part of my training, I was asked to draw a symbolic picture of how I saw my life at that present time. It was one of the first exercises that we did at the beginning of the weekend. Always eager to draw and paint, I was quick to create my life on a page. I drew a tree at the top of a mountain. Leading up to the mountain was a winding path. It was a sturdy enough tree with three branches. Each of the branches, to my cluttered thinking, represented a part of my life at that time. I thought of them as physical, emotional and spiritual representations of me. My branches were totally devoid of leaves and the tree looked like it was either dying or in its winter state. After I had finished the drawing, I reflected on the image with a certain amount of sadness. It looked an empty landscape.

Afterwards, we discussed what our images represented. I remember saying that I felt as if my life was fruitless and lacking in purpose. I remember thinking that I was not achieving my purpose, whatever that purpose was to be. She asked me to remember what I was feeling as the weekend continued.

The reiki training was like nothing else I had ever experienced. We did dancing to release our energy. I was amused at the loudness of the music and mesmerised by the twirling of her body. I was not someone who easily displayed anything in front of others, unless I was intoxicated with alcohol. I was self-contained, almost withdrawn in the expression of my emotions. Rhythmic dancing, letting the body free of its inhibitions, was an alien exertion. It was a dancing that left no room for ego. In order to take part properly, I had to inhabit my body fully and feel the music.

I was pushed to free myself of limiting beliefs. We rotated around the space of that small shed as if the rhythm of the dance was releasing a confined energy. It was a boundary-destroying experience. I began to feel what it was like to trust others with my full presence. I began to inhabit my body again and to see how good it felt to dance – to dance with freedom, to dance without self-criticism.

As the weekend progressed, we learned healing techniques and ways of holding space for another's health issues. We ate organic lunches in her kitchen and walked amongst the trees in the garden to connect with nature. It was a relaxing experience. Besides the intensive learning and the difficult moments of uncovering the true self, I was happier in that space than anywhere else at that time.

This Reiki Master had listened to my life for six months so she was well aware of my story of gender identity disorder. It was a knowledge that was nearly to come between us. Before she was prepared to initiate me into reiki I, she wanted me to declare that I was a woman. She said that in order for me to heal, I had to realise that my body was female and I had to embrace this truth. I cannot accurately express here how angry I felt with her at that time. I categorically did not want to say that I was a female. I was not ready to accept my outer femininity. I was still so attached to the label of gender identity disorder. I had told so many people at that stage that I could not admit to being a woman, even if biologically and physically it was a truth dictated by my genitalia.

I had tied myself firmly to not being a woman and inhabiting the wrong body. The reality was that I was nowhere near to healing that deep wound. As far as I was concerned, my Reiki Master was now my enemy. She was only seeing me as my outer shell and trying to force me to accept that existence as my only reality. I rebelled against her entirely.

It became a struggle between us. She kept pressing me to accept my femininity and I kept ignoring her. But she was insistent that she wouldn't initiate me unless I gave in.

It was said much like de Valera's 'empty formula' of 1927. The words spewed out from my mouth but I did not mean any of them and I could not wait to ignore them.

I shouted it out. 'Okay, I give up, I'm a woman.'

It was not from any conviction that I was female but because I wished to be initiated into the healing. Inside I was angry with her beyond words and my anger found the oddest expression. I literally started bleeding. From a pin prick of a mark just under my nose, blood gushed out into my cupped hands. It was funny at first but then it became rather scary as I couldn't stop it. The Reiki Master had warned both me and her daughter that, during the initiation ceremony, we might start coughing or sneezing or doing something odd, but bleeding had not been on her list. I went through a wad of tissues trying to stem the flow. When it all disappeared, there was no nosebleed or deep cut or broken sore but a tiny pin prick only just visible in the skin. It really shocked me at the time. Today I know it was a purging of sorts, a release. I had faced my first acknowledgement of the truth. I was in a female body, whether I liked it or not, and that body lived and breathed and bled as a woman.

However, the reiki training was to have more tricks up its sleeve than a mere shedding of blood. During the weekend, we also did a partly guided meditation. She verbally led us into a quiet place in nature and then left our quietened minds to produce the rest. On our return from the meditative state, we were asked to draw what we felt or saw in our mind's eye.

I have never been good at meditating. My mind refuses to stay quiet enough from the noise of everyday chatter and worries. It overthinks and refuses to relax. However, whether it was her soft tones or the smell of incense in the small room, as she stopped talking, my mind quickly drifted away. The wooden shed disappeared and, in its place, I could see armies driving their enemies across battlefields. These were huge armies, as in a Cecil B. DeMille film, thousands of men on horseback and on foot, wielding spears and swords. Castles and ramparts were sacked and destroyed and great rulers brought to their knees. As I saw the vision in my meditation, I could also hear poetic words running through my head:

> My name is Ozymandias, King of Kings:
> Look on my Works, ye Mighty, and despair!
> Nothing beside remains. Round the decay

Of that colossal Wreck, boundless and bare
The lone and level sands stretch far away.

My meditative state had internally brought forward the lines from 'Ozymandias', a poem by Shelley, which I had learned in school. It describes the ravages of time and the transitory nature of material things. It was a poem that always held significance for me. Maybe it was because my English teacher had asked me in my fifth year of senior school to come up to the blackboard and draw the poem as an image, or maybe it was because the notion of nothing having permanence appealed to me. Our bodies, castles, bricks and mortar are all temporary existences.

When we had finished meditating, we were asked to draw an image of our meditation. In my drawing I included the poem, but I also included an image of a pyramid with a large eye inside it. At the time it was not an image that I had ever to my knowledge seen before. I asked the teacher what it was and if it had any significance. She talked of the omnipotence of the eye, the essence of its power. Interestingly, it is an image that I have seen in a multitude of places since that weekend. I have seen it on the American dollar, in films and in books. Since starting a spiritual path, I have had images, numbers, songs, poems and books all serendipitously appear.

My meditative state gave me an insight into the nature of my own existence. No matter how much I fought with my body and hated its existence as female, it was not going to survive into the future anyway. It would wither and die and decompose. As strange as it might seem, that piece of knowledge was liberating for me. I knew from my meditation that one day I would be free of my body's limitations again. I would be back in the world of spirit and Christine/Chris would be gone.

At the end of that first weekend, we were again asked to draw a picture but this time how we saw ourselves, now that the initiation was over. I drew the tree again, but now the sun was out, the three branches of my tree had leaves and the picture looked far brighter.

At the time of my reiki training, I was a sixth year form teacher and the girls had the habit of buying their form teachers a present at the end of their final year. The gifts were always jewellery, chocolates or wine for the female teachers and ties, chocolate or wine for the men. The Monday after my reiki weekend, I was given a different present. One that brought us all to tears!

'Mrs Connolly, can you come to the form room? We have a presentation to make to our year head and form teachers.'

I walked down the school corridor ready to accept another bottle of wine or box of chocolates. The girls were always very good in thanking staff for their support, but it was usually difficult to purchase anything outside of the consumable gifts.

As we stood in the classroom, the group of girls smiled and clapped as the other staff members were handed out books, flowers, wine and chocolates. When it came to my turn, I was asked to leave the room.

'You need to come outside for your present.'

I was puzzled. Why could I not receive mine indoors with the rest?

It was a beautiful, crisp, sunny day and I was happy enough to get some fresh air before my next class. The class prefect stood in front of the rest of the girls, hiding something behind her back.

'We didn't know what to buy you. You are allergic to flowers. You said you are trying to lose weight, so that ruled out chocolates and wine, and we didn't want to buy you another book. You seem to have read everything. So we got you this.'

From behind her back, she pulled out a small tree in a pot. And not just any tree, but a tree with three branches, all of them completely individual. Two of them had been grafted on to the original trunk to create a tree bearing three different types of pear. As they handed it to me, I was so moved and affected by the synchronicity of the gift.

'I cannot thank you enough girls. It's the perfect present.'

They smiled, glad to have pleased me.

'At the weekend I was on a course, and on the last day we were asked to draw something to represent our life. I drew a tree.'

There was a sudden intake of breath from the students.

'A tree with exactly three branches, each one representing a different aspect of my life – you have just presented me with that tree.'

A round of applause broke out amongst the students and some of the girls cried. We had all just taken part in an amazing moment of serendipity, where spirit had revealed itself to all of us, but had also shown me that I was on the right path. In that one moment, I was without doubt, life was now magic. I felt so energised, like I was being plugged into some divine thread of existence that made my life far more significant than I had previously thought.

Sadly, three weeks later I was back to my 'doubting Thomas' persona –

doubting the ability of healing and failing to see the magic of serendipitous circumstances. It is a pattern that I have followed most of my life – elation to frustration. If there is a universal power and a host of angels, then they have all been extremely patient with me in the past. In retrospect, they have kept knocking at my door and I have kept opening it, greeting them, genuinely happy to meet them, but then forgetting their existence as soon as I have shut the door again, going back into the material world of everyday life. I have spiritual Alzheimers!

However, this spiritual path is a destiny that I have personally chosen. I have had so many occasions in the past where I have met someone and known, before they have spoken a word to me, their significance in my life. They have resonated with me on a level that I did not always understand but always recognised.

I have met people who have seen the Akashic records in their meditative states and psychic mediums who have talked about these records. I cannot tell you whether these things really exist in terms of irrefutable evidence but they do resonate with me, as I think the conscious soul knows the truth when it reads it.

In the past, I have learned of many spiritual things and walked away from them, perceiving them only as the notions of crackpots. However, over time, as dripping water eventually erodes the hardest substance, my hardest held beliefs have been weathered away by a stream of spiritual truths, and I know that this river is still flowing. Heraclitus of Ephesus teaches us this wisdom beautifully: 'No man ever steps in the same river twice, for it's not the same river and he's not the same man.' At this stage of my life, I was fairly certain that I had chosen an existence defined by gender issues but I did not know why. It was finding out why that made my life inconceivably better for me, my family and all those around me.

My reiki psycho-spiritual healer temporarily left her healing practice for a period abroad. She wanted to do some more personal training and most of her clients were doing well, or could be accommodated by other therapists. So I had to find someone else to complete my reiki training. Her leaving left me with a significant hole as I had attended her every week for over six months. It was a good break for me though as I was making a common mistake. I was blurring the lines between the healer and the healing. I was seeing her as the cure rather than the therapy that she practised and the spirit behind it. Stepping away from that situation was therefore important.

Chapter 30
The French connection

Finding a replacement teacher/counsellor/healer was a priority for me as I had come so far that I didn't want to go back to chaos. However, I turned my search towards books as the teachers in there seemed more dependable. I plundered bookshops looking for words that could enlighten me. I read books on Buddhism, Hinduism, Judaism and Kabbalah. I spent all my extra cash on CDs that connected you to mindfulness and journeying. My library was extensive but my learning was not experiential. I turned back to searching for a teacher in person. Through the internet I found a fascinating French woman who was more than happy to take me on as a trainee in reiki.

I went back to Stage I and started all over again, this time with a group of three. Some channelled energy powerfully, their hands hotter than sometimes bearable; others had hands as cold as ice and I felt little healing from their hard efforts. I was beginning to realise that not all vessels held the same amount of light or energy. If a person was 'out of sorts', then their hands were unable to channel. If a person was unburdened by life around them, the energy could flow through them powerfully.

I practised and learned reiki like a person possessed. Sometimes my hands were on fire and I felt I was getting somewhere. Yet, at other times, something was stopping me from believing that I could heal anyone with my hands. Something was telling me that I was nothing better than a charlatan if I offered healing to any of my friends and family. I was trapped in a fear that the others in my group did not seem to feel. They had faith in the process and faith in themselves. I had absolutely no faith in my ability to channel healing.

Learning reiki became about more than just finding a cure to my gender issues. I didn't think a cure was possible. I had become stuck in a place of non-acceptance. There didn't seem to be any label out there that fitted my feelings. I felt alone and very isolated. I still told people that I was gender identity disordered but I didn't really believe I was disordered anymore. Thus reiki was about being immersed in something new, to avoid being left alone with my thoughts. It was about leaving behind all thoughts and exploring the world of spirit. I felt better surrounded by people who were openly spiritual.

To avoid my fears of the future, I went once a week to reiki. My children supported me wholeheartedly but there was a little teasing. They were young and knew little about alternative healing. Now their attitude has somewhat changed as they have seen the impact of this healing in my own life. But they still tease me about magic mushrooms and joints of 'whacky tobaccy' as if my alternative life has been fuelled by psychedelia. It never has been. I think my non-participation in such activities has frustrated them. I think they would have almost preferred to see me as bohemian and liberal rather than stark, raving spiritual.

At the time of learning this second round of reiki, I was doing well in my teaching career and starting to heal my own life, without being tied to a lie. It was easier in many ways to heal because I didn't have to confront my sexual preferences living alone. I had the space to find a love for myself rather than being a person moulded for the love of another. As a married person, I had spent too many years being what someone else wanted. Sadly, I had always known that if I wanted to heal my life, my marriage would have to end. My husband could never have made that particular movement forward with me. Even wishing to live openly with my sexual preferences would have been too much for any marriage, so it was completely understandable. I couldn't conceive of staying with him and becoming the real me. So it was easier for both of us to acknowledge that we weren't helping each other by staying together. I do have guilt for marrying him, although I will never regret the two children that our marriage gave us.

At one of the practice healing sessions, my new French teacher asked us to heal each other on the plinth, taking it in turns to be the recipient. It is a wonderful feeling to have four people giving you their energetic healing, especially if they are all totally clean of their own issues. Your body feels suspended in love, lifted by their wishes to be effective healers.

However, my self-doubts were debilitating when it came to returning the healing. I had a demon sitting on my shoulder, constantly nagging me to see the 'non-sense' in the work. To my demon, there was no such thing as hands-on healing. Only conventional medicine could cure the sick. All alternative healers were nuts, and I was the only sane one by doubting it. The constant back-chat from my own head ruined the efficacy of my healing. In group training sessions, I would just ache to go home to my children, even though something had driven me to attend. However, as others had also left their homes and families on a Sunday morning, I felt guilty for being a fraudster with them.

One morning at a group healing, something different occurred. I was standing with my hands over a man's body when I caught a glimpse of myself in a big mirror that was hanging over the fireplace. Usually mirrors were the last place that I looked, as they showed my body as it was and shattered my mind's false creation. However, the image I glimpsed that Sunday morning stopped me in my tracks. I couldn't even breathe or move. I just stared back entranced. It was indeed my face in the mirror but it was removed of all pain and wrinkles, lines and angst. It was my face but it was beautiful, almost angelic. I saw myself free from troubles and worries, and released from stress.

I was bathed in radiance. I must have been there staring at myself for ages when the teacher, in a muted voice, asked me to concentrate on what I was doing. I wanted to explain to her that I had seen something special in the mirror but I decided that she would think me mad.

Although moments such as these are easy to discredit, and forget, a whole chain of seemingly connected, predestined events are more difficult to refute. These started to occur at the same time as another crash in my personal life.

Chapter 31
The journey

I had finished my training and was now a Reiki Master. I knew all the symbols and all the background history of the therapy, but something was still stopping me from practising. I didn't have faith in the power of healing. I was soon to be shown why this personal faith didn't exist and in the most startling of ways.

It began with a crisis. Yet again it revolved around a relationship. I had fallen romantically for a lovely, gay woman. She wanted to go out with me, but I felt that she didn't really understand who I was underneath my outer skin. She was like the men in my life – she saw my body as very important in our relationship, a body I was trying to ignore. She wanted to celebrate my femininity and I wanted to hide it. No matter how unattractive or irritating its existence was for me, it was what mattered to her. She was a lesbian and my physicality was important to her. If I denied her that physicality then I was upsetting her firmly attached label. How could she call herself a lesbian if she was tied to a woman, who claimed to be a man, and hid her femininity in favour of masculinity and didn't want her feminine body touched or acknowledged? Our short relationship made my life seem ridiculous.

Again, I put on copious amounts of weight in a vain attempt to hide my body. I was trying to attract someone who would not want me for my external appearance. Unfortunately, that decision just left me fat and unhealthy. In about three to four desperate years, I managed to put on about six stone. It was difficult to make out any particular sex when looking at me, except to see an amorphous blob. I was emphatically hiding my body and myself from the world. I have often met other people carrying far too much weight and wondered what aspect of themselves they are hiding.

Therefore, despite having a Reiki Master course under my belt, I was still a complete psychological mess and I went back to reading to find a cure for my malaise. I sought knowledge again from spiritual and philosophical books.

I came across a book by Brandon Bays, *The Journey*. It was a powerful story of self-healing and came with a list of weekends and seminars. I read it in one day. Two weeks later, serendipitously, a Brandon Bays weekend course was offered in Dublin. It was only the second time that her course had been offered in Ireland and I had just finished her book. What were the odds? It was surely no coincidence.

Brandon Bays wasn't giving the course herself but she would make a brief appearance through a video. It was enough to have me signed up and ready to go. I was not coping well with my gender identity disorder and I was beginning to do what the psychiatrist had warned me about years earlier – I was drinking too much to deaden the feelings that were erupting.

The Journey weekend involved talking about deep issues with a complete stranger and finding healing through an understanding of the personal causes of pain. I, unfortunately, could not get past the first 'hello'. The poor person who was dealing with me looked aghast when I told them that I had to leave the room, and probably the whole weekend. She frantically called for back-up and handed me over to a wonderful young girl called Catherine.

I know Catherine won't mind her name being mentioned here as she is a caring soul who is not in any way frazed by most things that have come her way. If I remember correctly she had a day job but doubled as a DJ at night. She was a very interesting person. She was also a very good facilitator and she managed to get me to spill the whole story about my life. I felt sorry for her at the time as she had to listen to a litany of failed relationships and self-harming and it was all expressed through a very negative energy. Tears constantly streamed down my face and I had to blow my nose frequently throughout the revelations. To say I was a mess was an understatement.

However, Catherine gave me more than a good ear. She also introduced me to shamanism. Through the course of our conversation, she had learned of my reiki interest and believed that I would gain a great deal from a weekend of shamanic healing. I had never really heard of it before. Strangely, through all of my reading, it had eluded me. I had a vague recollection of it from a documentary that I had watched as a teenager on the Kogi tribe of

South America, a documentary that I had never forgotten.

The tribe lived on the upper Andean slopes. They had originally lived in the plains, before the arrival of the Spanish conquistadores, but had migrated to the high mountains to be safe from the colonisers. For centuries, the Kogi tribe had maintained their indigenous way of life by living cocooned away from the outside world. However, in the 1980s they decided to come down from the high mountains to tell their story because their habitat was changing.

They had always allowed a few of their tribe to learn Spanish, in order to trade goods with the natives of the lowlands. In the 1980s, the Kogi elders sent their Spanish speakers to the city to look for someone to listen to their story. Through some strange channels of communication, their story arrived at the doors of the BBC who took a small crew, consisting of one cameraman and one interviewer, up into the rainforest where the tribe lived. They were to film their unique way of life and capture their indigenous knowledge on camera. It was a story back then which filled me with amazement. Their vision of life resonated with me deeply. It is now a story that I can completely relate to as it encompasses most of what I have learned.

The tribe claimed that they were 'Big Brother', part of the original dwellers on earth, and that they lived within the blessings and care of Mother Earth. They did not harm the earth as it was their eternal mother. They needed her to be happy and undamaged so that her fruits could give them life. They were very sexual in their explanation of their narrative. The earth was the seed of all femininity and thus extremely important to them. The Kogi carried around with them a ceremonial bowl in which they crushed cocoa leaves with a pestle-shaped piece of wood. The mortar, or bowl, represented Mother Earth, the womb, the feminine energy; the pestle or 'penis' fitted into the bowl and turned the cocoa leaves into something digestible. Thus the Kogi symbolised the symbiotic relationship of male and female. They explained that neither the pestle nor the mortar was productive on its own; one needed the other to produce. Their male leaders spoke of the importance of the feminine energy, of Mother Earth, of her nurturing nature.

In their story, the modern Western world, which had conquered and colonised their native environment, was known as 'Little Brother'. It was quite humbling to hear them talk about their 'Little Brother'. We were errant and bold but not irredeemable. The Kogi believed that we had a great deal to learn in our understanding of the world. Their message to their 'Little Brother' was that we had forgotten how to live in harmony with nature. We were behaving like spoilt children and damaging the environment through our selfish behaviour, destroying the womb of the earth that had given birth to us.

This tribe, even back in the 1980s, knew that climate change was happening because their Andean mountain habitat was changing. The snows were not as deep in the winter and the water, that this snow provided every spring to feed their plants and provide their sustenance, was not flowing as freely. Their world was changing and they blamed it on the mining industry that they saw in the valleys below them. Mother Earth was being stripped, raped and plundered, and her only method of survival was to fight back to preserve her own existence. It was a very sobering programme and I felt guilty for my part in their habitat's destruction as a greedy 'Little Brother'.

Now I was hearing of shamanism for the second time, from a stranger at a weekend course. I was curious to see if her shamanism had any relevance to my remembered documentary. Part of me was also afraid that it was going to be very alternative so I was more than a bit hesitant. However, Catherine sold it well. Her attractive personality helped, coupled with my desperation to move my life forward in any way, shape or form. I will forever be grateful to Catherine, as it was shamanism that was pivotal in transforming things for me.

The very next weekend after the Brandon Bays experience, with no more than six short days to think it through, I was in a car, heading into the Irish countryside with only a tent and a rucksack full of biscuits. I was less than six miles from my house when the panic started to rise in my stomach. I was a staid, middle-class teacher, what the hell was I doing going to a sweat lodge? I didn't even know what it was.

I also seemed to be one of the few going with a car. Most of them making the journey to the sweat lodge were much younger than me. So I was sequestered to give lifts to two others whom I had never met before. They were just as I imagined – flower power T-shirts, tie-dyed skirts, scruffy jeans, tattoos, piercings and bandanas. I had a jumper and jeans!

I felt like a fish out of water. I felt like their mother taking them to a camping trip. It was one of the most bizarre experiences of my life up to that moment. I sat there in my Seat Toledo and severely questioned my own sanity. I was even pathetically afraid that they would possibly kidnap me and take all my money for drugs or keep me as a slave on some hippie cult farm in Kildare.

Looking back, I couldn't have been with safer people. But at the time, the conversation that they were having in my car was like a different language to me. It was all about alien sightings and ghost experiences. I was so scared by the unfamiliarity of it all.

And the feeling of fear wasn't alleviated when we arrived at our destination, a ramshackle farm. I just wanted to turn my car around and speed back to civilisation. The arrival was less than exciting. There was no one around to greet us. I could see two men in the corner of a field putting blankets on an inverted, tepee-style building. They waved and smiled to us and we all waved back. My fellow travellers went over to a field with a totem pole in the centre and started putting up their tents around the edge. They seemed to know what they were doing, so I followed suit and crawled inside my two-man tent for comfort. I actually hid.

Within an hour all the hippie types had arrived and the place became one big hand-shaking, friend-hugging venue – men with beards and braids, girls with long flowing dresses and vegan-thin individuals. They were all healthy and tanned whereas I was pale, overweight and looked like a carnivore. They must have wondered what suburban stone I had crawled out from under. Of course, they were not judging me at all. I was judging myself, as was always the way, and I was judging them. In fact, they were extremely friendly, even coaxing me out of my tent for a cup of herbal tea.

When the shaman appeared, there was a genuine acknowledgement of a greater presence than ours. Dressed in jeans and a light blue T-shirt, he walked out of the farm house and those around me almost genuflected. His skin was dark brown from the sun, and weather-beaten to wrinkles. His eyes were piercingly blue. He had an air about him of someone with knowledge and gravitas. When he shook my hand, he held it overlong and stared into my eyes. It was off-putting. It was as if he knew something about me which I hadn't yet realised because I was too dumb to know it. He was part Native American and didn't glorify himself at all. He was a genuine shaman, but he would never have given himself that title. His name was Peter.

That first evening of the weekend I watched him perform a few small ceremonies to open sacred space for us all. Quietly and with great reverence for the work, he informed us of the nature of the weekend and what it meant to take part in the ceremonies. The first part of our time with him would be walking the medicine wheel. We were asked to walk the medicine wheel in our bare feet, for as long as possible, even until the morning if we could. It would be a time for quietness and reflection. We were not to talk to each other or even make eye contact. This was extremely important, he emphasised, as we would be disturbing someone else's journey into the self.

The medicine wheel was a field with a pole in the middle and some herbs scattered around the outside to create the shape of a large circle. At least it appeared that way to me. I was very cynical and, quite frankly, ignorant. I had taken up this weekend to see if I could find any way of coping with my life, and there I was, in the middle of the countryside, making judgements about other people's beliefs.

There was no food for us to eat that first evening. The others who had previously partaken of this type of weekend were ready for such fasting and had eaten a large lunch before leaving home. I had come straight from work and had only eaten a bar of chocolate and packet of crisps from a petrol station on the journey. I was very hungry.

We were told that we were in the process of fasting so that we could be ready for the sweat lodge the next day. My eagerness to jump into the experience had left me in the singularly difficult position of not knowing anything about the events of the weekend. I had done no research and was thus encumbered by my ignorance. I had to spend a whole night walking clockwise around a circle composed of sage and other elements, with a totem pole in the middle, whilst my stomach rumbled loudly. I was not to talk to any of the others on my trek, nor make any noise that would ruin their reflective experience. I was to walk in meditative silence. It was actually a wonderful night.

For seamless hours, I walked barefoot with nothing to do but contemplate the stars and the night sky. The cows in the surrounding fields became my friends. I gave them all names and told them my life story. I made up their responses and found them to be much cleverer than me. Maybe I was starting to talk to my inner self at last.

Every sound as I walked was amplified in my head through the absence of other things. My feet become one with the grass. I could not tell where my feet started and the grass ended. The sky, the clouds and the stars grew bigger and brighter as night-time passed. I expected darkness to rob me of my vision but my eyes grew accustomed to the lack of light. Fellow walkers almost disappeared as my mind swirled around and around with the flowing of the medicine wheel. I wasn't wearing a watch. My cynical mind had left it behind in Dublin, in case it went missing over the weekend.

I think I went to my tent at around two in the morning. I could nearly make out the time on my old Nokia phone with its small screen. At that stage I had walked maybe six hours. I was a novice at the medicine wheel and my feet ached, but I felt good about my attempt. Others stayed out until the sun came up and I could hear the swish of their feet through the grass as they ventured from the foot-worn paths on to fresh tracks. I could also hear the sounds of praying and soft crying from nearby tents and I wondered whether I had learned enough from the walking.

I was cold in my tent that night, colder than I have ever been in my whole life. The lack of food and the low night temperature were partially to blame. My body was racked with pain and the coldness was in my bones. It had entered through my feet as I had walked through the grass and had made its way up to my chest. No matter which way I turned on the thin camping mattress, or where I tucked my hands and feet, the coldness penetrated every inch of me. By the time the sun came up, I was near to tears and still awake. I had not slept. I had also cheated with food during the early hours of the morning and had eaten half a health food bar. I figured the lack of food had added to my coldness. I felt like one of the aesthetics I had been taught about in medieval history class, suffering out of a devotion to God. It was a suffering that made the warmth of the sweat lodge the following day even more divine.

The morning brought straggly, weary walkers out into the sun. None of us looked like we had enjoyed a good night's rest. I am also embarrassed to admit it now, but very few of them looked like people that I would have spent any time with less than a week before. My societal labels would have kept us apart. They were mostly from backgrounds unfamiliar to me, freer types with far less baggage. In fact, I was scared with the strangeness of my surroundings and the topics of their conversations. However, I felt less inclined to run home after a few minutes alone brushing my teeth in the morning sunshine. The familiarity of that simple act put me at ease.

The sweat lodge was ready for us. The shaman had been up early, lighting the fire, reciting his words and praying to the gods of his world. He was definitely a curious-looking man. His face seemed to change shape in front of you, looking different at every glance. He had eyes like an eagle, dark, small and almost hooded. His body was thin and wiry but undoubtedly strong. His skin was almost leathery from the time he had spent in the outdoors. His exoticism didn't frighten me as there was an aura around him that was intrinsically friendly and warm.

No more than any priest at an altar, the sweat lodge was his centre of spirituality and he took it very seriously. I was not going to be allowed to break the rules that he imposed, no matter what my fears. In his lodge, every man had to strip to the waist and wear shorts and every woman had to wear a skirt and a thin top, as the lodge would get very hot. There was no exception to this gender rule. The energy of men and women had to be allowed to flow by the wearing of suitable garments. A woman's physical energy could not be bound in a pair of shorts or trousers.

I tried to explain to him that I was not comfortable in a skirt but he just shook his head, looked at me with his eagle eyes and said that I would enter the lodge in a skirt or not at all. As far as he was concerned I was a physical woman. There was no other physical presence that he could see when he looked at me. The balance of male and female energies to him was sacred and he would not let it be overthrown by a rebellious mind.

I was furious. I had come away on the weekend to help me deal with gender identity disorder, not to have it pushed down my throat by a man who didn't know me. I wanted to tell him in no uncertain terms the degree of my anger but it felt as though the time was wrong. So I just walked away and worried that this weekend would be another failure. A woman who had listened to our conversation followed me. I can't remember her name now but her kindness was genuine.

'Do you not have a skirt with you?'

'No, I never wear one. I didn't know the rules of a sweat lodge. It's okay. I'm going home. I'm tired anyway.'

She put her hand on my arm. 'No, don't go. The lodge is really a wonderful experience and Peter doesn't mean to be harsh. He just has enormous respect for the old ways.'

She had a kind face but I was angry at any thought of being seen as a woman, or dressing as one.

'I'm not wearing a skirt,' I moaned. 'It's just not me.'

'I have a sarong. Will you wear that and come in with us?'

Could I refuse her kindness? Or waste my weekend? I swallowed my egoic pride and she lent me her sarong. At least it wasn't a skirt or a dress.

Oddly, I felt free wearing it as if I was unfettered by my clothing for the first time since being a baby. But I still didn't like being told how to dress, so I entered the sweat lodge in a temper and with a flash of anger aimed at Peter.

As we were instructed beforehand, we kissed the ground and entered the lodge on our hands and knees. We were only to crawl to the left upon entering, so we would not go against any flow of energy created within the lodge.

The ground was wet and grassy. The lodge was damp and dark. I felt like I was entering the portals of Hades. The fear grew in the pit of my stomach. For the third time that weekend, I wished I was at home watching the football or even reading a book about shamanism rather than experiencing it. I could taste the grass pollen in the air, mixed with earthy tones.

In silence, I sat as the lodged filled with half-naked bodies. It was cold in the lodge and I envied the man standing at the roaring fire outside. I didn't know at that stage that he was the fire-keeper. He would bring red-hot stones from the fire into the middle of our lodge. Four by four, he would shovel them in carefully; each time of their entering signified another direction of the compass, until the lodge participants had prayed to each of the corners of the earth.

The shaman, Peter, sat in the middle of the lodge just behind the pit of hot rocks. With incantations, unfamiliar to me, he began crumbling sage and other herbs in his fingertips, dropping them over the hot stones. Then from a small bucket by his side, he tipped cold water over them. The effect was like a very powerful sauna, and as the prayer rounds were completed the lodge grew hotter and hotter.

My body sweated like a pig. Sweat was running down my nose, into my mouth, down my chin and onto my neck, through my shirt and between my legs. I was a human puddle. Then the world started spinning and my lungs were aching and I felt the need to exit the lodge as fast as my weak body could take me. However, my personality isn't one for quitting. I stuck it out. Luckily for the rest of us some didn't and as the flap of the lodge was lifted back, it brought a gush of welcome, fresh, cooler air. Three hours later, it was all over and I had done my first sweat.

The grass outside the lodge was warm and dry. The sky above looked bluer than ever and the world seemed different. The shaman gently laughed at me and said that I had sweat lodge eyes; the eyes of startling intensity that would stare into the sunlight and blink furiously at the new world.

I just knew that I felt strangely different, inside and out. I felt like I had purged part of my soul in the lodge and had left a part of me behind. The sarong was soaked through and covered in mud. My T-shirt was stuck to my skin and my body felt like it was glistening with new life as if I had been birthed from the womb of the lodge. Strange feelings were running through my head. I had done this before but not in this lifetime.

Once I had acclimatised myself to the world outside the lodge, Peter took me aside.

'Are you glad that you did the sweat lodge? You looked unhappy coming in.'

I blushed slightly. 'Yes, I'm really glad, I enjoyed it. It was a really amazing experience.'

He smiled at me and held my gaze firmly with his steely blue eyes.

'You have experienced sweat lodges many times before you know, just not in this life.'

I was slightly taken aback. I had never met this man before.

'I actually dreamt about you last night, Chris.'

My blushing grew stronger.

'I met you as you once were, a long time ago. You were a powerful woman and we danced together under the moon. You must accept your femininity. It is part of you. The feminine energy is part of all of us.'

I didn't know what to say. He leant forward and took my hand. 'Make peace with your past.'

This was a difficult teaching to accept. It was not what I wanted to hear. Even when considering the reality of having past lives, I had wanted them to be male. But he was a strangely mesmeric man and I couldn't walk away from him without wondering how much truth there was in his words. Who had I been in past lives? And were they real?

We were all hungry after the sweat lodge, having starved through the ceremonies. The meal we ate that lunchtime tasted better to me than any food I have ever tasted. I had not eaten a meal for twenty hours and my stomach was achingly empty. My taste buds were ready for a feast. And I was given one. Although it was all vegetarian and organic, it was delicious. The colours, aromas and depth of flavours were all intensified by my hunger. For the first time that weekend, I also got to talk properly to some of the other lodgers.

'Hello, I'm Sandy.'

'Hi, I'm Chris.'

'The lodge was great wasn't it?'

'Yes I loved it, although I was almost too scared to go in.'

'It's your first lodge then?'

'Yes.'

'Mine too,' she smiled. 'What do you do for a living?'

'I'm a school teacher. And you?' Her reply was not what I expected.

'I've just started working as a psychic medium.'

Taken aback, I joked about it. 'Oh I've always wanted to talk to my granny.'

It was all we had time to say as someone started talking to her from across the table and our conversation ended as abruptly as it had started.

An hour later, during the washing up, she tapped me on the shoulder.

'Your granny is here, she wants to talk to you too.'

I looked at her askance. 'Are you serious?'

'Yes. Come outside to the yard where it's quiet and you can talk to her.'

We went outside into the sunny September afternoon and I sat beside her on a garden bench. If I tell you now that it was a moment that profoundly changed my life then I would not be overestimating it. She asked me not to talk or interrupt but to sit and quietly listen. For the next ten minutes she proceeded to name all my family, from my father to my sisters and my children. We even had a laugh over one of the names she mentioned. 'Who's Gary?'

'I don't know a Gary,' I confidently replied.

'Think about it carefully,' she said, 'you must know him'.

I shook my head again and she looked at me puzzled. Then her face broke out into a smile.

'It's your son. Your granny says it's your son.'

'But his name is Gareth?'

'Well that's close enough and anyway she has a funny accent that's difficult to understand.'

'That would be because she's Welsh.'

My granny had shortened Gareth's name, calling him Gar and various other shortened versions. In my willingness to see it all as a hoax of some sort, I had failed to see the obvious.

'You're going to have another partner in your life.'

'Really, that's good! I could do with some company again.'

However, my heart sank when she said the name.

'His name is Alex.'

'That's not possible,' I replied, thinking that I would never be with a man again.

'Well I'm sorry but it's the name your granny is giving me. Oh but wait she's changing it now into something longer, like Alexander.'

I didn't really want to know. I didn't want a man.

'Oh he's a lovely person. He will be with you as long as you live or as long as you need him.'

I nodded at her but was still fuming at having a man foisted on me.

'Your granny says not to be dismissive of the relationship though. You're going to think that it's not passionate enough. But it will be better than any relationship that you have had in the past. It will be kind and loving, gentle and supportive.'

'Well you can tell Granny that I would prefer the passionate kind thank you very much.'

'You are not to confuse true, long-lasting love with quick burning passion. This will be deeper, more meaningful.'

I looked at her and wondered whether she was making it all up, but she had listed my family's names as well as other details of my life with great accuracy.

'Okay, I'd better keep an eye out for this Alex then.'

'He's your twin flame, soul mate. You will know immediately when you meet him that he's your future.'

The psychic gave me other details that day, some of which I cannot remember as I had no pen or paper to write them down. Her conversation with me was brought abruptly to an end when she was told by her friend that their car was leaving.

'I'm sorry I have to go.'

'No problem, thank you very much for that.'

'It's a pity I have to go, your granny has more to tell you.'

'Oh well, she was always a good talker.'

'Here, I will give you my number. You must ring me. Your granny says it's important.'

It was at that moment my thoughts let me down again. Was I just played? Was her small reading just looking for clients for the future? However, the next time we did meet, she refused to take any payment from me and she gave me the most amazing hour, listening to her pass messages from both my grandmothers.

The sweat lodge weekend had been an amazing journey in more ways than the totem walk or the heat of the lodge itself. I had met a psychic medium, had my future partly told and had been given a glimpse into a past life. I went back to Dublin, with my younger new acquaintances in the car, and felt that I had undergone a significant episode in my life. Things would never be the same was the distinct impression that I took from the weekend in Kildare, and looking back I was definitely right.

Back in Dublin, I bought every book that I could find on shamanism and read them avidly but they were mostly concerning a different type of shamanism. The books were by a man called Alberto Villoldo who had trained with the shamans of South America. It was a shamanism that I felt a spine-tingling connection with but I didn't know why.

Chapter 32
Living alone with my children

At this stage, I was settling into a good life with my two teenagers in a new home. I had moved from the rental after only six months and bought a house close to my parents, which luckily was also close to my children's friends. It was a good solid house with a lovely big garden and a sunny aspect. I had been looking at houses for nearly a year, but when I walked into this house, I looked no further, as I could see myself living there. It was the oddest feeling. I stood in the dining area, in front of the large window, and I knew I would own the house.

A friend had given me the information on its availability. She had seen it in the papers and thought that it would be perfect for me because it was only two streets away from my parents and I would have the support that I needed. It was an argument that actually pushed me away from wanting to buy the house. I didn't wish to live in a similar house to my parents. It would seem that, after so many years of life, I had not achieved anything at all and I was back at home. So I stubbornly refused to look at it and house-hunted other areas instead.

Of course the house patiently waited. I drove past it one day, when there happened to be a viewing, and decided to take a look. The minute I walked through the door I was ready to buy, even though the rooms were not even the size or shape that I was looking for; but I could see them all in a different configuration. I would open out the kitchen and dining room into one big area and block off the front of the lounge from the back of the lounge, as it was a big sprawling room with a strange L-shape. The vision of living in the house was so clear that I went back to the rental, worked out my finances and put an offer on the house. There were seven other interested parties so I ended up in a bidding war. I had to pay forty thousand euro more for the house than the original price but I was not deterred. This was my home and I had to live there.

My parents were very pleased that I had bought a house so close to them. They had been very supportive on hearing the news of my broken marriage, although at first my father was quiet and tetchy with me. He came from an era where people worked through all the difficulties of their marriage and marriage was for life, as the vows declared. For my dad, 'until death us do part' was a literal expression. There was no escape clause in his marriage vows, no matter how difficult things became. However, he was living in a marriage with a woman whom he loved completely. He was not living a lie, as I was.

I had told my parents eventually about my gender identity disorder. That was one of the most difficult conversations of my life – trying to tell my parents that I was not their daughter, but a son. They were sitting at their kitchen table when I told them. They didn't say much. I left no space in my monologue to allow for a reply. I just kept talking, talking until every detail of my life was laid bare, until every strange notion I had ever had was graphically placed before them. I think they were numb by the time I had finished. But my mother started crying then – she cried quietly as if trying not to make a fuss.

'Why did you not tell us before? That's what makes me feel so sad. All the times that you must have felt so lonely, did you not feel that you could trust us to accept you?'

'I didn't know what to say, Mum. I wasn't too sure who I was.'

'Well you're not to worry. It's not a problem. Is it, John?' She looked at my father. He said nothing.

'I'm sorry, Dad.'

'It's okay.' He couldn't manage to say much more. He was stunned.

'Do your sisters know?' Mum asked.

'Susan does. She was very good about it. It's difficult telling Sarah over a phone.'

'Well, we love you anyway. You know that, don't you?'

'Yes, Mum.'

'Because you really should have told us before.'

The fact that I had not trusted her enough in the past seemed a horrible blight on her love for me. She looked down at the table and turned her ring on her finger.

'All those years living alone with this, it was wrong!'

'I know. I'm sorry, Mum.'

'No, I don't want you to say sorry. I'm so sorry. I just feel sad for you.'

My dad didn't say much. How could he? It was not part of his make up to discuss his feelings. His daughter, whom he loved very much, had just told him that she was no longer his little girl. She had changed the goalposts of their relationship forever.

However, it was something that my poor mum said that vented his rising irritation with the conversation. He was really not prepared to hear it from my mother.

'But I can tell you now that I always thought you were my little boy really.'

I couldn't believe what I was hearing.

'You were so different from your two sisters. I thought that at puberty, periods wouldn't happen for you. You would be different. We'd find out that there had been a mistake. You felt that too, didn't you, John?'

She looked at my dad for support.

'Don't be so stupid, Mair.' He left the table and walked away.

'He's just upset,' my mother said. 'Not with you, just with it all. Don't worry. He will be fine about it.'

She had never spoken a truer word. My father never gave me a problem at any stage after that first day. He supported me in all my decisions, financially if necessary, and always kept his silence on any problems that he might have had with my decisions or my revelations. I was just his Chris and he loved me.

And a couple of years later, he was the epitome of politeness and friendliness when I finally brought my new partner home to meet my parents. I admired him greatly for how he dealt with it. Until the day he died, he showed me nothing but unconditional love, from the first awkward moments of being told to the last days before he passed. He could not have been a better father in his acceptance of me.

I still admire my mother. Every day she hugs me and still listens to my issues, but now the issues are not about being gender identity disordered. I dropped that label as soon as I realised that I was not in the wrong body, and after I had learned to accept myself through shamanism.

Telling my children was equally as difficult. The words were so difficult to find. In some respect, I was killing off their long-held vision of their mother.

'I want you to know that no matter what I tell you now, I have always loved you both and always will, and I am also so proud to be your parent.'

Two apprehensive faces looked back at me.

'But not proud to be our mum?'

'Of course I'm proud to be your mum.'

'Really?'

'Yes of course!'

'But you just said that you want to be a man.'

'I wanted to grow up into a man when I was younger. I wanted to be born a male, I suppose, but I don't want a sex-change to become one. I just want you to understand that I am not a woman in all aspects of myself. Inside I feel like I'm male.'

The oddest thing about my conversation with them is that I found out that they were not overly surprised at all. They had both lived with me all their lives and knew me better than most people. They hadn't been fooled. I was always their alternative type of mother. I had never appeared mainstream to them. Although there is a huge gulf between thinking your mother is different to actually knowing your mother wants to be a man. The three of us had many long conversations about my gender issues but usually it was on a one-to-one basis as my children were of different ages.

My son, being an older teenager, wanted to talk about who I fancied. Did I fancy women? If so which ones? Had I done anything about fancying them? He was very factual and direct. Some of his questions were difficult to answer as I felt embarrassed but I had landed a bombshell on both my teenagers and I felt it only fair to answer their questions honestly, whatever those questions were.

My daughter was more outwardly emotional about it all.

'Did you want to have children?'

'I wanted to be a parent but actually giving birth was not a thing I wanted to do.'

'So did you want to have me?'

Her big blue eyes were so sad and filling with tears.

'Oh my God yes, I totally did. I didn't want an only child. I was looking forward to having you.'

'But did you want a little boy instead of a girl?'

'To be honest I did want another boy because I was scared that I would ruin bringing up a little girl, as I wouldn't have the feminine instinct to share with her. But as soon as I saw you I fell in love with you completely. You were, and still are, adorable.'

She started crying and I hugged her. She was more hurt by my news. She still needed a mother. She had already lost a father when my marriage broke up; she didn't want to lose her mother too.

'I will always be your mother, I promise.'

'You won't go away and come back different?'

'No, I won't. That will not happen.'

'But you're not happy being a woman.'

'No I'm not. But I have to learn to be happy being me, whatever that is, whether that is different from being either male or female!'

She seemed more assured although I knew it was so difficult for her to understand.

'The one thing I do know is that I will always want to be your mother. That will never change. I love you and your brother. You are the best parts of my life.'

As I tried to explain it all to my children it became clearer to me. I knew transitioning would fail to create the real me. I was just born to be a mixture of male within female and was beginning to understand living that way. However, although I told them that I was happy, I really had some way to go to achieve that outcome. I still had very difficult days. But I wanted them to believe it. I didn't want them to grow up thinking that their parent was a mess.

My children seemed to like our new home as much as I did, and naively I thought everything was on track with them. The house moves and separation had obviously been difficult but they seemed to be coping. However, they were just keeping it bottled up, and at one level they even blamed themselves for the break-up, even though it was something I had assured them had never been an issue. I had told them about my gender issues hoping that they would understand that my life was the irreconcilable issue between their father and me.

My daughter was not coping at all. I had not seen the tell-tale signs. I was stupidly not looking for them, and she was clever at hiding them. Eventually, she told me that she was finding life difficult and wanted to go to counselling. I had offered to take her for some counselling as soon as the marriage had failed, but she had not been ready to face the issues then, they were still too raw. She was also only nine at that time and really not at an age to deal with her feelings with someone outside of her family.

However, she pronounced at the age of fourteen that she was now ready. I was hardly surprised. She had gone through a great deal.

'Mum, I really want to go and talk to someone, please.'

'I know. I will find you someone and make an appointment.'

'No, Mum, not just anyone!' Her face was strangely stern.

'Yes, I know, I will find a good counsellor. No expense spared!'

I didn't have much money at the time but I knew it worried her that the counselling would cost. Money, or the lack of it, had become a bit of an issue, with my one salary paying for our house and all the bills.

'No, it's not the money, Mum. It's the person. She must be friendly.'

'She?' I questioned.

'Yes, she must be a woman. She has long, blonde hair, a big smile, isn't too old and is very friendly.'

I looked at Lindsay inquiringly. 'Do you know her already? Does a friend go to her already?'

She shook her head. 'No, I've never met her before, but she exists I'm sure. I can picture her.'

I started laughing, not out of disrespect but out of bewilderment. 'That's a very specific request, how in hell am I to find her?'

'I don't know but you will. You're my mum.'

Although I had been to a sweat lodge and other alternative healings, I was still sadly unaware of the wonderful work of spirit around us. I did not think I would find this counsellor. The universe already had the answer!

Two weeks later, a friend asked me to go to a 'Mind, Body and Spirit' fair in a local venue. I wasn't busy, and I liked the friend's company so I went with her. It was a chance to buy new books and possibly get incense and candles at a cheaper price than in the shops. What I actually found though was a complete surprise – I found the counsellor.

Walking through the hall, I saw a blonde, smiling, thirty-something woman looking back at me from a poster. She was a trained psychologist and available for counselling on all issues including weight problems, smoking and bereavement. I took one of her leaflets and showed it to my daughter.

'That's her,' she replied.

'Great,' I said, relieved. 'I will make you an appointment.'

Lindsay gave me a negative look. 'No, you go first to check her out.'

'What? Why? She's exactly like the counsellor you wanted.'

'No, Mum, you have to go to see if she's good.'

I declined at first but my daughter was, and still is, very persistent.

'You must go first. You can't send me to just anyone who might make a mess of counselling me.'

Three weeks later, I found myself outside the door of an unfamiliar house with the counsellor's leaflet in my hand, ready for my appointment. The problem is that I hadn't prepared any reason for being there. I couldn't tell her that I was only checking her out for my daughter. So I quickly scanned her list of expertise and realised that I didn't need any of them. I wasn't a smoker, didn't want to diet and hadn't been bereaved. The only one that I felt I could blag my way through was regression therapy.

I knew very little about regression and, barring the psychic medium's discussion with my granny, I felt that I had little or no knowledge of the afterlife, let alone other lives that I might have lived before. Serendipitously though, I had recently been given a book by Brian Weiss on the topic but had not yet managed to read it. So it was with quite a bit of interest that I lay on her plinth and allowed the earphones to be placed on my head. She also put a cover on my small finger to read my pulse on a monitor. It was all very space age and theatrical to my uncomprehending mind. She counted me backwards with my eyes firmly closed and then asked me what I had on my feet.

'I'm wearing sandals.'

'Okay and where are you? What's in front of you?'

All the answers that followed from my lips I firmly believed came from my creative mind; after all it was full of historical knowledge.

'I'm in South America, I think. I'm in a tribal area. In front of me I can see tepee-type dwellings and fires.'

'Good, what else do you see?'

'Oh God, it's awful.'

'Your pulse has started to race, Chris. What are you seeing now?'

'They're dying. All of them! They're dying. And there's nothing I can do. I can't stop it.'

'It's okay. It's fine. Can you tell me what they are dying from?'

'It's some disease, like smallpox. We are drumming drums, trying to keep the evil spirits away but it's no good. They are all dying.'

Tears were now starting to form in the corner of my eyes. I had felt very happy that day walking into her office and now I was in a strange state, with my pulse racing and my hands almost shaking.

'It's my fault,' I repeated.

'Why is it your fault? You didn't bring the disease to them, I'm sure.'

'I should be saving them though. I'm their shaman.'

It was there – the word from the documentary on the Kogi, the word I had encountered again in a sweat lodge.

'So what is a shaman?' she asked.

'A healer, a spirit healer, I think,' I answered.

'I think we should leave that picture of the past now as it is distressing you. Let's go to another time in that life.'

So I left the village of dying people with their wailing still ringing in my ears and the smell of death. I found myself instead in a house. It was Western style with a latched door and wooden beams. I was sitting at a long, oak table in the centre of the room, a pen in my hand. I was signing a treaty for the use of our tribal lands. The Europeans standing over me were uniformed and Spanish.

'Before you return from this past life, I want you go to your death.'

The scene changed and I was back in the same house, thirty years later. My body was laid out on the oak table and men and women were sitting around me, chanting and praying. I could almost smell sage burning in the room and hear the wood from a hearth spitting. I died peacefully.

'So what do you make of everything you've seen?' the counsellor asked.

I looked at her and smiled. 'Well it's a memory from a history lesson, isn't it? The conquistadores, the natives wiped out with smallpox, the death of a civilisation and its customs.'

She fixed me with a sharp look. 'Is that all you believe it is?'

'What else can it be, a past life?'

'Maybe. I'm not saying it is or it isn't, but does it explain anything that is happening in your life? Any issue you may be having?'

I took the monitor off my finger and sat upright on the recliner.

'Well something did cross my mind.'

'Go on.'

'I wonder whether this picture, whether fact or fiction, is the reason why I don't believe in the curing ability of alternative medicine.'

'Why? What's the connection?'

'Well, they all died because the shaman's alternative medicine didn't work. Although I suppose it was not seen as alternative medicine then. It was just their tribal beliefs and medicine. But maybe I have no belief in the power of spiritual medicine, due to this subconscious story in my head.'

It seemed silly after I had said it. I thought she would dismiss my theory out of hand.

'It's a plausible theory,' she replied. 'Maybe you should look into it more.'

The bigger part of me believed that I was rehashing a history textbook. After all, I had taught the Age of Exploration only weeks ago. However, other parts of my experience were not as easy to explain. My pulse had raced. I had cried. I had felt as though I had been watching something real.

Was I actually there? Was I in that village many years ago? Can we really carry issues from previous lives through into this life?

Chapter 33
A link to my past

Before she left me that day, sitting open-mouthed on the bench in the farm, the psychic medium had told me that I was definitely to come to her for a further session. She was adamant that my grandmother had more to tell me. It took me six months of nervously thinking about it before I got back to her, but she remembered me and we made an appointment. I sat on the couch in her mother's modest but comfortable home and wrote notes furiously as she sat opposite me, her head cocked to one side, listening to some voice out in the ether. She spoke very fast as if the words were coming at her rapidly from a place beyond, as if my relative was anxious to tell me everything that I needed to know and to convince me that they were there with very specific details.

Most of the messages that came were examples of things that had happened to me already. They were said in order to prove the existence of spirit, as they were easily verified. Other details were things yet to come – very bizarre and seemingly unconnected things which less than three months later became woven together in the most extraordinary series of events.

Both my grandmothers talked that day through the psychic medium in the small house in Kildare. I still have the five pages of their conversation with her – five pages, back and front, full of family memories, family names and future events. I could narrate them all here as they are interesting in their depth and lack of generality. To me they are all amazing, stunning and unbelievable in their accuracy of revealing my life.

This woman whom I had met only once before knew things about my family that even I had to cross reference with my mother. She could describe my paternal grandmother and her kitchen in colourful detail. She talked about her singing hymns whilst cooking over an old oven. She mentioned my granny's lost baby, who was with her now in the afterlife. She gave me details of future things that made absolutely no sense as they only came out as a string of random, seemingly disconnected words.

'Names, places and people often make no sense, but they will make sense in the future,' she said. 'Just scribble them down and some day they will make themselves known.'

I nodded my head and kept writing.

'The truth is important to you. It will become clear one day, your gran says. And you're going to meet a shaman.'

'That's already happened. His name is Peter.'

'No, it's a future thing, not past. It's not him, it's another man. You will meet him through painting. He's going to be important in your life. He will teach you what you need to learn.'

'That sounds interesting.'

'And there's a big house in the countryside.'

'Fantastic, will I live there?'

She rarely answered my questions, she just kept communicating.

'It's a large house, going to be important in your life. There's a name attached but I can't quite make it out. Something like Oak Dene or Oak Grove. You'll know it when it comes along.'

My mind raced forward to a majestic building in a lovely rural area as my future home. I imagined it double fronted, detached and sitting amongst beautiful trees and fields.

When I returned home to my own house, I read through all the notes that I had taken down. Some of them were so random and odd. There were at least two pages of words that I could not find any meaning to at all and I formed the conclusion that she was completely bonkers. These random words were written down after a rather worrying note concerning a car accident. I was going to be involved in this car accident, but I was not going to be hurt. She was very specific. There would be a red car and a white car involved. However, she reiterated that I was not to worry as I would not be injured. It was written before a list of unconnected words – roast chicken, herbs in the garden, children in a swimming pool and, most absurdly, the words 'born-again virgin'.

Reading through the pages, I definitely felt that they were all meaningless jumble, but I was worried about the car accident, especially as my son's friend drove a red car and drove too fast, as most young boys do. So I lay awake at night wondering how to keep my son out of his friend's car. I should have realised that fate cannot be altered. The car accident was to happen and there was nothing that I could do to stop it.

A few months later, I invited some friends down to my sister's summer house in Wexford. It was a difficult place to find so I offered to meet them at the nearest local garage to show them the rest of the way. One friend had already arrived, so I left her cooking dinner in the kitchen while I travelled the fifteen-minute journey to meet my other friend.

It was on a very narrow and winding stretch of road that the accident happened. Speeding around the corner, on my side of the road, was a red car. It was out of control and swerving everywhere. It narrowly missed running into the front of my car. It veered right across the road and plummeted into a ditch. The two men in the red car smashed through the front window with their flailing bodies. There was blood and glass everywhere. They had not been wearing seatbelts. A white van, travelling behind them, stopped abruptly and the man sat in his vehicle, almost stunned.

Covered in blood, the two men from the red car stumbled out of their damaged vehicle on to the road. One of them had blood dripping down his arm and he washed it carelessly in a puddle of water on the roadside. I got out of my car and went over to them, followed hesitantly by the white van driver. Neither of the two injured men spoke English. They were shouting and cursing and smelled of alcohol.

The white van driver eyed them angrily. 'Oh Jesus, I'm not staying here to help these two eejits. They're pissed.'

'Yes, but they're also bleeding,' I said.

'I'm sorry love but I have a dinner to get to and these two are not worth the time. They could have killed you driving like that. I'm sorry but I'm late for Sunday lunch. I don't think either of us should worry about them.'

He drove off down the road, leaving me with two bleeding, drunken men. I tried ringing an ambulance but there was no phone coverage. Eventually I managed to persuade the disorientated men to get into my car so that I could drive them to Wexford regional hospital. There was far too much blood coming from both of them to leave them on the road. One of them had a very deep cut down his forearm, which was gushing blood. I found a clean T-shirt in the boot of my car and wrapped it around the cut. Then I tied his arm up to the coat hook above the back door of the car. I remembered that blood flowed slower if elevated above the heart.

To be honest, I was in a bit of shock myself. I had so nearly been hit in a head-on collision, and here I was with two Polish men, who were badly disorientated, obviously drunk and definitely injured. The ride to hospital was very strange as the only noises they made were either groans or curses. I ditched my car at the emergency entrance and helped them into A&E. A nurse greeted me at the door.

'What has happened here?'

'These two have been in an RTA. They have lacerations to their arms and face, some contusions and possible concussion.'

'Are you a medic?' she asked me, helping one of the men into a chair.

'No, sorry, I don't know where all that came from. I've probably been watching too much *Casualty*.'

She smiled at me and asked the two men for their names. Neither of the men answered her.

'They're Polish I think.'

'And drunk,' she muttered, 'by the smell of them! Was anyone else hurt?'

'No, they just crashed their own car.'

'Okay, well thank you for bringing them in.'

I left them both behind in her care, losing a T-shirt and a coat in the process. The amazing thing about the accident was that, as I drove shakily back to the house, all I could think of was the notes that I had made from the psychic medium – a red car and a white car. When I reached the house, my friends had all arrived and one of them was putting a roast chicken in the oven.

'I hope you don't mind,' she said, 'but I took herbs from the garden for stuffing. Are you okay? You look pale.'

'Yes, I'm fine. I've just seen an accident.'

I described the cars, the Polish men and the hospital trip.

'You've had an eventful time. By the way, the children are in the pool having a swim before lunch.'

I didn't react to what she was saying. My mind was in freefall – car accident, roast chicken, herbs, and children in a swimming pool. I had heard it all before in a house in Kildare.

'Chris, are you sure you're okay? You look dazed.'

'It's the psychic's information. Everything I wrote in my notes is coming true.'

'What psychic?'

'One I went to in Kildare a while ago.'

I informed her of everything. My friend was amazed.

'So all that's missing is the "born-again virgin",' she laughed. 'Well that's probably me, knowing my luck.'

Lunch was lovely, the sun was out, the car accident was forgotten and the bottle of wine was making the day far more relaxed. The food was also wonderful. The roast chicken and roasted vegetables tasted beautiful, sitting in a flower-draped garden with a clear blue sky and baking sun. We were tidying up in the kitchen when the icing was put on the psychic cake. A girl who worked for my sister walked into the kitchen and started talking about her new husband.

'How are things with all of you?' she asked.

'Fine thanks. And how are you?' I asked in polite response.

'Well I'm a bit fed up at the moment. The husband is out night fishing all the time. Sure I might as well be a born-again virgin.'

There was not one person in the kitchen who did not stare at her in total disbelief.

When I went home from that weekend, I reread all the notes I had written down. It was not going to be too long before another page became true.

Chapter 34
Meeting Ash

I walked along the seafront in Dun Laoghaire towards Eblana Avenue. It was a beautiful evening. I could have gone for a swim in the Forty-Foot or for a walk down the pier, but I was going to yet another new experience. I was attending a Brazilian Light Energy Healing with the shaman from the sweat lodge. Although I had taken part in some odd things at this stage, I was still anxious about what I was letting myself in for. Except for Peter, who was taking the session, I knew nobody else there.

The room was usually used for yoga. It was empty of anything except for a light bulb, hanging limply in the centre of the room. I nodded to some people, already sitting on the floor, and found myself a quiet spot against a wall. I was nervous. There was no calming music on in the background but there was a strange air of anticipation. Opposite me was a thin man with long hair tied back in a ponytail. He had an interesting face, oval eyes and a wide mouth that smiled easily. I kept looking at him as he seemed familiar. I watched him for as long as was comfortably possible and then the ceremony started.

Peter walked in and gave us a background to the event. He stood in the middle of our group and then started chanting words, invoking spirits and bringing forward energy. Sitting on the floor, I was pushed back against the cold, plastered surface of the wall. I was almost bruised by the force. It was disturbing but also exhilarating. My mind rushed around into dark nooks and crannies, thinking of black magic and voodoo. Most of the other people in the room had experienced it all before so they were quite calm about it. But for me, the world was yet another bit stranger than it had been an hour earlier.

After the ceremony, Peter walked over to me. I was quite surprised that he had remembered me from the sweat lodge.

'It's Chris, isn't it?'

'Yes, nice to meet you again. That was a really interesting ceremony.'

'I'm glad you enjoyed it, such a powerful healing energy.'

There were people around the room, watching me talking to him. They all wanted to have a conversation with Peter. He was like their guru or sage.

'I want to introduce you to someone, Chris.'

I was surprised. Why was I important to him that he wanted me to meet someone?

'Chris, this is Ash. He is a very good painter but he is also an excellent shaman.'

The man who shook my hand gave me a big, warm smile. It was the man who had been sitting opposite me with the ponytail.

'Hi, Chris. Nice to meet you.'

Peter looked at us both happily.

'Good.' Peter nodded, as if he had completed some important business. 'Now Chris, I think you should work with Ash. He could train you in shamanism.'

I was perplexed. 'Uh, okay. Maybe at some stage. I'm really busy at work at the moment.'

But he hadn't waited for my answer. Peter was off spreading his lovely energy and wisdom amongst others. I was left with Ash still smiling at me. I fumbled for a topic of conversation to escape Peter's unusual suggestion.

'So you're a decorator then. I could do with someone to paint my daughter's room as it happens. I've just had the attic converted. It needs painting.'

'Where do you live?'

'Not far from here. Near the Rochestown Lodge.'

'I know it. I'm based in Dalkey at the moment. I could paint it for you if you like?'

I took Ash's phone number and contracted him to paint my house. He arrived early one morning while we were still in bed. I was half asleep and in my pyjamas when I opened the door to him. I invited him into the kitchen and offered him a cup of tea before he started work.

I was totally unprepared for what happened next. As I stood in front of him, holding out a cup of tea, he placed his hand on my shoulder.

'It wasn't your fault those people died in that village. It wasn't your fault at all.'

I just stared at him, open-mouthed.

'What do you mean? How the hell can you know?'

'They were ill with smallpox. There was nothing you could have done. You were their shaman but you couldn't have saved them. Do you understand?'

Did I understand? Of course I didn't. I was stunned. My mind was reeling. I didn't know him. How could he know what I had told a counsellor in regression only a few weeks earlier? I stood looking at him in silence but there were, strangely, a few tears in my eyes.

'How could you know that, you weren't there? How could you know?'

He simply looked at me and smiled. 'My spirit guide told me.'

'A spirit guide?' I asked incredulously. My legs were shaking and I felt very nervous.

'Yes, my spirit guide.'

'I really don't understand.' My mind was still racing, uncomprehending.

'My spirit guide is with me all the time,' he responded. 'I don't know you so I can't tell you these things. This is all from him. It's a reassurance. You were not to blame for their deaths. You have to forgive yourself.'

'But I don't understand. I told a regression therapist about a village. I told her the natives all died. I said that I had been their shaman. But you can't possibly walk into my kitchen and know all this.'

'But I did because it's all real. You were obviously there and spirit is telling you not to carry the blame for their deaths.'

Obviously! How was any of this obvious?

The kitchen seemed a very ordinary place in which to have such a very extraordinary conversation. I was a history teacher, born in Wales, brought up in Ireland, living thousands of miles from South America. I had no knowledge of the work of shamans, bar the time spent at the sweat lodge with Peter and the Brazilian Light Ceremony. This was all ridiculous. Where had the real world gone? Was I still in bed dreaming?

Life suddenly appeared to have yet another layer, a subtext, something more exciting and magical than I could ever have imagined. Although my grandmother had given me a strong understanding of the spiritual, it was a solid, conservative, church-based faith. I was not prepared for all this. It was mind-blowing. It confirmed the existence of spirits, reincarnation and shamanic beliefs all at once.

'So I'd better drink this tea and paint your room,' he said, as if he hadn't dropped a bombshell at all.

'Yes but what does all this mean for me?' I asked.

But I didn't wait for him to answer me. My mind was in a state of euphoric amazement. 'Will you train me, Ash? I want to know these things for myself. For example, do I have a spirit guide?'

'Yes.'

'Who is it?'

'That is for you to find out. And I will train you.'

From that moment onwards, I tried to open myself further to the world of spirit. There are still times when I head back to the safety net of my old world. However, it has lost its sheen now and appears dull and unrealistic beside this new one. The new world has the expectation of magic and mystery, gifts and prophesy, healing and alchemy. It is a world that I used to read about in the books of Paulo Coelho and Deepak Chopra but now it happens to me. I am part of it.

Chapter 35
Spiritual shopping

A weekend of Doreen Virtue added to the new spiritual world that I found myself inhabiting. Before this weekend, I was cynical about most believers in angels despite having read some of Doreen Virtue's books. She was too American and flash for me and believers in angels were women of a certain age with an almost innocent view of the world. However, she talked with such enthusiasm about the existence of angels that she was very convincing. But I still found myself sitting there, looking at the people around me and thinking they were 'suckers'. In fact, at heart I was jealous of their firm belief in the angelic realm, envious that they could see or understand something that I was unable to envisage.

Doreen Virtue talked a great deal about the job descriptions of most angels. One angel in particular stuck out for me, Archangel Michael. This was probably due to the fact that my friendly psychic medium had insisted that Archangel Michael was always around me; I had found this difficult to believe at the time. The description of him was of a mighty heroic type, fighting off all demons and problems with his sword, and forging a better world. His power and strength, in the face of adversity, struck a chord with me.

I found parts of the show fascinating and other parts a bit embarrassing. At one stage, we had to turn around and find a random audience member to partner with for psychic work. I was rather worried about this, as I had no great wish to hold hands with an unknown person and pretend to read their mind, or give them a future prediction. I felt a fraud even attempting it, but I did.

I sat opposite a stranger and held her hands and attempted to do as Doreen Virtue had instructed us. We were to open our minds and not filter any thoughts that came through, but to speak them out, no matter how ridiculous they seemed. I told my partner, a middle-aged woman, that she was looking to buy a new car and that she was not to buy the red one but to go back to a different garage and buy the blue car. I even gave her the name of the garage salesman. I was stunned by how much I had to tell her and I presumed that I was making it all up from my vivid imagination. However, she looked at me equally stunned and said that she had been looking at cars during the week and was considering a red one but had been worried about its mileage. She had seen a blue car at a garage managed by a salesman with the name I had given her. However, as he was an acquaintance of her husband she had decided not to buy her car from him as she didn't want to appear to be looking for a favour. She would now reconsider that decision. She was amazed that I had even mentioned the red car. That made two of us!

The Doreen Virtue show provided further strange occurrences and I left well-versed on all the angels. Ms Virtue instructed her audience not to leave the angels for special occasions but to call upon them whenever we felt the need. A shopping trip with my daughter a few days later gave me my first opportunity to check out angelic powers.

At this stage, when I thought or spoke of 'angelic powers', it was still very tongue in cheek and very cynical, despite the experience of the Doreen Virtue afternoon. Trouble with my car CD player gave one angel in particular a chance to show his worth. The player was in the boot of the car and held ten discs. It kept jumping every time the car hit a pothole in the road, which on Irish roads was a regular occurrence. My daughter and I were driving to a new shopping centre to look for skiing clothes. On the way to the shops, the track we were listening to continuously jumped, driving me nuts.

'Oh for Pete's sake, I hate this bloody CD player.'

'You should get a new one, Mum.'

'I can't afford one, honey.'

The CD jumped again and I said, 'Archangel Michael, find me a new CD player and cheap!'

Lindsay laughed. 'Are you mad, Mum? Angels don't exist and if they did you can't go around demanding CD players off them. I'm sure you'd have to pray in a church or something.'

'Yeah, well,' I laughed. 'I heard all about Archangel Michael last weekend and he seemed to be kick-ass so he can get me a new CD player and a car wash while he's at it.'

The pair of us laughed and sang along to the continually jumping track. As we drove up to the ski shop, we noticed a queue outside the shop next door. I looked at the window to see what it was selling. All I could see were large signs announcing a grand opening at ten o'clock. It was ten to ten.

'Lindsay, hop out and go and stand in that queue while I park the car. Quick.'

'Why? We don't even know what that shop sells.'

'Well, why not?' I replied.

I joined her in the queue after parking the car. The lady in front of us was anxiously looking at the shop doors waiting for them to open.

'What's the queue for?' I asked.

'They're giving out vouchers for half-price off,' she replied.

'What do they sell?'

'Bikes,' she said. 'I'm hoping to get one half-price for my son for Christmas.'

Lindsay tugged at my arm. 'Mum, we should go then.'

I was just about to turn away when the door of the shop opened and a sales person came out holding vouchers. The first ten in the queue were to get vouchers for 50 per cent off anything in the shop, except for the bikes. The lady in front of us was number eleven in the queue so we turned to go away. The man who was second in the queue took his voucher and came to the lady in front of us and offered her his voucher.

'I was hoping for a bike,' he explained.

'Me too,' she replied. They both turned towards me.

'You're in the queue next, do you want the voucher?'

For some reason I said yes, although I had no clue what else lay beyond the shop doors. At the entrance, I asked the salesperson.

'Excuse me, what do you sell here besides bikes?'

'Car parts,' he replied, 'and car radios and CD players.'

My daughter and I looked at each other in disbelief – CD players for cars!

There were hundreds of makes on offer in the shop, most of which were too expensive, even with the voucher.

'Can I help you, madam?'

The label of madam I hated. I had to swallow my annoyance to reply to him.

'Yes, I need a cheap CD player.'

I knew I only had around €80 to buy one, as I had to buy skiing clothes too. There was one CD player that I liked on the shelf, but at €160 I still couldn't afford it.

'Now this one's good,' he said, pointing to the make I had been eyeing.

'It's too expensive, I can't afford that.'

'But madam, you have the 50 per cent off voucher.'

'But this is already reduced by 50 per cent. Surely you can't use the voucher on it too?'

'Well, yes you can.'

My daughter and I looked at him incredulously. 'You mean it's now only €80 and it was €320?'

'Yes,' he replied.

We went to the sales counter immediately, our purchase under our arms.

'Can I have your details please, madam?'

'Sorry, what for?'

'The machine needs to be installed and we need to make an appointment for you.'

'Oh okay.'

'Installation is usually €50 but today as it's opening day, we are doing it for free.'

Of course you are, I thought. Archangel Michael is watching over this.

'You also need to purchase the connector to attach the CD player to the dashboard.'

There had to be a moment of failure. Everything had been too good to be true. 'How much?' I asked.

'Forty-five euros,' he replied.

It looked like the purchase was going to be too expensive after all, but I let him search behind the counter for the right connector.

'I'm sorry,' he said, 'we only have one left and it's out of its packaging. Do you mind if we use that one and of course charge you nothing?'

So now I was getting €50 off installation, €45 off the connector cable and an originally priced €320 CD player for a mere €80, a total price of €415 worth of technology.

I handed over my €80 and looked at my daughter. Her smile was enormous as she softly said, 'Archangel Michael, Mum!'

If we needed any extra proof, it came when we went to leave the shop. Standing at the door, on the way out, were two girls dressed in short skirts and tight-fitting tops, wearing the shop's colours. They were handing out a free car cleaning kit for the first ten customers to leave the shop with a purchase.

My daughter and I laughed all the way home. We had shared the strangest of mornings. I don't know whether my daughter even remembers it now. Maybe she puts it down to coincidence and maybe the euphoric excitement we felt on that day has been worn away by cynicism. I hope that this story still resonates with her and she doesn't become the doubting Thomas that I have been.

Thus, the spirit guide in my kitchen with Ash was not the first time that I had been shown the existence of a spirit world or an angelic realm. Indeed there had been many occasions previously but they were all chalked off at the time as being coincidences or forgotten in the light of the next practical day. The story of Ash and his spirit guide is very important to this book as he was someone who helped me significantly in healing the rift within. My gender identity disorder would take on a very different aspect with his help.

I would come to understand my present existence as just one of many existences that I had lived on this planet. And that all these existences were interwoven and linked by a universal thread. In understanding this and seeing some of the past lives in my shamanic journeys, I further understood why it was very negative to invest my energy in the problems of this one existence. It was important to see the bigger picture.

The question I was asking now about my label of gender identity disorder was not how I could heal or physically alter it, but why I had chosen this issue for this lifetime. What lesson was I here to learn in this non-binary gender existence?

Chapter 36
Training with Ash

Ash decorated my house and then he agreed to do some healing work on me. Sessions were held in a tin shack over the market stalls in Blackrock – a small room with a corrugated iron roof, up a rickety flight of stairs. He rented the space from a woman who read angel cards and was also an intuitive and hypnotherapist. Her name was Mary Kennedy. Although I saw her in this space with Ash, I never really conversed with her except to nod 'hello'. She was always busy with clients and I was always busy with Ash.

The corrugated room was always cold in the winter months of my first sessions. A small fan radiator gave the only warmth so I would sit there in my coat and wait for the room to thaw. It was typical of all my other forays into the world of alternative healing. Most of the genuine healers that I had met did not earn enough money to rent luxurious spaces. They usually worked out of basements and garages, sheds and church halls. So yet again, I was looking for healing and answers from a person with no medical training in a less than salubrious venue. I questioned my sanity. However, Ash was a wonderful shamanic practitioner and my healing from long-held illnesses was quickly achieved through his soul retrievals and illuminations.

I stretched my boundaries of trust when I first worked with Ash and my mind was full of dubious thoughts. However, once on the plinth, I was transported to a different place. The world became quieter and the raindrops on the corrugated roof disappeared. The sessions were all about healing my subconscious from the wounds of this life and past lives.

My small, spiritual grandmother appeared. Ash saw her first but he didn't tell me immediately. When I later mentioned her, he said that she was there often and that she was a very important spirit in my life. Just like the psychic medium, he could describe her perfectly, which startled me considerably. I used to look around the small room hoping to see her but I never did. Over a series of weeks in that cold little room, I was helped to release a great deal of pain from my body.

Frequently, I cried on the plinth. I made it a prerequisite of my visit to bring extra tissues with me. However, I always tried to cry silently, as my mind was still telling me that any other form of crying was too feminine and I didn't 'do' feminine.

Ash told me that he had been trained by Alberto Villoldo and that he would be quite willing to train me in the ways of South American shamanism. The circle was closing. I had read Alberto Villoldo's books after my first meeting with Peter in the sweat lodge, and Villoldo had trained the man who was now prepared to train me.

Ash said that shamanic training was not for everyone and that his spirit guide had to confirm to him whether I was right for training. I must have been ratified, as we began my training a few weeks later with the direction of the South – the way of the snake, Sachamama. For someone who was at complete loggerheads with my own body, the physical healing of the South was a bumpy ride.

In South American shamanism, the student is brought around all four directions to learn the medicine wheel. Each direction is represented by an animal and is associated with a different aspect of life. The South is the realm of the physical and represented by the snake which slithers close to the earth, and thus embodies our physical connection with Mother Earth. In the direction of the snake, the student heals physical wounds. In the snake, my eczema and asthma disappeared. My arm lost the red rash and infected spots. It didn't itch anymore and it didn't bleed with cracked skin. I was astounded. I also had two years of school teaching without missing one day, for the first time in my career. The way of the South was very powerful for me.

After the South, I travelled into the West for emotional healing with the spirit animal of jaguar, known as Otorongo. This animal embodies our challenges with the emotional problems of life. As the jaguar stalks prey so we stalk our fears and devour them. I found the West very challenging as I had years of emotional baggage from my self-imposed label of GID. Crying was the least of my worries. I couldn't think straight at work during this time. I was constantly feeling emotional. It took longer to get me through the West than the South. I ended up well-stalked by jaguar.

But I was still enjoying my training. The power of being in the learning of the West showed me that illnesses were the products of emotional baggage from either the past or the present. My body was full of the scars of emotional pain. Gender identity disorder had given me illnesses associated with emotional unease. Ash was to help me in the first and second layers of healing them. However, the universe was to show me that there were always deeper layers to go through.

Time spent with Ash was precious. Learning 'one-to-one' was expensive but it was also very illuminating and well worth it. My doctor's bills disappeared. At each step, I saw practical proof of the theories that I was learning. I would read shamanic books all week, then at the weekend I would travel to Ash and he would show me the work in action: soul retrieval, journeying, extractions and spirit guides.

I collected stones on the beach for my mesa – a cloth which is folded to make a bag in which the shamanic practitioner keeps their amulets, power stones and sage. In other words it is his or her medicine bag. However, I was not very respectful of mine as I had little or no connection to it. Despite trying to be a good student and following all instructions given, I didn't take my mesa seriously as a medicine bag and I rarely took it anywhere with me. The bag and I had a strange relationship.

Ash had moved from his rented accommodation in Dalkey to a house in the countryside, about eighty minutes from Dublin. It was set in a beautiful area – rolling hills, green fields and hedgerows that were full of flowering plants and studded with trees. Travelling down to his house was a happy drive from the city streets of Dublin. We had become quite close as teacher and student and I trusted Ash with my shamanic learning. He was a patient and methodical teacher who knew how to encourage.

In the direction of the North, my regression therapy life caught up with me. The North is the realm of our ancestors, the lineage from where we originate. It is represented by the little hummingbird that makes long journeys, or also the big brown bear that stands his ground and fights his foes bravely. In the North, I was to journey into my past lives and into my ancestral line to heal the lineage. I never managed to leave the North with my first period of training with Ash. My ancestral path was where the healing of my GID was to be achieved but it was not going to happen easily. It was healed in the revelations of that same past life in South America but it did not happen with Ash. It was to happen later.

In each direction, certain processes take the student through the training of the medicine wheel. I am not going to write down all the processes in this book. Others have already written of them and I wish to keep some of my training a respectful part of my journey. However, as part of my training, I did attend sweat lodges almost once a month and I was to see and feel things that I had never experienced before. The lodges were a powerful part of my training and I did leave huge chunks of my past behind in their wet, steamy wombs. Later I was lucky that my new partner came to some lodges with me, which took away my fear that my alternative preoccupations might keep us apart.

When I left training with Ash, stuck in the North, my old fears came back and I put my mesa on a shelf and left shamanism behind. I lost some of my stones and forgot most of the teachings he had given me. I know looking back that I was still holding on to the problem of guilt associated with the work of such medicine – the guilt of losing a tribe that had died of smallpox. It might not have been a conscious guilt but it was there below the surface, colouring my ability to believe in my efficacy as a potential shamanic practitioner.

I think Ash knew that we were coming to an end as teacher and student. He told me on our second last meeting that he did not think that he had much more to teach me and that I had learned nearly everything he had to share. I was confused as I hadn't finished the North or journeyed through the East, but I did feel that we were ending our association for a reason. Our paths had to veer away from each other in my journey to spirit.

I now understand that what is good for one person is not necessarily good for others at that time. Ash had his own path to follow and I had mine. And I had to understand that there is no perfect master in our quest for enlightenment. In some ways I had become too reliant upon Ash, as I had with my first reiki teacher; I had to learn not to give my power away to any individual, no matter how good they were at their teaching. Along our path, we meet many wonderful teachers and they are all equally important in helping us find our own way.

We are all stumbling through the debris of our past lives and our present disillusions. We may be at different stages in the learning curve, but even our teachers are still learning. I used to put my teachers on pedestals, a dangerous thing to do. Now I walk beside them, hoping to learn but not to follow blindly. I also hope complacency never sets in or fills me with the arrogance of feeling that I know everything.

For well over a year, I spent nearly once a fortnight with Ash, at first in the corrugated market building and later in his new home in County Kildare. I was to be reunited with him over three years later when I understood all the lessons of the North.

Chapter 37
Pippa

Due to my training with Ash, my relationships were changing. I was becoming stronger about my preferences, less dominated by the needs and wishes of others, and more capable of speaking my mind. People also came into my life that reflected my new passion for everything shamanic and healing. I was attracting people that resonated with my new life.

One person in particular came a long way to influence my future. Her role was far reaching, given the limited amount of time that she spent in my company. Her name was Pippa and her accent was unmistakably Australian. She was a fiery, five-foot-one-inch, pocket rocket of positive energy and creative force. She had left Australia with the sole purpose of shaking up her life.

From a narrow perspective, it looked like a mid-life crisis. Tired of the circumstances of her life in Perth, and the stress of looking after others, she just left everything behind for a sojourn in the cold and damp of Ireland. Her father had originally come from England so Pippa did have some notion of life on the edge of Europe. She gave up her work, said goodbye to her family and headed off with no position or accommodation arranged. She joined the staff at the school where I worked and we soon struck up a friendship, based on the fact that she was heavily into crystals and their healing powers. Pippa also believed in past lives and was enthralled by my story of the regression session with the psychologist and Ash. I could talk to her about everything alternative and she understood.

In the course of our conversations, I told her that I had learned reiki and was now learning shamanism. She had gone to alternative healing back in Australia and was eager to be my first guinea pig. I was not as eager to practise on her. But she was persuasive and I was soon setting up a plinth in my back room and giving her the full attention of all my learning so far. The results were very positive for her. A bad shoulder, brought on by too much computer work and repetitive typing, was immediately relieved, much to my amazement. She had been receiving almost weekly physiotherapy on the shoulder since coming to Ireland. However, after just one session on the plinth, it was seemingly better. She went back to her Friday physio and was told by the surprised woman that the knots in her shoulder had gone and her muscles were totally relaxed.

I naturally believed that Pippa's faith had provided her with the healing. I was sure that my part in it was limited. I had just provided the plinth. However, it was not just her muscles that healed on the plinth. She often went on incredible journeys through space and time. She saw the past, the future and even past lives. Sometimes, she did not reveal the stories she saw, especially those involving me, as she felt that they would interfere with my future. She was a wise woman.

However, her place in the transformation of my life was not just in assuring me of the power of alternative healing. She said that a friend of hers needed healing and asked if I would help her. Pippa had only been in the country a short time and she was already sporting more friends than I had after a lifetime. Alexandra was a much younger woman than both Pippa and I. Initially, I did not want to take her on as a client. Alexandra had no interest in alternative therapies and seemed totally uneasy with the idea. In Alexandra, I saw a complete refusal to trust the healing work and I was afraid to fail her and prove her doubts correct.

However, Pippa persisted, so I gave in and put Alexandra on the plinth. The results were more than either of us could have imagined. The death of her father many years before had become traumatised in her hip; the long-term pain was released with just one healing session. Her very quiet, almost apologetic personality grew into confidence as the wounds of her past healed. But of more consequence for me was how her obvious healing affected me. I had believed erroneously that Pippa had almost healed herself on the plinth, but this young woman had no obvious connection to the spirit world. She was completely trusting in me to help her. It gave me more confidence in the work.

Alexandra's session also showed me another aspect of her role in my life that I had totally missed. Looking down at her face in the middle of a healing session, her face changed before my eyes. I recognised her and felt strangely moved. It is a difficult thing to explain but often a face being healed changes, as the energy of the healing is passed through the body. It is as if their soul self comes to the surface and shines through, and their outer skin, which reflects the worry and pain of everyday life, is dismissed. Ash once told me that working at shamanism would make me look younger as it would rejuvenate my mind and body.

So that day, when Alexandra came for healing, I saw much more than Pippa's quiet, shy friend. I saw a soulmate from many years ago. My friendship with Alexandra developed out of her session on the plinth. We had a connection that neither of us could put into words or could acknowledge at first. Indeed I tried hard to walk away from our deepening relationship, fearing being hurt again, of loving someone who would reject my body and thus reject me.

However, we were not allowed to walk away from a preordained destiny. Brian Weiss tells one amazing story of two people who attend his psychiatric room as patients. They both describe the same events in past lives but from different characters in these lives. Brian Weiss realises that he has two people who have spent many past lives together, now coming to him independently; neither one knowing that their soulmate is attending the same doctor. He worries about how to get them to meet each other as he has confidentiality to observe. He tries making their appointments one after the other in his office so they could bump into each other and possibly spark an interest. All his methods of trying to introduce them to one another fail. However, both of them are delayed in the airport one day and recognise each other from his waiting room and the romance blossoms. It is a beautiful, heart-warming story. All of Brian Weiss' books are powerful in their proving of past lives.

Pippa was to be the Brian Weiss of my awakening.

Alexandra and I started meeting each other as friends. On one occasion, out at dinner, we described a house that we saw in our mind's eye. It was situated in France. It had a view, down a sloping hill to the sea below. It was a three-storied farmhouse with a large room, an old fireplace and books in the alcoves on each side. It was a very clear picture that we painted and we were very exact in its description. As we both saw the same house, we believed that we were co-creating it out of similar likes and dislikes. I remember how happy I was at the time to think that we had such a great deal in common.

Not long after Alexandra and I had envisioned the house, Pippa and

Alexandra went out for dinner. They sat and talked of nothing in particular, but then Pippa started to describe a house in France. Alexandra recognised it. It was our house and Pippa's description was unerringly accurate. She described the same bookshelves either side of the fire, the same fields leading down to the sea and even the same flowers in the garden.

Alexandra rang me immediately. She was angry.

'Chris, did you tell Pippa about our conversation?'

'What conversation?'

'I really don't like having a private conversation repeated.'

'Alex, what conversation?'

'The one about France! Pippa has just described our French house perfectly.'

'What? She can't have! I haven't told her.'

'You must have. It was exactly the same.'

'But I didn't.'

We were both puzzled. Where had she got the information from? Pippa was soon to provide the answer to the conundrum.

The same night as her dinner with Alexandra, Pippa went back to her rented room and ended up having a journey to a past life. It was something that she told me happened to her occasionally. She would have almost trance-like visions of things. In this envisioned past life, she was in the same farmhouse in France, living with her father, younger siblings and a stepmother. I was her father and Alexandra was her stepmother. Pippa had been able to describe the French house in exactly the same detail as Alexandra and I because we had all lived there together in a past life. Pippa had seen us all clearly – the father, the daughter and the stepmother.

When Pippa told me of her vision I presumed that it was a mere creation of fiction. In fact, even Pippa herself had problems believing it as real. I could not get my head around it, even though I had encountered proof of a past life with Ash and the dying villagers in South America. However, this was stranger than strange.

'It must have happened, Chris,' Pippa said. 'It's why we became such good friends so quickly. It's why I was sort of jealous when I introduced you to Alex and you spent more time with her than me. She was my stepmother. I didn't want her to marry you in that past life.'

'But that's a crazy thought,' I said.

'Yes but maybe I have come all this way to get you back together again because I tried to keep you apart before as her stepdaughter.'

'It's really freaky, isn't it?'

Today I am sure that our antipodean friend arrived in our lives to matchmake, and bring Alex and me together. She had insisted that I heal Alex on the plinth. I believe, whether rightly or wrongly, that Pippa was making up for her attitude in that past life in France, when she had been jealous of my new wife and had tried to come between us. Whatever the reason, she had travelled a long way from Australia to bring two people in Ireland together.

When Alex and I became partners we did not tell many people about our relationship, to preserve it from the scrutiny that others might force upon it. However, Pippa knew before us, she had seen us together on my plinth in one of her journeys. She had guessed, before it had become a reality, that we would be together. The three of us took trips together in her time in Ireland – one to Wexford and another to Madrid. We all enjoyed each other's company and it was a very happy time.

After a year and a half, Pippa left Ireland and went back to Australia. She had completed her purpose and went home happily to a new future. I still miss her constantly, even though she was only here a short time. We were definitely connected more than this story has expressed. She is one of the most spiritual people that I have ever met. An interesting aside is that she actually shares the same birthday as my daughter in this life – they were both born on 15 July – another very odd coincidence considering her role in my past life.

Luckily, due to the healing that she had received on the plinth, Alex accepted the alternative nature of my life. She is still very supportive of my interest in shamanism and has in the past come with me to meetings and sweat lodges. This is naturally a source of real comfort for me as I often have trouble understanding the reality of all the alternative areas myself. Alex, on the other hand, is from a spiritual background, where angels are not easily dismissed. She has a conventional religious upbringing, but at least it expects the spiritual to exist. With my upbringing at home, there was quite a degree of agnosticism, even pure atheism from some quarters.

Chapter 38
The greatest lessons

It was Alex who helped me break away from my reliance on Ash. Our paths were diverging and I couldn't see this. I enjoyed his company and the wonderful shamanic ways that he was teaching me. Ash had been working on my acceptance of my body for what it was – a female body. However, I riled against such a viewpoint. I was still stuck in the battle of my male ego for survival, and the destruction of my feminine side. Ash wanted me to acknowledge what was real and understand the existence of a genderless spirit inside my feminine body. He wanted me to accept my feminine side, not battle with it. However, it was the last thing that I wanted to do. I had told my closest friends that I was GID and thus I had to stay loyal to that label of seeing myself as a male within a female body. I couldn't go back to them and say that I was fine in my body after all and that it had all been a big mistake.

However, the universe had other plans for me. It was not going to accept my hiding from the truth for much longer and so it threw a spanner in the works and it showed me the truth about my outer shell in a way that really hurt. There is no need to mention names here. People come into our lives and press our buttons. They are sometimes wonderful people with others, but jar with us. The people I met at this stage were necessary in my life. They achieved something very important for me. They held a mirror up and I didn't like what I saw and I ran away from it. I thought I was running away from their misogynistic behaviour, but I was actually running away from my own negative beliefs about being a physical woman. I saw women as negatively as they did, but I just didn't realise it.

When Ash had lived in Dublin, his work with me had been a real flow of knowledge and progress. In the tranquillity of the countryside, this all changed with the development of a relationship for him that altered his approach to shamanism, as much as it altered me. He became associated with a group that saw a particularly strong character as their teacher, a man whom I could not gel with. He ran a series of sweat lodges in the Irish countryside. This new self-appointed guru held very strong views on the role of men and women, roles that I could not accept.

Again, I was hitting the same barrier that I had with Peter in that first sweat lodge. This guru saw me as a woman and insisted on treating me that way. Whereas Peter had treated women with equality and respect, this man exuded a different feeling towards women. It was a treatment that was less than equal to the men he surrounded himself with. In the sweat lodge, he continually had men seated around an inner circle by the fire, whilst the women were seated around the outside, removed from the heat or glow of the stones. A considerable number of men visited his lodge and he felt that it was so important to see men get back to their roots. Of course he was accurate in this, but the energy of the universe is an important balance of male and female. When either dominates the other, the result is negative. His lodge became a haven for men and boys who then dominated the procedure and didn't allow the energy of the women to co-exist. The women were almost submissive, none of them expressing their powerful energy. They had no place in this lodge to be their true selves. The guru held court and did so with little respect for the feminine energy. He talked the talk about the male and female, but he did not practise what he preached. It was a huge turning point for me.

He was my reflection. It took me a long time to realise it. I had thrown out the power of the feminine from my own life and exalted the power of the masculine. I was completely out of balance. It was no wonder I had been left in the North, in the ancestral path. I had not gained any higher perspective on life. I could not sit in the East, with eagle, living with such biased thoughts. I obviously was still living from the wounds of my ancestral path. The problem was that I still had no idea as to why my ancestral path was one that rejected the feminine. This last piece of the puzzle came a few years later.

I found my position of inferiority with this man unacceptable. He saw me as a woman, as my body expressed itself, and I was given the same place of subordination as them. I hated that treatment and he did not like that I did not respond to his lodges and what they had to offer. But I refused to be lesser than the men in the lodge. Yet he was in my life for a purpose.

Ignored and treated as just another woman, I now found an empathy and sympathy for the feminine side that I had buried. He was bringing up such anger in me by his response to the feminine. But his response was only a reflection of my own anger at being a woman. I wished to be a strong male energy, safe from all threats and attacks. This man, by refusing to accept the male part of me, drew out the darkest issues in me. At one stage, I even revealed in his lodge my whole story of the woman in me that I was attempting to kill. I opened up about my GID label and told them all that I believed I was a man trapped inside a woman's body.

His reply was so difficult to absorb: 'Thank you, sister, for your honesty.'

Thank you, sister! Had he not listened to one word that I had said? Sister, really?

The words stung my ears. What part of 'gender identity disorder' had he not understood? In his lodge I felt that I was back in a world that I wholeheartedly wanted to escape, a world where women were subservient to men, where the Catholic church's patriarchal system was still living and breathing but in the guise of shamanism. I went home and scoured the books, looking for indigenous shamanic cultures with a male-dominated core, but could not find one. In every single one there was a definite equality in their power, the union of Mother Earth with Father Sky, of the symbiotic relationship of one with the other.

Ironically, I later learned that the group, dominated by that powerful male, dismantled their sweat lodge and moved it to a new piece of grass. They believed that it was not a hot lodge, as the ground that it stood on held the wrong energy and that the space inside was too male. They were somewhat on the right path. The energy that they had created was unbalanced. They needed to allow their women to have an equal status in their lodge, to create a better place to honour their shamanic roots.

There was no place for me in such an unbalanced society. Indeed it was pushing all my buttons, as I was equally unbalanced but refusing to see it. They praised Mother Earth, the feminine that had nurtured all life, but they did not seem to support the energy of their own women. Ash and I parted ways not long after my debacle with the guru. I didn't like Ash's friendship with such a man. It was my issue and not his. Alex had come to the sweat lodge with me and she was equally as disparaging of the leader.

'He doesn't seem spiritual to me,' she said. 'He's too full of his own importance and he talks down to women.'

However, there was another aspect to the lodge that drove me away from it, an aspect that amongst the details that I recount here still frightens me.

I was sitting at the back of a lodge, almost behind Ash, as the ceremony commenced. I was following the process to the best of my ability and taking it seriously, but the anger in me that day regarding the male domination of the space was rising. Anger has no place in a sweat lodge. I should never have taken such energy in there with me.

As I sat on the ground cold, my body not heating from the air around me, I felt a very strange feeling going through my back. It was as if all my nerves were tingling with an unpleasant sensation. There immediately followed a feeling of nausea and a desire to flee the lodge. When eventually we came out into the sunshine, I felt completely unstable and not myself. I babbled all the way home in the car.

Luckily Alex had come with me that day and was doing the driving. I even stopped to buy a bottle of red wine on the way home, even though I drank white. (At this stage of my life I actually drank alcohol infrequently as it affected my ability to meditate and reduced my energy).

Back home, the strange behaviour continued. I opened the wine, poured out copious quantities for myself and drank it far too quickly, all the while talking oddly and out of character. My children looked at my partner with disbelief. Who had she driven home from the sweat lodge for dinner?

In a moment of clarity, I realised what had happened and rang Ash. He confirmed my fears and said that I had been entered by a spirit, the spirit of an old hag. This frightened me. Today I am still not sure if that was the correct explanation or if the anger in the sweat lodge had simply released the darker feminine side of me. Either way, the whole experience left me reeling and I have only been to one sweat lodge since. They are wonderfully healing places but the opportunities have not arisen.

Between the strong male guru and the sweat lodge hag, I left the group and the teachings of Ash. It was not his fault what had happened that day. I had attracted and created the entity myself, but I was unhappy with the dynamics of the group and the world according to the guru. I needed to find myself another teacher.

Ash taught me a great deal and I am forever grateful for his part in my journey. He is a powerful healer and has a kind heart. I think he knew that our paths were to diverge. He was often frustrated at my lack of belief in the work of shamanism and my considerable doubting of the processes. My soul had not healed from previous incarnations and that needed to happen for any shift in consciousness to take place. I was still trapped in a story that I didn't fully understand and it was all about that smallpox-ravaged village.

Chapter 39
Life with Alex

In my personal life, everything was coming up roses. The beautiful woman that had agreed to go out with me was eleven years younger, very pretty and really intelligent. There was nothing about her that jarred with me and I was always happy in her company.

Every opportunity we got we travelled together and further cemented our relationship. In my self-acceptance, her role was paramount. I obviously still believed that I was in the wrong body and had informed her of my GID early on in our friendship. She had not batted an eyelid but had taken it as the most ordinary circumstance in the world.

Being with me as a partner was something that she had worked out in her own head before it had even happened. She had gone through the problems that it would cause, including the fact that I had two children, and she had worked out that there would be many issues that she would have to face from being with me. First and foremost, there was my obvious lack of a male body. She had never been with a woman before and she did not in any way see herself as a lesbian. As far as she was concerned she was, and still is, heterosexual.

In fact, this was to be her biggest stumbling block. She knew that other people would label her lesbian or bisexual if they saw her with me; this still annoys her. She does not feel the label reflects her position at all. She sees me for who I am – a male inside a female body – and she treats me as Chris, a person of no particular gender. For Alex, gender does not matter. It's the person inside that she sees as important.

Maybe it was because we had lived together as a married couple in a past life that she reacted with such total acceptance. I cannot say exactly what has determined her responses to me but I do know that society likes to give her labels for her behaviour, and sometimes these labels are very inaccurate.

For my part, I had always worried about being with any woman because of my lack of male physique as I did not want to be touched as a woman. However, with Alex all this worry seemed to quickly fade away as I never felt like a woman physically with her. Maybe I too was responding from a reflection of our past life together. Or maybe it was because she accepted me for the person I was – not a body or a mind on their own but a triumvirate including the soul.

Being with Alex brought me to a better love of myself. I didn't feel as angry with my own body when I was with her. She, more than anyone else in my life, seemed to know and understand the inner me. She reacted to this inner me with huge empathy, but she also kept telling me that my outer body was beautiful too. It was as if she didn't care what package I came in. She was just in love with Chris. It still is such a wonderful feeling. No one else before had ever treated me this way. They had always wanted to define me. Her approach was so important in the healing of my world.

During our first summer together, we travelled to Spain. Luckily we both liked the same type of holidays. Neither of us enjoyed crowded beaches, overlooked by white apartment blocks and hotels, so we booked a little one-bedroomed, old-fashioned, cortejo high up in the mountains overlooking Malaga. With the azure blue sea in the background, we swam in a small pool, under a canopy of bougainvillea, and relaxed away from everything.

It was a beautiful location but very isolated. Access to the site was a long trek across dusty, untarmacked roads up very steep hills. I had rented a Volkswagen Golf which had unfortunately come with a low spoiler. Gingerly, I drove up the grit roads, scraping the ground in places. The journey was quite off-putting and the roads were so steep and dangerous that we decided to stay in situ for the whole week, reading and taking in the view. Luckily, we had brought nearly enough food to last us seven days. The rest of our water, wine, fresh fruit and vegetables were delivered to us by our landlord, a lovely Spanish man with very little English. He owned two plots of land and kept goats for a living.

It was a beautiful escape from life and one of the best holidays that we have spent together. We had no one else to talk to and we learned so much about each other. It was also the first time that I took off my clothes and went skinny dipping. With Alex, I felt comfortable inside my own body. I loved the feel of the cold water on my skin and the freedom of being unclothed and naked to the world. I have stripped bare many times since– in Thailand, in Greece and even in Wexford, but always when totally alone. It is when I feel safe.

By the time our week was over, Alex and I were closer than ever. We didn't go back to Madrid straight away. We stayed and rented another house in the Alpujarras. This area of Andalusia is mountainous, remote and dotted with old white-washed villages, 'Pueblos Blancos', which are Berber in architecture and very distinctively Moroccan. It is a stunning landscape. We travelled through it for a week, enjoying the fresh mountain air, the wines of the region and the famous *jamón serrano* from Trevélez.

When we came back to Dublin from that holiday, we were already spending most of our time in each other's company. Moving in together was the next obvious step and a very important one. My family had been accepting from the start. It was easy for them as they had come to terms with my stance on my sexuality and gender. They also had seen me at my lowest, in terms of relationships – my failed marriage and failed attempts to be with women. They were extremely happy that I had found someone who accepted me completely for who I was. It also helped that my partner was a lovely person – friendly and warm, even though shy at first.

It is one aspect of our relationship that I have had to learn to be empathetic about. I am not shy. I can be very extrovert when given the right circumstances. I do not particularly have a problem sharing my views with the world. We are diametrically opposed in this way. Alex would prefer not to share her views with anyone, except close friends. Sometimes I wish to party, or be out in a crowd, and she would prefer reading or watching TV, just the two of us. She is a quieter person who was raised in a quieter household. Even though she had more siblings than I, her house was a quieter domain. It has been good for me, learning to share my life with someone who needs a quieter world. It has helped as our quiet holidays have given me the time to meditate and practise shamanism, without prying eyes. We do not always holiday alone. We have been on many holidays with my family who have shown a wonderful understanding and acceptance of our relationship. We have always felt totally accepted by them.

Alex has helped me understand the importance of family in my life. When I was growing up, I had kept my sisters and parents outside of my private thoughts and feelings. I had not shared my GID with them and had cut them out of my emotional responses to life. Alex helped me to change all this – she encouraged me to ring them, visit them and interact with them. Without her, I would have isolated myself quite easily. In some respects she is the archetypical daughter-in-law who keeps her husband informed of family birthdays, Sunday lunches and health issues. She tells me to ring my mum, my sisters and my children. It is sad to admit this truth, but I am quite capable of falling out of circulation and into my hobbies.

It is important to have good family in dealing with emotional issues in life and I have been totally blessed with my family. I have also found that the more I share with them, the more I receive in return. They were unable to help me in the early days when I bottled things up and kept things to myself. Alex has helped me share my life with them.

However, there was one aspect of my life with my partner that used to always worry me in the early days. 'Would you like me to have a sex change so that our relationship is normal to the world and we are not mislabelled?'

'Don't be silly.'

'But wouldn't it be easier with your family if you were with someone who was a man?'

'You are male, just not in the usual body.'

'Yeah, I know but wouldn't it be easier if I was in the right body?'

'Maybe, but my family would still find fault with your age, your Protestant background, even your separation. I don't think anyone would be good enough.'

'Yes but it might help if I changed. I would do it for you.'

'Well then you're a wally! I didn't fall in love with a person in a man's body. I fell in love with you. And you could change into something I wouldn't love so much if you took hormones. Seemingly they make you more aggressive at first. You're bad enough as it is, with the fast driving and impatience. Imagine how you would be testosterone-fuelled.'

She looked at me and laughed.

'Look Chris, joking aside. I don't want you to change your body. I told you before, I thought through all the problems I would face before we even started going out together. I knew what I was letting myself in for and I thought that you were worth it. So stop worrying. Our names, genders, age and skin colour are not who we are. They're just labels. I love you, the Chris underneath all the labels.'

Alex and I have lived together now for seven years. At first we lived in my home with my children and that was a comfortable enough arrangement, except for the times that my children wanted their friends to come around. In those first years, we had to tell my children not to introduce her as my partner and there were other times when Alex did not want to face their questioning looks and just went home for the night to her house. I found this difficult as I wanted to live the truth. I wanted to be open with her. However, I had taken over thirty years of my life to even discover the truth, so it was not fair to expect someone else to live it so quickly. But we have to respect the people in our lives for the position that they adopt and the fears that they have. We cannot ride roughshod over their needs because we have a personal epiphany. Alex taught me a great deal about curbing over-exuberance. I had to learn to temper my enthusiasm about showing my true nature. And if the truth be told, I was also unready for many of the questions and looks that our relationship might bring. I had to learn to recognise boundaries.

So our first years together were difficult in this respect. However, when we were alone, the true depth of our bond could be really enjoyed. I have had the happiest years of my life with Alex. When I say the happiest years, these are not to denigrate my experiences with everyone else in my life; my children have brought me so much happiness too. In this parental role, I could not have been happier with the relationships that we forged. I would trust my children with anything. They are two good, moral people with loving hearts. However, as a life partner, Alex is my happiness, as I am completely myself with her.

Eventually we both realised that taking our relationship to another level meant releasing ourselves from the confines of my house. Alex bought a home and within a year we were happily cohabitating. Luckily, my children are adults now, with degrees, careers and futures of their own. They do not need to live with me but they know that I am there for them if they ever need anything, and we see each other often. I know that they both laugh sometimes at my vision of the world, and I am sure they will be slightly embarrassed at elements of this book but they will understand my reason for narrating them. It is my truth, not theirs, though I think they are already way ahead of me at their age which I suppose is the nature of evolution.

Chapter 40
Dunderry Park: The last piece of the jigsaw

A small, rural village sits in the middle of rolling countryside, littered with the history of an ancient Ireland and shrouded in Celtic paganism and druidry. The village is a mere two roads which intersect at its centre, dotted with one or two pubs, houses, a garage and a church. A small drive out of this quiet village sits the imposing edifice known as Dunderry Park, nestling amongst fields of grass, bordered by trees.

It is a Georgian manor house, replete with a large, painted wooden front door, set back from a series of steps, adorned with finely chiselled pillars. The front door opens into a warm and welcoming entrance hall with a large fireplace and paintings on the wall. Doors lead everywhere from this central hub – an office to the side with old tall windows and bookcases; a large entertaining room with a high ceiling and decorative moulding; a dining room, painted in a warm red, with windows overlooking a green lawn and bushes; lastly an inner stairwell with winding bannisters leading up to the many bedrooms that make this country house a retreat of some size and grandeur.

There is no Protestant ascendancy, old school gentleman, living in this glorious pile of bricks, nor is there a nouveau riche family. Dunderry Park belongs to the Oak Tree Charitable Trust and is managed by a wonderfully eloquent former psychiatric nurse called Martin Duffy. He is one of the most admired people that I have ever met as he is inconspicuous in his work and lacking in the ego of some shamanic teachers who have become so much to so many. Martin is an average-build bald man with expressive eyes. When I first met him, he had a penchant for wearing a wide-brimmed hat and a small leather waistcoat with a white shirt. He was very dapper looking and not as I had expected. He was not adorned with tattoos, piercings or any other New Age accoutrement. When he talked, the words were delivered calmly and coherently. His teachings were always backed by his personal experiences of shamanism from across the world. Sitting amidst a circle of listeners, he would fill the room with interesting anecdotes. However, he had also worked for the Health Service Executive for many years, and thus he knew the healing world from both sides – mainstream and alternative. He was a shamanic practitioner who had straddled both worlds equally for many years. And yet he had no doubt in the efficacy of shamanic work and that fact always impressed me.

The word Dunderry is from Gaelic and refers to the oak groves situated around the house. It was a place that I found on the internet when I went searching for somewhere to continue my shamanic training. It is the centre of Irish Shamanic Studies. Martin Duffy is a permanent resident in the house and he is helped by Annette Peard, one of his first students and also a Druidess. I owe a huge debt of gratitude to them both for the help they have given me in finding the final piece of my personal puzzle.

However, my journey to Dunderry Park did not have the most auspicious start. I wrote to the centre by email asking if I could begin midway through one of their courses, as I already had some knowledge of shamanism behind me, and did not feel that I was a beginner. I was barking up the wrong tree. Their teachings were based on shamanic ideas from across the globe and they were not particularly attached to one specific genre.

The home-based Celtic shamanism and druidry were deemed as very important, but Martin firmly believed that there were core teachings in all strands of shamanism that were equally important. He believed a student could become bogged down in the dogma or practice of one type of shamanism and that shamanism had to be a personal growth into healing. It was the shared wisdom of all shamanic teachings that impressed him. I suppose it is rather like a Christian believing in the core principles of faith, rather than the strictures of either Catholicism or Protestantism as a narrower definition.

Thus my previous, very specific South American training with Ash was not going to give me any bonus points in future training with Martin. I had to start my training all over again. Whereas Ash used the rattle to take me on journeys into the shamanic realm, Martin relied on the shamanic drum. I soon found that the drumming did not resonate with me. In fact it turned out that drumming irritated me beyond reason.

My first weekend at Dunderry Park was a huge departure for me in every sense. Firstly I had to share a room with other people, and they were all women. I was unable to dress or undress in front of them. I took frequent long trips to the bathroom, armed with clothes. Secondly, I was learning in a group of thirty or more whereas I was used to having Ash to myself, and the individual attention that brought. I was uncomfortable in group sessions. I looked uneasily around at the others in the room and my mood was quite black.

However, Martin was an excellent facilitator. He knew how to put the group at ease whilst controlling the ebb and flow of conversation to allow for a quiet, reflective environment. He was a consummate teacher, something of course which I really appreciated.

This first weekend was an introductory weekend to shamanism. I learned many different aspects of shamanism from the South American to the North American, the Celtic and even the Mongolian. I realised that many of the people in the sessions with me had gone through their own difficult emotional upheavals, and I was not the only one looking for healing. There were many sitting in circle with me who had gone through abuse and other traumatic life events.

The training was given in a huge room which stretched almost from the front to the back of the building. It was an imposing room with very little decor to distract the mind. Six large windows gave a dual aspect to the front and the side of the house. Every vista was of trees or plants. On the floor was a carpet, and well-lined curtains gave a cosiness to the place, as well as drowning out the light when journeying was undertaken. All participants sat on bean bags around the room, to create a large circle, headed by Martin. An altar, of specifically important pieces of nature, crystals and figurines, as well as candles, sat prominently in the middle of the room, laid out upon a cloth. A shamanic drum was situated nearby, standing on edge, waiting to be awoken by the wooden drumstick leaning against it.

The shamanic drumming and journeying of that first weekend should have been an opportunity for me to take part in an alternative reality – a way into a deeper experience. Journeying is a shamanic process, common to all shamanism, whereby the practitioner travels to other realms through the constant rhythmic beat of a drum or a specific rattle speed. Every other person in the room seemed transported by the rhythmic beating, the echoing sound of the stick against the taut surface of the drum. But my stomach churned with its incessant beat and I kept feeling sick.

By the end of the weekend of 'Introduction to Shamanism', I had failed to journey for myself but I had learned so much that I still wanted to continue the experience. I signed up for a whole series of weekends to learn at a deeper level. It was this decision to fully commit myself to a year of training that broke open all my fears.

I made some very close friends at Dunderry Park who provided me with support throughout my training. One of them was to be my 'roomy' for the first full training weekend – a small, South African girl called Jo-Anne. She was the perfect roommate for my first weekend. She was warm, funny and very empathetic. We talked until two in the morning the first night, and she didn't even bat an eyelid when I had one of my terrible nightmares and vaulted over her bed in the early hours of the morning, in a bid to reach the door and freedom.

Sitting in group session that first morning was very tough. Many of the group seemed to know each other, and they paired off to partake in the practices. I had no one to pair off with as Jo-Anne was already taken, so I looked desperately around the room for another person. A woman, with a very dark countenance, was sitting in the far corner, almost brooding. I didn't recognise her from our arrival the night before and I didn't want to be paired with her. She seemed so black and depressed.

The dark woman and I were paired off together and Siobhan is now one of my closest spiritual friends. She went to Dunderry Park very fearful of what might come out of the training and it showed on her face. We were given an exercise to do whereby we had to journey for the other person into the lower world and bring back a message for them. I was worried about doing it as I had not found listening to the drumming easy. It gave me headaches. Martin told us that we were not to report on anything negative that we encountered, as we might interpret it badly or put our own negative thoughts on to our partner. We were told to leave our attitudes outside the door and to bring only good thoughts and energy into our work.

I had failed to journey for myself but now I had to do it for someone else. Probably because I didn't want to let Siobhan down, I tried very hard to complete the journey. I cannot go into the details here as they are personal to her, but the journey was extremely successful and I ended up in a past life which had affected her into this present life. It was a recent past life and she was dogged with its negative overtones.

I had been told not to tell her anything negative but I decided with her permission to tell her what I saw, the good and the bad, especially as I was actually there with her in that past life. Siobhan and I had shared a past life, where neither of us had behaved with a great deal of courage for our convictions.

When I told Siobhan, her reaction was amazing – not only did she understand what I was saying but she totally believed it. The details fitted perfectly with her issues and fears in this life. It also helped her better understand a medical condition she suffered. It helped her to see that it might have a route in this past life.

What Siobhan and I learned that first weekend of training was to impact on us both. Neither of us felt that we could turn our backs on shamanism and what it had to offer. I also learned that I had a power animal with me. It was a big brown bear. There was also an eagle, but the eagle was flying high above me, circling, not landing. The bear resonated with me as I had often seen one in the sweat lodges with Ash. In fact, at one sweat lodge a member of the lodge had told me that they had been given a name for me – Little Singing Bear. When I was told by Siobhan that there was a bear standing beside me and an eagle flying around me, I knew that I was in the right place in Dunderry Park and that my progress would come from healing the ancestral line and understanding the issues of my past lives.

I knew I had an issue in the North. It was why I had not been able to move out of the direction with Ash. I believed it was possibly causing my gender issues in this life, but I didn't know why. I seemed to have a refusal to recognise the importance of the feminine energy and its importance in the balance of the world. I couldn't actually admit to myself that I was living in a female body. I couldn't own the reality of my own body. I kept telling people that I was in the wrong body.

Part of me knew that I would not be able to heal my ancestral line if I didn't accept my feminine body. It was a hugely difficult step forward for me to own my physical body. Since the age of five I had rebelled against my feminine gender. I had invested so much time rebelling against it that to change that particular chip, and reset my ideas, was tantamount to telling myself that everything that I had thought and believed for fifty years of my life was wrong.

I had huge difficulty in expressing this. I only wanted to believe that I was a man in the wrong body – that I should have been born male. I didn't want anyone trying to explain to me that I was just a person, with a male interior and female exterior, and that all of these were just labels anyway as my spirit was genderless. Of course now I do understand. My body is female and I was born with it. I did not have the wrong body. I just had the wrong way of looking at it.

During my time at Dunderry, I found this acceptance of my female body the most difficult to achieve. I was hell-bent on telling people that I was a man and that my body was my problem. They were equally polite and understanding but also spiritually very attuned and already knew that I was making a mistake. My body was not wrong. My time in Dunderry was hugely important because I had to face the significance of this balancing of the male and the female, and I had to learn that the feminine energy was equally as important. I had to ask the feminine back into my life.

The two people who showed me the importance of balancing yin and yang were Martin and Annette. They are rather like the yin and yang of Dunderry. However, even in my dealings with these two people, I saw the inadequacies of my view of the world. When there was any splitting of the group into two, I always wanted to stay with Martin. I preferred being in his energy and loved his male way of looking at things. I felt more comfortable in his presence. However, I was to realise that my views were negatively based, not positive. I actually had a negative attitude towards being with Annette. There was a voice in my head that told me she would not be as good at teaching. This voice believed that she was just a female and that I would not learn anything from her. I saw her as less powerful and less capable. I was naïve, condescending and bullish in this assumption. Stripping back the layers of my life, I found the voice of my father from my early childhood, giving out about women. I also found the stereotyping that I had grown up with societally. However, there was another level to my own sexist attitude that I was yet to uncover.

As my time in Dunderry progressed, I saw the real strength of the feminine energy through Annette's work. I saw the nurturing, caring side but also the strong, protective, fiery woman who could battle through all issues with great fortitude and honesty. Now I have enormous respect for her as a shamanic teacher and person. I have grown to love her as I have grown to love my own feminine energy. My journey with Annette is captured beautifully by the first century philosopher, Plutarch: 'what we achieve inwardly will change outer reality.'

In further training weekends, I became very close to Siobhan, Jo-Anne, Angie, Shane, Richard, Patricia, Johnny and many others. We learned from each other, as well as from Martin and Annette. However, I was still having trouble with the drumming and during one weekend of training I reacted very aggressively to the beat.

It was late on a Saturday night and we were doing a purging of our fears around a fire. The idea is to meditate on the many fears that you have in your life and then collect pieces of wood or flowers or any symbolic offering from nature, tie them together in a bundle and throw them onto a purging fire. I threw my offering into the fire to the sound of loud drumming and then my heart lurched and I literally fled the room. The drumming had made me feel so sick that I couldn't stay any longer in the house with the others. I was very embarrassed by my actions. I felt as though I was being a drama queen and creating a fuss that would bring unwanted attention to me. But the overwhelming feeling in my stomach was of so much fear and sickness that I couldn't stay. As I opened the front door and bolted for the fresh air, all I could see before my eyes were hundreds of people dying. All I could smell in my nostrils was the burning of fires and the stench of death. The drumming and smell of fire smoke had taken me back.

If I'd had my car keys at that moment, I would have driven home and never returned. I was a history teacher in a secondary school, an ordinary person. How could I visualise a past life just because of a few drums? My mind was angry with me for being so ridiculous. What was I thinking?

But as I stood outside the large Georgian building, in the dark country night, I knew these things were real. A tribe had definitely died all those years ago, and they had drummed relentlessly when the dying had started. Through my instruction, they had taken to drumming, night and day, to call in the healing spirits, to save themselves.

Standing on the forecourt of Dunderry Park house, I could feel so clearly their deaths and with it the grief of those days. Tears started streaming down my face. Martin came out to see if I was alright. He said only one thing when I told him of the tribe and the drumming.

'If it happened it was not your fault.'

I went to bed early that night while the others watched a documentary. I was physically sick all night. I sweated, I was nauseous and I had a headache. The next morning, it was all gone. I was not only feeling better but I felt that I had been partly released from some old wound – a pain that consciously I had never known existed.

Previously, I would have convinced myself that what happened that night in Dunderry was merely a hallucination, born out of tiredness or stress or some other plausible reason. However, I had been told in my own kitchen by a man I barely knew at the time that it was not my fault that those people had died in that past life. I had been given proof that the village was not just a figment of my imagination.

Before I left Dunderry that weekend, I went to the crystal shop. I found a small, black-blue stone and picked it up. I asked the woman what it represented. It was the stone of the power of the eagle and of the shaman. I thought it was an apt stone for me to find.

The drumming in Dunderry had started to unblock the direction of the North. The past life that I had lived in that village was opening itself up, and I partly understood the message that I had to learn from the deaths of those villagers. I was not to blame for their deaths – the power of healing comes from spirit, and shamans or healers are just the conduit.

Oddly enough there was another message in this tribal past that I was not to learn until another visit to Dunderry Park. There was a message on the power of the feminine energy and its place in creating a balanced world, but I was not ready to hear it. I was still too aggressive towards my own feminine energy. I still hadn't realised that I wasn't gender identity disordered, but actually perfectly ordered and I was mislabelling.

Chapter 41
Breathing into balance

It took me three years of weekending in Dunderry Park to find most of the last pieces of my puzzle. I financed myself through all the courses, happy with everything that I was learning. I returned home more inspired and energised after every trip. I completed the Shaman's path, the Advanced Shamanic course and the Shamanic Practitioners' course before finally finishing with a Shamanic Counselling course. All these I attended while teaching full-time and in the last two years I also had the extra job of Deputy Principal. I found my training invaluable in this last role. Dealing with parents and students is a tricky situation, so I often found myself asking my spirit guides to help me calm down an angry parent or frustrated child. I also asked for help in keeping me cool-headed and focused on the real issues of any presented problem.

However, although my relationship was going wonderfully, and my work was going well, I was yet to leave the North on my shamanic journey and a huge stumbling block was to fall in my path as I was still refusing to see the truth about my life.

There is no place for complacency on the shamanic path and when I had finished my courses in Dunderry, I had notched up the experience without totally living it. I had become a shamanic person in theory rather than in practice. I had learned the way, even talked the way, but I did not walk the way. There was still something holding me back. I just didn't know it. And it was related to my label of gender identity disorder.

I still had an issue with the efficacy of the work and even with the validity of its healing abilities. The shift in my attitude and the removal of the final blockage came during a Holotropic Breathwork weekend. The process of Holotropic Breathwork was discovered by Dr Stanislav Grof, a psychiatrist and one of the founders of the field of transpersonal psychology. The description of this breathwork is outlined on his institute web page: 'Holotropic Breathwork™ is a powerful approach to self-exploration and healing that integrates insights from modern consciousness research, anthropology, various depth psychologies, transpersonal psychology, Eastern spiritual practices, and mystical traditions of the world.'

It is a technique that uses breathing and other elements to allow access to a non-ordinary state of consciousness. In this non-ordinary state of consciousness, the soul can experience its own birth into its present body or go even further back into past life situations, where issues can be resolved and healing attained. It is not to be gone into lightly. The holotropic weekends are run under the most careful supervision, with a group of trained individuals ready to help and support each attendee. I was lucky enough to take part in three holotropic weekends down in Dunderry, but one in particular was to have a profound influence on the way I saw my life.

During every weekend in Dunderry, new relationships are forged through sharing a room with different people. This particular weekend I was given a roommate I had never met before. She was a woman from the countryside and a person of a completely different background. Ashamedly, I saw her as yet another Annette, a nice woman who would have nothing to teach me about my shamanic path. I was still exalting the teachings of men, whilst denigrating the teachings of women. With everything that I had learned through weeks of courses and teachings, I had still not completely healed this rift in my thinking. I was showing a gender bias that was very sexist. The Holotropic Breathwork was to make me whole as the name signifies.

Before the holotropic session, each participant is given instructions about their breathwork. The participant is advised to stay on their yoga mat for safety reasons, as injury could occur if they start moving around. However, when the music started for the breathwork, I found it extremely difficult to stay still. I found myself almost writhing on the floor in a bid to contain my energy. Eventually, I broke with protocol and sat up on my knees and began holding up the wall behind me with both hands. It was almost a struggle in my mind to stop this solid wall from falling down. I was near to tears as I was envisaging all the stones starting to crumble and the rocks falling about me. I could feel the end of a civilisation.

Oddly, I was also aware that I was a woman in this holotropic regression.

I was strong and capable and shamanic. As much as I tried, I could not stop the walls from crumbling down. Eventually I lay back down on the mat and I just cried. I cried for all the people who had been lost through bloodshed and wars. I cried for the eternal mother, Pachmama, who had been scarred by the greed of men and their unfettered attack on the planet's wildlife and biodiversity. I cried for the raped women in India, the controlled women in Afghanistan and the murdered women in Salem. The experience seemed to last hours and I was exhausted. In Holotropic Breathwork the participants are given a sitter who looks after them. The sitter provides tissues and water and watches over the breather. But there are also the facilitators in the room, who walk around to assist where necessary. I asked for assistance by putting up a hand. Martin came to assist me.

'I need you to hug me,' I said, my eyes red and my voice almost hoarse. 'But I need you to hug me as a woman.'

It was the only thing I wanted at that time. I wanted to be hugged for my feminine body and for my female self. It sounds odd writing this, but what I had done in the holotropic was to share the vision of pain that all women had endured, but especially the pain of the shamanic woman who had lost her tribe in South America from smallpox. Martin gave me a very long and very comforting hug.

When the Holotropic Breathwork was finished, we had a session about our experiences. I told the group that I had been in a past life in a Peruvian city, Cuzco or Machu Picchu, and I had mourned the death and destruction of that way of life – a life that had been conquered and plundered by Spanish conquistadores. It had been a life lived in harmony with the landscape, without plundering the earth for its riches, but respecting the earth for its nurturing and cradling of mankind. It was also a life in which I had been a woman.

The jigsaw pieces started to fit together for the first time. I had always thought that the shaman who had lost their tribe was a powerful man. But I had been a powerful woman in that life instead. Her tribal medicine and spiritual power had not been able to stop the destruction of her civilisation. She had watched them all die, and she turned her back on that way of life. She had decided that it was powerless in the face of Western cannons and a patriarchal church. She saw the male energy as being more powerful. Thus in my future lives, I had turned my back on the feminine energy as being powerless and incapable. I had focused my energy on the power of the male energy, with its ability to mould the world to its choosing.

This may seem a very big jump to make, but I had learned through my shamanic training that the soul has wounds from past lives and carries the knowledge of past lives within its consciousness. For the first time, I believed that my gender identity disorder was bound up in this past-life history – a shamanic woman who had lost her tribe to a Western patriarchal power, had lost her belief in her natural medicine and thus decided to pledge her future to the power of the Western world and its masculine energy. She had literally turned her back on her medicine.

Later that day, I was given further proof from spirit that I was on the right track in my thinking. My roommate, Carol, was to show me a very emphatic sign. In the quiet of our bedroom, she took out of her weekend bag a small chunk of rock and handed it to me. She had been in the session group and heard my story of the tumbling Incan walls. It had resonated with her immediately. She had visited Machu Picchu only that year and had brought home two pieces of rock with her from the ancient stones, purchased from a local shop. She had felt drawn to bringing one with her on the weekend. She knew it was for someone in the group, but she didn't know who. When she took it out of her bag and said that it was obviously meant for me, I cried. Here was a woman that I had never met before, giving me a piece of stone from a wall that I had envisaged holding up with my bare hands, during a Holotropic Breathwork.

For Carol, it made her weekend more complete, as her gift of the small stone was so significant. For me, the piece of rock was proof that the feminine part of me had died that day with the destruction of a powerful civilisation. My refusal to be feminine had found a new depth of origin. Later, I talked to Martin about everything that had happened, especially my female shaman.

'I saw her before,' he said. 'She was feral and lived in the forests with animals around her. She had a powerful energy.'

The oddity about this story is that I have always been allergic to animals and preferred the coast to forests and nature. However, after this weekend I lost a great deal of my allergic reactions to animals and became far more comfortable in the wilds of nature. I also brought back a better understanding of the power of the feminine energy. I felt less aggrieved about owning a feminine element to my psyche. I also felt less aggressive towards my body. I could accept it.

My friend Pippa once told me that my life was a microcosm of the macro story being played globally – a strong masculine force, riding roughshod over the ground, the feminine body of Earth. I was incapable of seeing how important it was to represent both energies and balance both equally. Of course I had not listened to her, but I should have, as she always saw such illuminating things on the plinth.

When I returned from Dunderry that holotropic weekend, the lyrics of the first song I heard on the radio made me smile as they totally reflected my weekend. The words from Bastille were no coincidence.

> And the walls kept tumbling down on the city that we loved, great clouds rolled over the hills, bringing darkness from above, but if you close your eyes, does it almost feel like nothing changed at all. And if you close your eyes, does it almost feel like you've been here before.

Well I had closed my eyes that weekend and the walls did tumble down. And I reckoned that I had definitely been here before!

Nothing is permanent, not my house or my body. It is all, as the quantum physicists tell us, just energy rushing around at different speeds and gathering together to create different entities. And if this is so, then there is no disorder with me being in this body. It is only an impermanent vehicle, to give me the opportunity to experience this world from yet another viewpoint. How much easier is it to find acceptance for ourselves and free ourselves from our labels, if we realise that our bodies are only temporary vehicles?

Chapter 42
Opening to the new: 2012

Becoming one has been a difficult journey. As Bertrand Russell stated: 'In all affairs it's a healthy thing now and then to hang a question mark on the things you have long taken for granted.' Our ancestors did think the world was flat once!

I can assure you that there was a time when my thoughts were so far from the ideas that I have penned in this book that they would have seemed completely alien to me too. I was brought up in a logical, ordered world. Life was one of fixed certainties based on rational thought. There was no mysticism to it. It was well defined and well structured. It was also well mapped out.

So I have been literally dragged, kicking and screaming, into this new consciousness. Sometimes I find the things that have happened in the past ten years hard to believe. The Newtonian world of measurable, quantifiable physics has been torn down, and I find myself sitting in the colourful world of quantum physics, looking up at Heisenberg's Uncertainty Principle on a blackboard and marvelling at the places this new science has taken us: parallel universes, black holes and time travel – there is no certainty to the old physical world view anymore. Everything is conscious energy in flux.

On New Year's Eve 2011, I went down to Dunderry Park again. This time Alex came as it was also my birthday. According to many it was the dawning of a new age, as the year 2012 approached. In fact, many of my friends saw it as the beginning of the return of shamanism, when the healing of the world would happen because the natural forces of yin and yang would be brought together in balance, rather than in competition. For me it was twice as important, as I also felt that I was balancing my male and female energies. I had decided that my masculine energy, wrapped in a feminine exterior, was not to be fought against anymore but embraced as a unique existence, no less worthy than any other gender.

So I ushered in this new paradigm on New Year's Eve in the most spectacular way. Surrounded by forty other like-minded spirits, I broke an arrow against my throat chakra, symbolically breaking the hold of old fears and negative actions, and then I walked over hot coals to take the next step into my new life.

With the embers burning brightly in the December night air, I walked four times over the scorching ground, my soul assuring me that I had nothing to fear. The first walk across was for my own needs. I walked to release the lost shamanic woman in me and rekindle that feminine energy that had once been a healer.

Through past lives and soul interconnectedness, I have learned that we are all healers, as we are all in possession of the same access to abilities. It is about what we choose to ignite within ourselves in our time spent here, and what we choose to ignore. Before, as a gender identity disordered person, I had basically embodied this imbalance of the masculine over the feminine energies.

With the second walk, I trod on the hot, grey coals for the healing of all my relatives and their happiness and success in the year ahead. This walk I took mainly for my mother who had lost my father the previous July. I felt that she needed the loving support of the universe at this time, facing her first year since marriage without my father by her side.

His death had come from cancer. It was a summer death. I had sadly left for a holiday in Greece, island hopping. Luckily, as I might not have made it back in time, there was a strike in Greece and Piraeus was shut down so we could not travel out to the remote islands on our list. We managed to find a flight from Athens to Crete instead. On a beautiful, golden beach, I was given the news that Dad was very ill and in hospital. Had I been on a remote island, I wouldn't have got home in time. Even so, I had to wait two days for the next available flight. It was the longest two days of my life. Unfortunately, my son was in Boston and my daughter was in Amsterdam. She had just started an InterRailing trip with school friends.

We all managed to make it home in time. Susan and my brother-in-law were amazing during this difficult time. They paid for the care Dad needed to die at home, in the peace and quiet of his own house, with his family around him. A bed was placed in the middle of the living room and all of us sat around him while he slipped in and out of consciousness. It was the first time that I had ever been present for a death. We played Welsh hymns on a CD player and sang to him, hoping that it would help him pass. In the middle of the hymns, we all were given a reminder of the presence of spirit. Suddenly, the lilting, haunting hymns were replaced with a ballad called 'Two Little Boys'. It wasn't on the CD we were playing. Mum looked shocked. It was the song my father and his best friend, Mick, had sung together many times when a bit inebriated at parties. We all laughed. Mick was there, helping Dad cross over. So when I walked across the hot embers that New Year's Eve, I did it for my mother and the husband that she had lost six months previously.

The last walk was the hottest, as the embers were raked for the final time. I took this walk, as we were instructed to do, for the whole of mankind. My blessing for us all was that we would find the balance of the masculine and feminine energy required to heal our planet at this amazing time. However, I didn't walk this final path alone. With her hand in mine, I walked the fire with my partner, Alex. It was the most wonderful way to bring in the New Year, as we stepped into 2012 together on this final walk.

When I awoke the next morning, it was 2012. The year the Mayans, the Incas and other ancient civilisations had prophesised as being a year of great significance. The sun was splitting the sky and the world felt new and exciting. Having asked the night before for the feminine energy to come back to me, I decided to take my first trip of the New Year to the centre point of feminine energy in Ireland, to the womb of Neolithic origin, a place older than the pyramids of Giza. I went to Newgrange.

Tombs such as Newgrange are symbolically the epitome of feminine energy, the long outer passage leading into the inner womb where there is no light except the flooding of the male energy of the Sun which enters into the tomb at certain times of the year, right up to the top of the circular interior. Newgrange gives an insight into the spiritual beliefs of our ancestors, of beliefs that have honoured the feminine as much as the masculine and have seen the importance of the two in harmony for procreation. The Goddess had as much place in this ancient world as the God.

I had often been to Newgrange but had never stood inside its central tomb. As a claustrophobe, I had just managed to enter a few steps, only to be too scared to go any further. In previous visits, the dark womb-like interior of Newgrange with its oppressive grey rock had all been too much to face.

However, that New Year's morning, having broken the arrow and walked on hot embers the previous night, the significance of the fears left behind gave me the opportunity to stand in one of the centres of Irish feminine energy, happy to feel enclosed by its solid walls.

Newgrange has more than 150,000 visitors a year and there are always around twenty people with you on each guided trip into the tomb. That morning, the trip before ours had around twelve and the trip after us around twenty. I could not have entered the small passage with all those people. I would have felt suffocated. However, I was given what I needed. Only a young American couple were with us in the tomb, making five in total with our young female guide.

I stood inside the darkness of the ancient tomb and I felt a deep peace spread through me. I felt a surety of purpose that would hopefully see me through the rest of the exciting year.

Epilogue

I am on the right path now.

In the past, I had created a persona for myself based solely around my love of the male energy. My world was dominated by the desire to embody this energy. To the psychologists and psychiatrists, I was gender dysphoric but, in truth, I was simply completely out of balance. I had written the feminine off as not being part of me. However, in the last year I have reaccepted the feminine whilst keeping a firm hold of my masculine side. I am balanced.

I no longer work as a Deputy Principal in the education system. I left due to stress but the time away has given me the chance to publish books and learn more about shamanic healing. In the future, I would like to work with people who are gender identity disordered or confused about their place in society: so many of us have trouble dealing with labels, and finding our path through the trauma of growing up. We need to learn to look on labels as impermanent and unimportant. We need to challenge labels others give us that don't define our reality.

The issue of the body's physique is not important if you walk away from the concept that image is everything. It is not the body that defines us but our behaviour within this body and our own ability to see beyond the outer physique. This is how many physically impaired men and women have managed to rebuild their lives after losing limbs or losing the power over those limbs. They have not allowed their body to put limits to what they can achieve or what they can do. We tend to refer to their courage as the human spirit's ability to overcome all obstacles. It is that amazing spirit inside of us all that needs to be recognised.

In 1994, in her book *Illuminata*, Marianne Williamson wrote: 'As a species, we are pregnant with a higher form of life. Pregnancy is a feminine force, and we are sourcing our new power from an ancient and more feminine energy. As we reach the end of the millennium, the Goddess makes a return to our consciousness ... the feminine ascends, rising up within us, working through us as we seek a more internal power.'

There are countless individuals at this moment in time revolting against the bodies that they were born into – men seeking to look feminine, women hoping to change to masculine. Maybe the learning for all of us is to find respect for the balance of both these polarised energies in harmonic existence. We all have masculine and feminine energy within us. It is acceptable to be both. It is healing to keep both. It is only the outer body that reflects a gender and sometimes even this outer body does not reflect just one gender.

I finished my journey through the shamanic directions. I went back to Ash only this year, to the South American training, and learned the teachings of the East. We had a wonderful weekend and I was presented with a mesa and a new rattle for my continuing journey. The East is symbolised by the eagle which takes you to a higher perspective. It was a really powerful weekend and I was so happy to finish my training with Ash. He is such a good shaman and kind man.

I was also happy to be finally through all four directions. I have now at last decided to open a healing room for shamanic work. I know the potency of shamanic healing. Through this ancient therapy, I have been healed physically, mentally and spiritually. Studying shamanism, and being with healers and teachers, has released me from limiting labels.

I think that we are far too quick in our modern society to label ourselves and limit our lives. Our schools are rife with labels for our children who have not yet found their true essence. If students find school boring, we label them with a wide variety of psychological and developmental issues, and we quieten them down with chemicals to make them conform. It is an aspect of our education system that I absolutely oppose. In thirty years of teaching, I have rarely seen a child who cannot learn or thrive in a classroom that is open to their individuality. But unfortunately most of our classrooms work to a standard child not a budding genius.

We are not our bodies. They are just the vehicles to carry us through life. There is no such thing as being born in the 'wrong' body. It is just being born into a different body, with a possibly unique identity. If you don't like that body and it clashes with the way you feel and think, then go ahead and change it, but don't describe it as the wrong body. Just call it the way it is – I am a man inside a woman's body and I would prefer to change the outside to match my thinking on the inside. But don't call it the wrong body, because that is negatively expressing an existence of life that can work perfectly adequately for other people.

The philosopher Schopenhauer once wrote that, 'Every truth passes through three stages before it is recognised. In the first it is ridiculed. In the second it is opposed. In the third, it is regarded as self-evident.' I have ridiculed the truths in my life, but now they are self-evident in my holographic picture of life.

Today I live very happily with my partner and I do not care what pronouns or words are used to describe me. They are just labels and we are all so much more.